HONOR BEFORE GLORY

HONOR BEFORE GLORY

The Epic World War II Story
of the Japanese American GIs
Who Rescued the Lost Battalion

SCOTT McGAUGH

DA CAPO PRESS

NOTE TO READERS: Throughout the book, battalions are identified with their regiments; for example, the 1st Battalion of the 141st Regiment is shown as 1/141. Military time (using a 24-hour clock) is also used throughout the book.

Designed by Trish Wilkinson
Set in 11.5 point Adobe Garamond Pro by Perseus Books

Cataloging-in-Publication data for this book is available from the Library of Congress.
ISBN: 978-0-306-82445-6
ISBN: 978-0-306-82446-3 (ebook)

Published by Da Capo Press, an imprint of Perseus Books, a division of PBG Publishing, LLC, a subsidiary of Hachette Book Group, Inc.

For more information, please contact the Special Markets Department at the Perseus Books Group, 2300 Chestnut Street, Suite 200, Philadelphia, PA 19103, or call (800) 810-4145, ext. 5000, or e-mail special.markets@perseusbooks.com.

10 9 8 7 6 5 4 3 2 1

To Marjorie,
who shows me every day
how to fight life's biggest battles
with spirit and style

CONTENTS

ORGANIZATIONAL DIAGRAM AND MAPS

PREFACE

EVERY DAY IS VETERANS DAY FOR ME. IN 2004 I BECAME THE founding marketing director of the USS Midway Museum. I work with and welcome veterans of all stripes aboard the museum in San Diego every day, including World War II veterans. More than 1.3 million visitors a year join them, to walk in their shoes for a few hours and experience service and sacrifice for America aboard an aircraft carrier.

I see World War II veterans approach a teenage U.S. Marine who graduated from boot camp earlier in the day to thank the youngster for his service. I listen to Vietnam veterans sharing their prisoner-of-war (POW) stories with visitors from around the world. I see Afghanistan veterans roll aboard in their wheelchairs. You would pass most of these veterans in the grocery store and have no inkling how much they have sacrificed for America.

I've discovered how so many of these otherwise "ordinary" Americans were remarkably brave under horrific circumstances, how they somehow maintained their humanity when surrounded by barbarism. Honoring the legacy of those who served and sacrificed for our nation has become my passion. Their legacy must be preserved for future generations.

Honor Before Glory is my seventh book and was the most difficult to write. The story begins a few months following the attack on Pearl

Harbor when America incarcerated more than 100,000 Japanese Americans living in Seattle, Los Angeles, San Diego, and elsewhere only because of their ethnicity.* Remarkably, a year later thousands of them volunteered for combat in a segregated army. Some served with the 442nd Regimental Combat Team (RCT) in Europe, and others reported to the Military Intelligence Service in the Pacific.

This is the true story of just one of the remarkable feats of the 442nd: the rescue of a battalion surrounded by Germans on an obscure mountain ridge near the German border for nearly a week. It is the story of how the 442nd succeeded where other battalions had failed. The 442nd not only reached 211 surrounded men but by the end of the war also became the most decorated regiment of its size in World War II.

Honor Before Glory chronicles the best of America and, in some ways, the worst of the nation. I hope readers will pause and reflect on an American spirit that spawns incredible bravery and one that allows discrimination and hatred born of fear and revenge. This book is largely based on previously unpublished and rarely seen oral histories recorded by the men who were there. It builds on other chronicles of the 442nd with new insights from those who often fell bleeding on a remote mountain ridge in eastern France in World War II.

To be sure, this is not the big story of World War II in Europe. It is a small story—a single rescue mission—that tells a much larger story. And that is the story of the millions of Americans who fought and sacrificed in Europe—each man's sacrifice for a larger cause. It is the story of Japanese American citizens' devotion to duty and their acceptance of sacrifice for a country that for a time considered them enemies. It also sheds light on a postwar debate that has simmered for decades. Some came to question the use of the Japanese Americans'

---

*Contemporary accounts at the time called it the "evacuation" or "relocation" of Japanese American citizens, without due process, into guarded camps on prairies and in deserts in a hysterical response to the attack on Pearl Harbor.

combat regiment, questioning whether their commanding general treated them as dispensable "cannon fodder" or relied on them as one of the army's bravest and most accomplished regiments.

Nearly all of the participants have passed away or are in their nineties. More than one hundred of their oral histories recorded in the last decade of their lives are a treasure trove, as are obscure army documents. Spending nearly a week on the ridge where the rescue mission took place and working with two French residents of the Vosges Mountains who are experts on the mission were invaluable. There was no substitute for personally examining the length of the ridge where the rescue mission took place or for sitting in the foxholes dug by 442nd soldiers more than seventy years ago. To look down and see both American and German machine-gun cartridges in the same foxhole was chilling.

This is the story of young Japanese American men in a remote forest, in their foxholes, at the aid stations, on suicide charges, and in the command posts. Their legacy was one of unparalleled service and sacrifice, one man at a time, for a greater cause.

CAST OF CHARACTERS

Seventh Army

Lieutenant General Alexander Patch . . . Commanding officer

VI Corps

Major General Lucian Truscott Jr. . . . . Commanding officer
Major General Edward Brooks . . . . Commanding officer

Germans

General Hermann Balck . . . . Army Group G
General Friedrich Wiese . . . . Nineteenth Army
Lieutenant General Wilhelm Richter . . 716th Volksgrenadier Division
Colonel Walter Rolin . . . . 933rd Grenadier Regiment
Major Franz Seebacher . . . . Commanding officer,
                                      201st Mountain Battalion
Captain Erich Maunz . . . . Commanding officer, 202nd
                                      Mountain Battalion

36th Division

Major General John Dahlquist . . . . Commanding officer

Colonel Charles Owens . . . . Chief of staff (later
commanding officer, 1/141)

Colonel Oran Stovall . . . . Commanding officer, 111th
Engineer Battalion

Lieutenant Colonel Fred Sladen . . . . . . Operations officer

Lieutenant Wells Lewis. . . . . Aide to Dahlquist

143rd Infantry Regiment

Colonel Paul DeWitt Adams . . . . Commanding officer

141st Infantry Regiment

Lieutenant Colonel William Bird . . . . . Commanding officer

1st Battalion, 141st

Colonel Carl Lundquist . . . . Commanding officer

Lieutenant Martin Higgins. . . . . Company A

Lieutenant Harry Huberth . . . . Company B

Lieutenant Joseph Kimble . . . . Company C

Lieutenant Gordon Nelson . . . . Weapons company

Lieutenant James Gilman

Sergeant Jack Wilson. . . . . Rifleman

Sergeant Harold Kripisch

Sergeant Edward Guy

Sergeant James Comstock. . . . . Communications

Staff Sergeant Bruce Estes. . . . . Rifleman

Private Robert Camaiani

Private Joe Hilty

Erwin Blonder . . . . Forward observer

Eason Bond . . . . Rifleman

Burt McQueen. . . . . Rifleman

Al Tortolano . . . . Rifleman

442nd Regimental Combat Team

Colonel Charles Pence . . . . Commanding officer
Lieutenant Colonel Virgil Miller . . . . . . Executive officer
Tech/4 Victor Izui. . . . . Medic
Colonel Jimmie Kanaya . . . . Medic
Tech/4 Kelly Kuwayama. . . . . Medic
Staff Sergeant Jim Okubo. . . . . Medic

100th Battalion, 442nd

Lieutenant Colonel Gordon Singles . . . Commanding officer
Lieutenant James Boodry . . . . Operations officer
Captain Young Oak Kim
Sergeant Harry Kamikawa
Staff Sergeant Itsumu Sasaoka
Sergeant George Suyama
Private William Yamaka
Sergeant Al Takahashi
Chaplain Israel Yost

2nd Battalion, 442nd

Lieutenant Colonel James Hanley . . . . . Commanding officer
Private Kenji Ego
Private George Sakato

3rd Battalion, 442nd

Lieutenant Colonel Alfred Pursall . . . . . Commanding officer
Private Nobuo Amakawa
Captain Joseph Byrne . . . . Company commanding officer
Private Barney Hajiro . . . . Rifleman
Sergeant Lawrence Ishikawa
Tech Sergeant Rocky Matayoshi . . . . . . Scout
Sergeant James Oura

Private Mutt Sakumoto . . . . Scout
Private Shuji Taketomo
Private Kenji Takubo
Private Jim Tazoi
Private Rudy Tokiwa . . . . Messenger
Private Ernest Uno . . . . Radioman
Tech Sergeant Jim Yamashita
Private Matsuichi Yogi

522nd Field Artillery Battalion

Lieutenant Baya Harrison. . . . . Commanding officer
Captain Moyer Harris
Corporal Nelson Akagi . . . . Forward observer
Lieutenant Susumo Ito . . . . Forward observer
Private Kats Miho . . . . Gunnery corporal
Staff Sergeant Don Shimazu . . . . Forward observer

405th Fighter Squadron

Captain Gavin Robertson. . . . . Pilot
Major John Leonard . . . . Pilot
Lieutenant Robert Booth . . . . Pilot
Lieutenant Edward Hayes. . . . . Pilot
Lieutenant Milton Seale . . . . Pilot
Lieutenant Paul Tetrick . . . . Pilot
Lieutenant Eliel Archilla . . . . Pilot

Note: Some ranks listed reflect the final rank upon discharge or retirement after a career in the military.
Source: Sons & Daughters of the 442nd Regimental Combat Team.

36TH INFANTRY DIVISION
ORGANIZATIONAL DIAGRAM

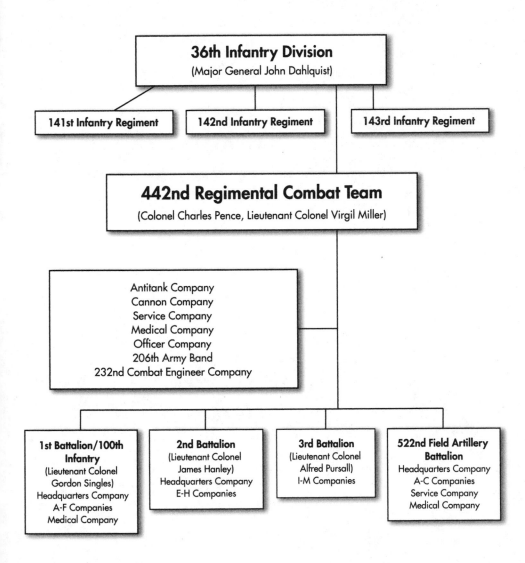

36th Infantry Division
(Major General John Dahlquist)

141st Infantry Regiment

142nd Infantry Regiment

143rd Infantry Regiment

442nd Regimental Combat Team
(Colonel Charles Pence, Lieutenant Colonel Virgil Miller)

Antitank Company
Cannon Company
Service Company
Medical Company
Officer Company
206th Army Band
232nd Combat Engineer Company

1st Battalion/100th Infantry
(Lieutenant Colonel Gordon Singles)
Headquarters Company
A-F Companies
Medical Company

2nd Battalion
(Lieutenant Colonel James Hanley)
Headquarters Company
E-H Companies

3rd Battalion
(Lieutenant Colonel Alfred Pursall)
I-M Companies

522nd Field Artillery Battalion
Headquarters Company
A-C Companies
Service Company
Medical Company

Source: 442 Veterans Club (Sons & Daughters Chapter of the 442nd RCT), http://442sd.org/category/442nd-organizational-chart/.

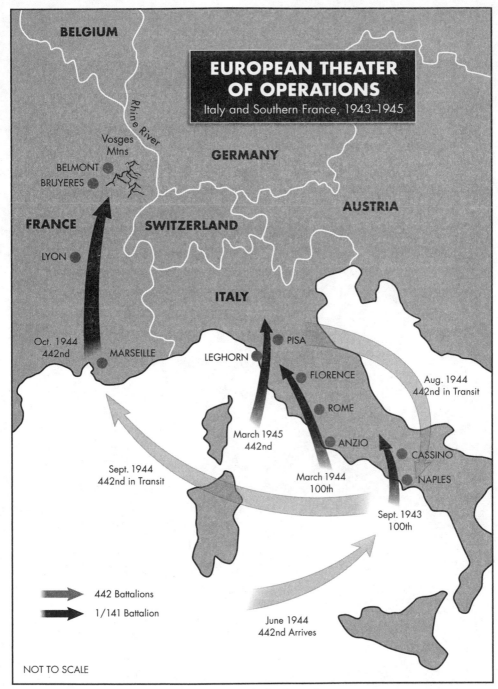

European Theater of Operations, Italy and Southern France, 1943–1945

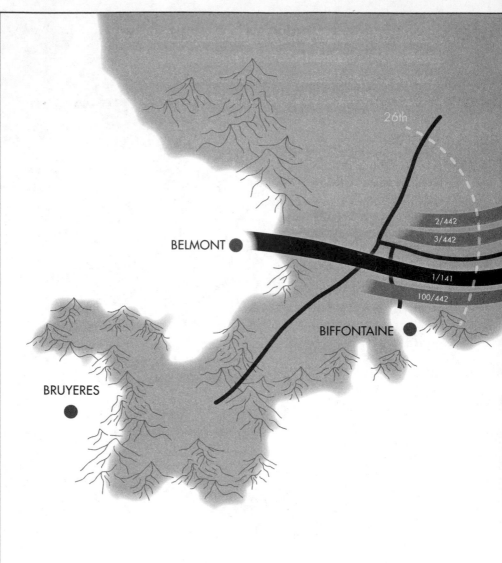

26th

2/442

3/442

1/141

100/442

BELMONT

BIFFONTAINE

BRUYERES

LOST BATTALION
RESCUE

October 24–30, 1944

Lost Battalion Rescue, October 24–30, 1944

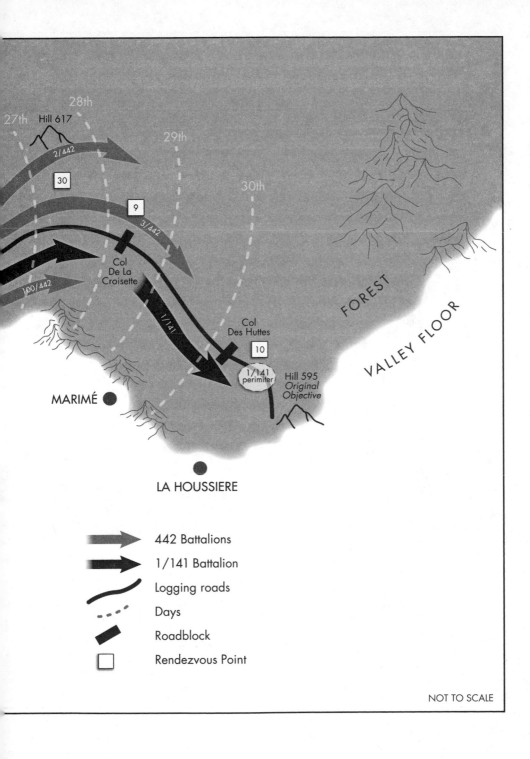

27th
28th
Hill 617
2/442
30
29th
30th
9
3/442
Col
De La
Croisette
100/442
1/141
Col
Des Huttes
10
1/141
perimiter
Hill 595
Original
Objective
MARIMÉ ●
LA HOUSSIERE ●
FOREST
VALLEY FLOOR

442 Battalions
1/141 Battalion
Logging roads
Days
Roadblock
Rendezvous Point

NOT TO SCALE

GO FORWARD

West Torrance High School, California

One suitcase, each family, all else left behind
Dignity, freedom, liberty: were those left too?
Trapped, alienated, segregated, confined
Stripped from their red, white, and blue.

Is this the American way?
Citizen or alien? Friend or foe?
Should I fight or should I stay?
Are you a yes-yes or a no-no?

Yet the great sea crashing against the shores
Grasping, clasping the land of both of homes
Engulfed in sweat, sorrow, and war
Treated like monsters in this world we roam.

Our freedom and families we defend
Don't take back a single stroke
Never give in, until the final end
We all stand strong: "go for broke."

I, a Japanese American, stand free today
Thanks to the sacrifice of those before
The courage of every soldier, every child, every Nikkei
Who plowed through the demands of war.

Go, go, go, forward, go forward
Fight for our freedom, liberty, our pride
Never take another step backward
Strength in every leap, every march, every stride.

Courtesy of the Go For Broke National Education Center.

PROLOGUE

H̲e̲ ̲r̲e̲e̲k̲e̲d̲ ̲o̲f̲ ̲c̲i̲g̲a̲r̲e̲t̲t̲e̲ ̲s̲m̲o̲k̲e̲,̲ ̲w̲e̲t̲ ̲w̲o̲o̲l̲,̲ ̲f̲e̲a̲r̲,̲ ̲g̲u̲n̲p̲o̲w̲d̲e̲r̲, rubber, and sweat. So did the others in the primitive foxholes and trenches they had dug nearby. No one had showered in days. To Matsuji "Mutt" Sakumoto, everything stunk on the morning of October 30, 1944, in the Vosges Mountains of eastern France. For nearly one hundred hours he had battled German machine gunners, snipers, and artillery in near-constant rain almost cold enough to become snow. For five days he had fought from dawn to dark and then had lain sleepless in waterlogged trenches as German artillery pounded his position through the night. A hot meal had become a distant memory. Yet images of mangled bodies and body parts in trees were only hours old.

Hundreds of men had been killed or wounded in less than a week on the rescue mission. Vicious fighting had limited each day's advance to little more than the length of a few football fields. But all that mattered to Sakumoto's commanding general was reaching the American battalion from Texas that had been surrounded by the enemy somewhere in the dense forest ahead. No matter the cost, Sakumoto and his 442nd Regimental Combat Team had to rescue them. His unit was limited to Japanese American soldiers, commanded only by Caucasian officers, in a segregated army. To Sakumoto and others, that stunk, too.

THREE DAYS EARLIER LIEUTENANT ROBERT BOOTH'S THUNDER-BOLT aircraft had approached the remote ridge where the trapped battalion had dug in. The surrounded troops had exhausted their food and medical supplies. They were critically low on ammunition. His mission was to resupply it from the air. As he made a treetop approach across a valley from the southwest, it became obvious the dense cloud cover ahead on the ridge would make the airdrop impossible. He had pulled hard on the stick to get his aircraft's nose up. He flew into the thick clouds and perhaps had become disoriented before his aircraft exploded on the side of the ridge.

On the same day a few miles away, Nobuo Amakawa and a comrade had charged a machine-gun nest that had pinned down their unit. His bravado was so unnerving that the Germans abandoned their post. More heroic deeds followed that day and the next, before he was shot in the neck and died of his wounds two days later. Amakawa was twenty-two years old. He would be awarded the Silver Star, Bronze Star, and Purple Heart.

Even though he wasn't a medic, Kenji Takubo had crawled fifty yards across open ground to aid a wounded soldier during the rescue mission. He hauled the man onto his back and then crawled thirty yards through enemy fire to a more secure position. A few hours later Takubo died in a shower of wooden daggers when an enemy artillery shell exploded in a fir tree almost directly above him. Takubo was twenty years old. He would be awarded the Silver Star.

Early on October 29 infantryman Takeyasu Onaga had felt an ache deep inside. Another suicidal advance loomed, the latest in a series of impossible orders that had been passed from foxhole to foxhole before dawn. He turned to a buddy and offered him his weapon if he died. Later that day Onaga lifted a tree off a wounded comrade to free him and then single-handedly destroyed an enemy machine-gun nest. When wounded in the neck, he ran across open ground to a medic to keep him out of danger. Onaga then lay down and bled to death. He was twenty-three years old. He would receive the Silver Star.

Now Sakumoto and others were perhaps a few hundred yards from the surrounded battalion. Before dawn his group had included Joseph Laurence Byrne, a lanky New Yorker of basketball-player height who was deeply respected by the Japanese Americans he commanded. He was one of the few Caucasian officers for whom many of his men would have given their lives. But the combat veteran had stepped on a mine a few hours earlier and was killed instantly. He was twenty-seven years old.

The logging road on the ridge that Sakumoto and the rest of the 442nd had followed was now tinged red with the blood of Japanese American citizens. Two years earlier, in the hysterical days following the attack on Pearl Harbor, many of them had been forced into internment camps on desolate prairies and in deserts of the West, only because of their ethnicity. Now they were dying while their families remained behind barbed wire.

These men had died not on a mission of great strategic significance but one of isolated rescue. It was a mission some officers and enlisted soldiers openly criticized at the time. Others questioned it in the decades that followed, including the commanding officer of the men Sakumoto and the rest of the 442nd had been sent to save. It was a rescue mission that epitomized the extraordinary World War II combat record of the "Go For Broke" regiment.

Sakumoto reached for a cigarette.

CHAPTER 1

A STRONG FORCE WILL FOLLOW

First Lieutenants Martin Higgins and Harry Huberth stared at the map of the Vosges Mountains of eastern France on October 23, 1944. After seven weeks of near-constant battle, they had learned that the 1st Battalion, 141st Regiment (1/141), would spearhead an advance onto a seven-mile ridge where the Germans had been dug in for weeks. Later in the day the battalion would depart from Bruyères and Belmont, two towns southwest of the ridge. A logging trail would lead Higgins, Huberth, and the rest of the 1/141 east toward an increasingly desperate enemy dug in deep in the mountainous forest.

Higgins and Huberth could imagine what they would do if they were defending the ridge. They would make the enemy's advance through this part of the Vosges as costly as possible at the onset of winter. Battlefield doctrine would call for booby-trapped roadblocks to force the attackers into minefields; machine guns would be positioned along routes the advancing enemy troops were forced to take to bypass those minefields. Foxholes would conceal the ridges' defenders until those troops were only yards away. Terrain would be used to the defenders' advantage, by holding the high ground with crossing fields of fire and preparing fallback lines of defense in case they became necessary.

They would wage a battle of attrition from dug-in positions and count on the mountainous terrain, dense forest, cold, rain, and mud to sap the attackers' strength and combat effectiveness. Their artillery would pulverize known resupply and medical evacuation routes. Further, they might hold some units in reserve for a counterattack on both flanks of the ridgeline if the advancing troops overextended themselves.

The ridge was in the southern Vosges Mountains, a range that extended ninety miles, north and south. The Vosges ran largely parallel to the German border, which was about twenty miles to the east. The west–east ridge was a relatively narrow stretch of dense forest with a slight bend to the southeast. It was rarely more than three hundred yards wide, most of it sloping gently to the north, where it met an endless series of ridges and hills that constituted the rounded mountain range far to the north.

The south side of the ridge fell away precipitously, almost cliff-like in some areas, nearly three hundred feet to a valley filled with farms. The slope of forty to forty-five degrees made a direct climb up from the valley below difficult, and the density of the forest made it nearly impossible. Any attempt would exhaust a man in minutes. Logging roads carved across the southern face offered the only reasonable access onto the ridge for the valley's residents.

One decent road rose from the valley floor onto the ridge. It started in Biffontaine, a ravaged French village of about forty buildings at the southern foot of the ridge. A tall gray church at the junction of three streets dominated Biffontaine, a battered building pockmarked by machine-gun sprays that had torn chunks out of its stone facade and massive wooden front door. To the south wheat and cornfields, now stubbled and dark brown following the summer's harvest, stretched for miles. Small stands of barren trees, sturdy stone farmhouses, and stately barns throughout the valley were connected by rutted paths made muddy by October's rains. Germans controlled the valley and the ridges surrounding the valley.

A single logging road ran the length of the ridge. Side roads, little more than paths cut through the forest from the north and south, climbed up onto the ridge and reached the main longitudinal route, like veins in a leaf. It was a rugged forest with only a handful of narrow trails. The 1/141 would have limited ability to maneuver. The officers would have to guard against surprise flanking attacks. The likelihood of an ambush was substantial.

Higgins spoke his mind at the briefing. "If a strong force does not stay close to the 1st, a gap could form which the Germans might easily exploit and surround my unit," the former horse soldier told Lieutenant Colonel William Bird, the commanding officer of the 1/141. Higgins greatly admired Bird, who had been wounded in battle less than two weeks earlier.

"A strong force will follow, move out," said Bird.[1]

THE DAY BEFORE, A UNIT OF THE 100TH BATTALION, 442ND Regimental Combat Team, had advanced across part of the same ridge, not far from the 141st's present position. It rode toward death atop growling tanks, toward the same enemy positions that now worried Higgins and Huberth. Germans were hunkered down behind boulders, in ravines, and in makeshift burrows in the misty morning forest, probably on both sides of the trail, the Japanese American soldiers suspected. Surely, their tanks' grinding rumble and exhaust would give the Germans plenty of warning. They would be poised to open fire in an instant.

The men had already endured brutal and chaotic fighting. For some men, it was their first week in battle, and some units had advanced farther than others. A hundred yards could create a dangerous gap that the Germans might exploit. When units found themselves in danger of being separated, others were sent forward to establish contact and reestablish the line of advance. Staff Sergeant Itsumu Sasaoka, Sergeant George Suyama, Sergeant Harry Kamikawa, Private William Yamaka, and the rest of their platoon were riding on the tanks to reach a unit that needed to be reinforced before the advance toward Biffontaine could resume.

German riflemen first heard the tanks approaching and then smelled their exhaust drifting through the trees. Seconds later they centered their crosshairs on the Japanese American soldiers as they appeared alongside or on top of their light tanks. Some soldiers flinched when the first shot clanked off a tank. A split second later the forest erupted on both sides of the trail. German infantry attacked from all sides. Part of the initial burst ripped into Sasaoka, who had crouched on the last tank of the convoy. As his uniform turned crimson, he hung onto the tank's machine gun and "directed a hail of bullets in the enemy positions in a last desperate attempt to prevent the other members of his platoon from being subject to the lethal enemy crossfire."[2] Weakened by blood loss, Sasaoka fell off his tank, landing hard on the forest floor. Another man took his place and sprayed the forest with suppressing fire. Pistols, rifles, and machine guns grew hot when Suyama, Kamikawa, Yamaka, and others returned fire as the firefight intensified. They could have jumped off the tanks toward cover, but most did not.

The tanks had rolled ahead as the firefight stretched to more than a half mile. Four Japanese Americans were knocked off their tanks. No one could afford to stop and come to their aid. The Americans pushed deeper into the forest as night fell. When the trail narrowed and choked off the tanks' advance, the reinforcement platoon jumped off, fought through the German positions, and reached the other members of the 100th who had been threatened with annihilation. Now the commanding officer of the 100th, Lieutenant Colonel Gordon Singles, could concentrate on Biffontaine, at the southern foot of the ridge, his battalion's objective.

The next day they reached the valley hamlet. The Americans advanced from house to house, routing Germans out of cellars, steeples, attics, and garden sheds. Despite three German counterattacks, Biffontaine fell to the Americans about the same time as the 1/141 was preparing to head out on its patrol. The 100th had lost more than 150 men in taking Biffontaine. Itsumu Sasoaka, George Suyama, Harry Kamikawa, and William Yamaka were among the losses. Sasoaka,

Kamikawa, and Yamaka had been captured by the Germans; no one could find Suyama.

Although Higgins and Huberth would not have to worry about a German assault directly from Biffontaine as their men assembled, the inherent danger of their mission had been only marginally lessened. The exact strength of the enemy on the ridge remained unknown.

HIGGINS HAD JOINED THE UNIT ONLY A FEW MONTHS EARLIER. He had grown up in New Jersey, the son of a devoted Boy Scout scoutmaster who taught his scouts military-style close-order (marching) drill. At five-foot-seven, Higgins was deemed too small for football but was a solid basketball player who was quick to make friends in tough neighborhoods and drove a Model A to the Jersey Shore on outings. Higgins was Irish, didn't run from a fight, and loved horses. He had joined the New York National Guard in 1939 after earning a degree in economics from St. Peter's College. After graduating from officer candidate school in December 1942, Higgins was assigned to the 10th Cavalry, the famed "Buffalo Soldiers." His father had raised a son who was uncommonly confident, self-reliant, and spoke French.

Early posts had included Camp Lockett, east of San Diego. On horseback Higgins patrolled sage- and manzanita-covered mesas and dry washes clogged with ironwood trees along the Mexican border. On those patrols he had met and teamed with Harry Huberth, who shared Higgins's love for horses. Huberth had dreaded the prospect of becoming an infantryman as war approached. He had used his New York family connections to find a sympathetic army recruiter who got Huberth assigned to the cavalry.

On February 10, 1944, their unit loaded onto trains bound for Camp Patrick Henry, Virginia. From there the USS *General William Mitchell* had delivered the men to Casablanca, Morocco, in March. That same month they learned the unit would be disbanded. World War II had little need for horse soldiers. Higgins opted for a combat assignment rather than stay with what would become a logistics unit. Huberth was told he was being sent to the infantry when his request for an armored unit was denied. They joined the 141st Infantry Regiment from Texas, a veteran combat unit. Both would fight their war from foxholes, not saddles.

———— ◆ ————

HIGGINS'S PATROL WAS PART OF THE MUCH LARGER ADVANCE BY THE VI Corps that had reached the Vosges foothills in late 1944.* Beginning with the Normandy invasion in June, massive Allied armies from the North and South had driven the Germans out of western and central France after four years' occupation and pushed them back nearly to the doorstep of Germany. If the 141st and the rest of VI Corps could break out of the Vosges to the east, they could drive across the Alsatian plain, where American armor, air, and artillery would be more effective, and reach the Rhine River on the German border. That reality wasn't lost on the Germans. The seemingly impenetrable Vosges Mountains could become their last line of defense if the Germans were to keep the Allies out of the fatherland.

Adolf Hitler had ordered that the Vosges be held at all cost, in part to buy time for the Germans' Ardennes Offensive, better known as the Battle of the Bulge, in two months' time. In addition, rumors circulated that a miraculous secret weapon was being developed by the Germans that would change the direction of the war. The German military had only to dig in and keep the Allies out of Germany.

Beginning on October 15, Operation Dogface called for the VI Corps to capture Bruyères, in the western foothills of the Vosges, and then cross the mountains and capture St. Die, along the Meurthe

---

* The VI Corps comprised the 3rd, 36th, and 45th Infantry Divisions. The 36th comprised the 141st, 142nd, and 143rd Infantry Regiments as well as the 442nd Regimental Combat Team. Each regiment was organized into three infantry battalions, plus supporting engineer, medical, and artillery units.

River, a week later. St. Die was an industrial, road, rail, and communications center. The 36th Division's assignment was to secure the VI Corps' southern flank. Higgins's objective, the end of a ridge overlooking the villages of La Houssière and Corcieux in the valley to the south, would enable the 36th to monitor German positions that could threaten the VI Corps' right flank.

To reach that objective, the commander of each squad, platoon, and company of the 1/141 likely had only two things on his mind on October 23 as he prepared for the patrol—his unit's tactical objective and the predilections of his men. Higgins, Huberth, and the other officers needed to know which men in their companies tended to lay down wide swaths of fire before clearly identifying an enemy target. To make matters worse, American units in the region had suffered from a shortage of mortar and artillery ammunition for several weeks.

It was also critical that they know which men in their units might fall prey to human nature and rush to a wounded buddy's aid. When they did, two men were sidelined. Soldiers nearby might have to widen their field of attack or defensive line to make up for the loss. When that happened, the ranks would be thinned and the unit's firepower lessened.

Some commanders could be harshly candid in their assessment of each soldier. In the final briefing before combat, they gathered their men, looked each man in the eye, and reminded him of a habit or tendency that might jeopardize the mission or the men. If everyone knew everyone else's strengths and weaknesses, some commanders said, it improved the unit's overall situational awareness and combat strength.

As the departure hour approached, the company commanders could not allow themselves to think of the casualties that might begin in less than an hour. Instead, they had to be ready and available to inform their men if they received critical last-minute information. No commander wanted to hold new information about enemy placement or firepower that he had been unable to disseminate before a patrol.

JUST BEFORE NOON ON OCTOBER 23, THE THREE COMPANIES OF the 1st Battalion moved out of Belmont, a village to the west of the ridge, where the entire 141st Infantry Regiment had assembled and briefly rested.* Each company had been assigned to a single farm, with one farmhouse designated as the regiment's command post. Higgins's battalion moved to the western end of the ridge, picking a member of the French Resistance, Henri Grandjean, and a local woodcutter, Pierre Poirat, as guides.

A wall of forest towered nearly three hundred feet above them as they approached the western foot of the ridge. They skirted along the edges of the farm fields along tree lines in the event German artillery found them and they had to take cover. Then, stringing out on a logging road, they reached the ridge's high point of just over seven hundred feet in elevation. If it weren't for the forest that enveloped them, Higgins would have had a commanding view of the valleys to the west and south as well as along the entire ridge to the east.

Rain peppered Higgins's Company A as it took the lead and advanced on paths between stands of towering fir trees. The forest floor was relatively flat and barren, so the Americans made good time—too good, as the afternoon passed and all three companies continued east. Then, shortly after sunset, Higgins's company took heavy enemy fire. Soon German artillery began pounding his position into the night, forcing him to fall back, as Company B, commanded by Huberth, and Company C, commanded by First Lieutenant Joseph Kimble, caught up. It wasn't until 2125 that they dug in for the night, carving slit trenches in the forest floor in search of rest.† They had advanced four miles on the logging road, much farther than they had expected.

---

*Each infantry battalion is organized into four companies. Each company is composed of platoons, which in turn are organized into squads.

†A slit trench was the length of a man's body, shoulder width, and perhaps eighteen to twenty-four inches deep. It enabled him to lie flush with the ground, presumably out of sight and somewhat protected from shrapnel.

The patrol jumped off again at 0700 the following morning. Higgins and the other company and platoon leaders of the 1/141 faced a German roadblock first thing in the morning, composed of downed trees that were probably booby-trapped and reinforced with land mines in the immediate area.

It was the latest obstacle the 141st faced after more than two months of near-constant fighting since Operation Dragoon, the amphibious landing on the French Riviera on August 15 as part of the Americans' 36th Division. Major General John Dahlquist, a man new to combat, commanded the 36th Division. From the moment Dahlquist went ashore that day near Marseille, he had been in hot water with the commanding officer of the VI Corps, Major General Lucian Truscott Jr.

Operation Dragoon's objectives had been to seize the strategic ports of Marseille and Toulon along a forty-five-mile stretch of the Côte d'Azur between Agay and Cavalier-sur-Mer from the Germans' Nineteenth Army. Once ashore, Truscott's VI Corps would proceed up the Rhone Valley toward Lyon. Hemmed in by the Provençal Alps to the east and mountains to the west, Truscott's force would advance north-northeast across a series of undulating plains and ridges on both sides of the Rhone River. Rapid advancement north from the Riviera could cut off German armies in western France as they retreated east toward Germany. A successful landing could also draw German troops away from Normandy, to the north.

Inexplicably, in the middle of the first day's landing, Dahlquist had decided to go ashore with an aide and climb onto an outcrop to observe the afternoon's landings. He apparently took no radio equipment with him. When unexpected enemy fire stalled the landings, General Truscott on the USS *Bayfield* could not reach Dahlquist to discuss the situation. A meticulously planned amphibious landing on several beaches—which had begun that morning with thirteen hundred bombers pounding the coastline—could unravel by midafternoon. As Truscott's frustration heightened by the minute, a navy admiral in charge of the landing craft implemented a contingency landing plan in Dahlquist's absence to keep the highly choreographed landings from falling behind schedule.

Truscott never truly forgave Dahlquist for being incommunicado, later saying that achieving some of Operation Dragoon's objectives had been pushed back by at least a day due to Dahlquist's poor judgment. Truscott grew even angrier with Dahlquist when he learned that Dahlquist had sent the admiral a thank-you note for making the tactical decision in his absence.

Truscott and Dahlquist could not have been more different in background, temperament, and reputation. Lucian K. Truscott Jr.'s gravelly voice filled a room. He reminded some of a bantam rooster who ruled without question and could be a son of a bitch if that's what the job required. The superstitious Texas native favored a leather jacket, his "lucky boots," and a white scarf. The son of English parents, Truscott grew up in Norman, Oklahoma, and taught school for six years before enlisting in the army in 1917. Truscott never saw combat in World War I and held a number of cavalry posts following the war. He was a blunt, driven, and ambitious officer, famous for his "Truscott Trot," which was a forced march of nearly four miles per hour instead of the conventional two and a half miles per hour. The Truscott Trot covered thirty miles in eight hours instead of the standard twenty miles.

At the start of the war, he had held a post in England. A year later he commanded a task force in North Africa and was said to have attracted the attention of General George Patton. Later in Italy, General Mark Clark had refused to release Truscott for transfer to the Third Army command, calling him too valuable to the Italian campaign.

Dahlquist, on the other hand, had forged his career mostly sitting down. The University of Minnesota graduate had also served during World War I without seeing action and then was assigned to various posts in Germany and the Philippines. In 1937 he was attached to the Planning Branch, Personnel Division, War Department General Staff.

Tall and soft, he held bureaucratic posts early in the war before being promoted to major general in 1943 and taking command in 1944 of the 36th Infantry Division, where he would face the enemy for the first time.

Dahlquist couldn't seem to find his way out of Truscott's doghouse. A few days after the landing, Truscott had felt compelled to give Dahlquist written instructions on how to deploy his troops to keep three retreating German divisions from escaping farther toward Germany. Truscott was livid because Dahlquist had erroneously reported that his units, including the 141st, were in position to halt the Germans' retreat.

Four days later Truscott had decided to fire Dahlquist, as the German army appeared to be slipping by Dahlquist's men in a trap set by Truscott. "John, I have come here with the full intention of relieving you from your command. You have reported to me that you held the high ground north of Montelimar and that you had blocked Highway 7. You have not done so. You have failed to carry out my orders. You have just five minutes in which to convince me that you are not at fault," wrote Truscott in his memoirs.[3]

Dahlquist explained that he had been given faulty field information when his troops had mistakenly taken a position on Hill 300 instead of a nearby hill that overlooked Highway 7.* Further, he pointed out, the enemy had cut his supply line at one point. But now he had four artillery battalions and a roadblock in place. The retreating Germans outnumbered Dahlquist's unit, but Dahlquist now held a strategic position to inflict maximum damage on the retreating enemy. Dahlquist believed that he had done as well as he could under the circumstances. Truscott wasn't fully convinced, but he left Dahlquist

---

* Hills and high points on military maps were named for their elevation. Along with precise coordinates and the twenty-four-hour clock, numbers were the universal language of military strategists.

in command. In Truscott's view, Dahlquist had allowed too much of the Germans' Nineteenth Army to escape.

By the middle of October, the VI Corps had pushed more than four hundred miles to the northeast and had reached the southern half of the Vosges Mountains. But now that same German army, commanded by an expert tactician, held the high ground. He had evaded Truscott's trap earlier with enough firepower to establish a line of resistance in the Vosges.

———◆———

THE GERMANS' GENERAL FRIEDRICH WIESE AGAIN STOOD IN THE way of Truscott, Dahlquist, Higgins, and Huberth. He had taken command of the severely undermanned Nineteenth Army only two months before the Allies came ashore on the Riviera. He had been ordered to prevent the Allies from landing along the four-hundred-mile coastline of southern France. Now his mission was to stop them in the Vosges.

Meticulous, analytical, and an expert in American battle tactics, Wiese had fought in World War I on the Eastern Front. After leaving the army to become a police officer, he returned to the military in 1935 to command a battalion in the 116th Infantry Regiment. Early in World War II he had been part of the Polish and then French campaigns and once again had fought on the Eastern Front. An adept battlefield tactician and enthusiastic National Socialist, his intense grayish-blue eyes, lean frame, and overall fitness made him a proto-typical Aryan officer who was both feared and respected. He had risen from battalion to army commander in only five years of war.

Wiese's primary asset in southern France had been a well-fortified coastline. Hundreds of concrete bunkers had been carved into hillsides. Nearly every approach to landing beaches was laced with crossfire emplacements. Thousands of mines had been laid in the surf. The Germans, however, had not made the same kind of commitment in the troops they had sent to southern France. Many units had received poorly trained reinforcements. Wiese inherited either inexperienced boys or unfit veterans from the Eastern Front, many of them captured Polish, Georgian, and Ukrainian soldiers who didn't speak German. Prisoners of war, foreigners, derelicts, and inexperience of recruits were the hallmarks of the German defense force. An exception was the 11th Panzer Division, known as the Ghost Division. It was renowned for its vicious fighting while enduring brutal losses in several battles on the Eastern Front. It had been transferred to southern France the month before Wiese arrived.

When he had taken command of the Nineteenth Army, Wiese had an estimated eight divisions plagued by critical shortages of fuel, transport, and other supplies. Some units relied on horse-drawn carts, wagons, and bicycles. After failing to prevent the Allies' amphibious landing, by mid-October he had ceded hundreds of miles of French territory. He had escaped with his makeshift army and was now entrenched in the Vosges Mountains.

HIGGINS, HUBERTH, KIMBLE, AND 272 MEN PREPARED FOR THE day's advance in bone-chilling rain early on October 24. Most carried only a day's supply of food and ammunition. Surely, rear-echelon supply personnel and the 141st's command post would keep up with their advance, even if it was into a forest that had little more than muddy logging roads and game trails.

At about the same time, another regiment in the 36th Division began to assemble near Belmont. The 442nd Regimental Combat Team and Higgins's 141st Infantry Regiment represented opposite ends of the American spectrum in 1944. The 141st held a familiar World War II lineage: a federally activated Texas National Guard unit intensely proud of its lineage. Meanwhile, the 442nd was the political creation of a segregated army and America. Commanded by

Caucasian officers, it comprised almost entirely Japanese American citizens, many of whom had been incarcerated in the months following Pearl Harbor only because of their heritage. Then, about a year later, young men like Jim Okubo, Barney Hajiro, and George Sakato were given the opportunity to volunteer to fight for their country. Some left families living in internment camps. Others said good-bye to families forced to vacate their West Coast homes and move in with friends or relatives in other states.

Less than two years earlier, Okubo had been supporting his Japanese American family by working for salmon fishermen in the Pacific Northwest before attending Western Washington University. His father operated a restaurant, and his mother sometimes assisted births in the neighborhood as a midwife. The generally reserved youngster had a quick, engaging smile that made him easily likable. He and his siblings had pledged allegiance to America every day in school. But that loyalty meant nothing to a vengeful America following Pearl Harbor.

On December 10, 1941, Federal Bureau of Investigation director J. Edgar Hoover sent President Franklin Delano Roosevelt a detailed report, illustrating where and how 1,212 Japanese Americans had been arrested in the two days following the Pearl Harbor attack. The letter provided no information on why the Japanese Americans had been arrested. While some advisers to President Roosevelt cautioned against falling victim to racial hysteria stoked by columnists such as Walter Lippmann, a campaign to incarcerate most of the West Coast's Japanese American citizens had ridden on a rising groundswell of hatred and vengeance in early 1942.

A *West Seattle Herald* editorial stated, "The government should initiate instant and drastic orders sweeping all aliens, foreign and native born, so far inland that we can forget about them for the duration [of the war]."[4] U.S. senator Harley Kilgore agreed when he wrote to President Roosevelt, "It is my sincere belief that the Pacific coast [sic] should be declared a military area which will give authority to treat residents, either aliens or citizens, as camp followers and put them under military law, permitting their removal, regardless of their citizenship rights, to internal and less dangerous areas."[5]

On February 19, 1942, President Roosevelt signed Executive Order 9066, authorizing the incarceration of more than 100,000 Japanese American citizens, mostly from the West Coast, in desolate internment camps in the wastelands of Arizona, California, Wyoming, Idaho, Utah, Colorado, and Arkansas. Dry lake beds, deserts, wind-swept prairies, and Indian land were appropriated. Truckloads of plywood, tarpaper, and barbed wire soon arrived in a race to build prison-like barracks for American citizens convicted of no crime. Within a few months, the West Coast was virtually cleared of Japanese American citizens.*

One morning in early April, posters had appeared on telephone poles, community bulletin boards, and storefronts in the Seattle area. Kenzo and Fuyu Okubo, along with Jim, eight brothers and sisters, and ten thousand other Japanese American citizens in Washington, had only a few weeks' notice to liquidate their lives. Their children were pulled out of school. Every working member of the family lost his or her job. The Okubos' possessions were reduced to a few suitcases. Everything else—personal belongings, family heirlooms, bulky valuables, clothing, even photo albums—was left behind. It was all in the custody of a sympathetic Caucasian neighbor, hastily sold at a fraction of its value, or simply abandoned.

Nearly all of the evictees had done nothing illegal, much less having had anything to do with Pearl Harbor. But America's simmering anti-Japanese sentiment that had festered since the turn of the century knew no bounds in early 1942. They had endured employment racism, school desegregation, and laws that prohibited real-estate ownership. At an assembly area, the Okubos learned they would be sent to a

---

*Japanese Americans constituted 40 percent of Hawaii's population. They were not forcibly relocated, as they were seen as less of a threat in view of the massive military presence in Hawaii. Plantation owners also vigorously opposed relocation because they relied heavily on Japanese American laborers.

hastily constructed camp in a nearly deserted and largely barren region of Northern California, a place of such abject desolation that America could easily pretend these neighbors had disappeared, perhaps forever. Thousands of American citizens were herded into community centers and county fairground buildings, hoping their families could remain together when they reached their final destination.

Overcrowded railroad cars carried the Okubos and hundreds of others under guard to Tule Lake, California, in May 1942. The collection of drafty wooden buildings that were twenty feet wide and one hundred feet long resembled a prison work camp. The Okubo family lived in a single five-hundred-square-foot room and was prohibited from cooking its own food. The federal government spent forty-five cents a day to feed each of them. Shortages abounded, including medical personnel. Jim Okubo learned the camp hospital was to be avoided at all costs. Keep the door closed in the family's war against dust. Take good notes in class because schoolbooks could not be taken to the barracks. Don't make trouble and bring shame on the Okubo family.

As the evictees coped with an uncertain future under confinement, a new debate developed in Washington, DC. Should Japanese Americans be allowed to volunteer for the army? Secretary of War Henry Stimson had vehemently opposed the idea, and a committee of senior officers wrote that "Japanese ancestry tends to place them in a most questionable light as to their loyalty." U.S. Army chief of staff George Marshall, however, would accept Japanese American volunteers. Others favored using Japanese Americans only to the extent that their language skills were required.

Nearly a year later, on February 1, 1943, President Roosevelt settled the matter when he authorized creation of the 442nd Regimental Combat Team. The president decreed:

> No loyal citizen of the United States should be denied the democratic right to exercise the responsibilities of his citizenship, regardless of his ancestry. The principle on which this country was founded and by which it has always been governed is that Americanism is a

matter of mind and heart; Americanism is not, and never was, a matter of race and ancestry. A good American is one who is loyal to his country and to the creed of liberty and democracy. Every loyal American citizen should be given an opportunity to serve his country wherever his skills will make the greatest contribution.[6]

He made no mention of America's incarceration of Japanese American citizens without due process. Jim Okubo and others could volunteer for a segregated combat unit open only to Japanese American soldiers that would be commanded mostly by "regular army" Caucasian officers.

Army recruiters in Hawaii were tasked with finding fifteen hundred Japanese American volunteers among the ashes of the attack on Pearl Harbor. An estimated ten thousand young men volunteered. On the mainland, Japanese American volunteers also easily exceeded their share of what the army needed for the four-thousand-man 442nd. Some were assigned to the Military Intelligence Service to become interpreters, interrogators, and analysts in the Pacific.

Jim Okubo had volunteered for his nation's army on May 20, ten days shy of his twenty-third birthday. After basic training at Camp Shelby, Mississippi, he was assigned to Company K, 3rd Battalion.* Nearly a year later, on May 1, 1944, the 442nd's 2nd and 3rd Battalions filled several transport ships at Hampton Roads, Virginia. On June 2 they arrived in Naples, and eight days later they joined the 100th Battalion near Rome. The 100th had been in battle for nine months and had earned a stellar reputation for bravery. In mid-June the 100th was attached to the 442nd as its 1st Battalion equivalent. It

---

*The 442nd was divided into multiple units. The Headquarters Company included command, antitank, medical, cannon, service, and officer units as well as the 232nd Combat Engineer Company. The 100th Battalion comprised Companies A–F. The 2nd Battalion comprised Companies E–H. The 3rd Battalion comprised Companies I–M. The 522nd Field Artillery Battalion was also attached to the 442nd.

retained its 100th designation, however, in recognition of its out-
standing combat record. That same day the 442nd was attached to
the 36th Infantry Division under Dahlquist's command.

Throughout the summer of 1944, battles continued day after day,
as the 442nd's battalions advanced north along the Italian coast, leap-
frogging one another, flanking German positions, and capturing Suv-
ereto, Belvedere, Pastina, Luciano, Sassetta, and Leghorn. The army
took notice and at its highest level decided to publicize their battle
record. "I have just been advised that action has been initiated in the
theater to obtain full press, still, and newsreel coverage of both Japanese American units now overseas. Several top writers have been assigned to features and stories on these units, and in addition the Army
Pictorial Service now has crews at the front with these units. Files will
be completed and shipped within the near future," wrote Colonel
Harrison Gerhardt in the secretary of war's office.[7]

Soon articles appeared in military and domestic newspapers. "From
a curious experiment the Army has received an unexpectedly rich re-
ward. A group of sinewy oriental soldiers only one generation removed
from a nation that was fighting fanatically against the U.S. was fighting just as fanatically for it," wrote one reporter.[8]

BETWEEN JUNE AND SEPTEMBER, JIM OKUBO HAD FOUGHT A
personal war against death. As a medic he had treated his first battle
wound within hours of his first firefight in Italy. Under enemy fire he
had learned to instantly assess a wounded man. He could identify the
sucking sound of a collapsed lung. He knew how to pack a wound
with sulfa, administer morphine, and tag the man so medics in the
rear would know he had been given a painkiller. Okubo had rou-
tinely raced onto the Italian battlefield under enemy fire, armed with
little more than plaster adhesive, scissors, bandages, iodine swabs, a
tourniquet, morphine syrettes, safety pins, and balm for burns.

Barney Hajiro was a member of Company I in the same 3rd Battalion and was typical of some of the young men in the 442nd who had been drafted. While some had volunteered out of a sense of patriotic duty, others like Hajiro had yet to find a purpose in life. The high school dropout possessed limited job skills and dim prospects before receiving his draft notice. He had grown up in a family so poor that he drank soda only on New Year's Day. He had spent his childhood on a sugar plantation in Hawaii. His parents worked ten-hour days in the fields for one dollar. They saved enough money to send him to a Japanese school, but in the eighth grade he had to drop out and work to help support the family.

At five-foot-seven, he was uncommonly tall and liked sports, especially the eight-hundred-meter run. He dreamed of running in the Olympics. But he had turned down a scholarship to high school in order to support his family. At twenty-one years of age, Hajiro had hitched an overnight ride on a cattle boat from Maui to Honolulu to find a job. Employment prospects were meager. He became a dishwasher and worked in a fish cannery during the summer. "Anything to survive," he later recalled.[9] Hajiro had watched Pearl Harbor fires burning in the hours following the attack.

Hajiro had been drafted into the army in early 1942. He was assigned first to an engineer unit. He was prohibited from carrying a weapon due to his ethnicity and had been ordered to dig ditches at an airfield. He hated it and volunteered for the 442nd at the first opportunity, in March 1943.

In basic training Hajiro had learned to fire the deadly but flawed Browning Automatic Rifle (BAR). Its thunderous recoil often made its operators flinch, reducing accuracy. He had discovered the BAR had a limited ammo capacity and that changing a damaged barrel was a slow, cumbersome process. Those were hardly ideal characteristics, as Hajiro had tried to imagine the difference between a training-camp firing range and perhaps a dozen unseen enemy soldiers firing back at him. In Italy Hajiro learned how to cut Germans apart with this BAR.

And he saw how his German counterpart could do the same to his friends.

Enemy fire melted some of the barriers between the Japanese American soldiers and their Caucasian officers. As the 442nd approached the Arno River, Hajiro saw a Caucasian military police officer in a street fight with an Italian. The short-tempered Hajiro joined the fray, throwing punches in defense of "someone I would never have helped if I had seen the same fight in New York City."[10] He was court-martialed for fighting with a civilian. It was his second conviction.

His first court-martial had come during training, when he fought with a cook who had refused to save some food until Hajiro completed his shift watching German prisoners harvest peanuts. He had hated life at Camp Shelby, especially the chiggers and poison ivy. He had been a messenger because of his running ability. Hajiro was heartbroken when his first court-martial included a transfer from friends in Company M to strangers in Company I and assignment as a BAR man for good measure. Now, after two months of fighting in Italy, Hajiro defended Caucasian police officers with his fists at the edge of enemy territory.

After crossing the Arno River on September 6, Okubo, Hajiro, and the rest of the 442nd had been pulled off the line. The bloodied regiment arrived in Naples by land and sea. They had been transported north to engage the retreating Germans and had driven them another forty miles back to the far side of the Arno River, near Florence, at an exorbitant price. Nearly 25 percent of the 442nd—more than twelve hundred men—had been killed or wounded in less than three months' fighting.

Replacements from Camp Shelby had soon joined them. Sometimes a replacement reminded a battle veteran of a buddy he had seen killed or carted off the battlefield only days earlier. One replacement was George Sakato. Named after a samurai, he had endured a sickly childhood while growing up in Colton, a railroad town in citrus country east of Los Angeles, at the foot of the San Bernardino Mountains. It seemed he caught every cold and flu bug, while his parents ran a pool hall and bathhouse (three tubs in a room behind two barber chairs).

Sakato hadn't been interested in much more than lunch and football as a boy. He had been held back a year in school, partly because he liked to ditch school with a friend and drive to Santa Monica or San Diego and then return by the end of the school day. After barely graduating high school, he went to work in a butcher shop. On December 7, 1941, he had turned on the shop's radio and learned of the attack on Pearl Harbor. "Oh my god, now what are we going to do?" he had asked no one in particular.[11]

He had tried to volunteer for the air corps six months earlier but ended up in the army. The thirty-day trip to Europe had wrenched his gut continuously.

———◆———

ON SEPTEMBER 25, OKUBO, HAJIRO, SAKATO, AND THOUSANDS of men boarded four troop transports in the Naples harbor. A small cadre of destroyers stood at anchor nearby, their crews building up steam for imminent departure. The weather had turned angry, the roiling sea pitching the armada to one side, then the other. For many like Sakato, the seasickness they had endured between America and Europe returned in an instant as they headed toward France.

Once they landed near Marseille, they loaded onto cramped and wet boxcars that carried the 442nd north into a land of destruction. Years of German occupation, followed by the American assault from the French Riviera, had turned a serene land of forests, farms, and countless villages—each with a steeple that had dominated the community's horizon and life for centuries—into a gray, barren, and charred landscape.

It had become a broken land. Mangled vehicles, shattered farm carts, and bloated animals turned black by fall's rain and cold littered farm fields. Those fields still in production had been stripped of their wheat and corn. Many trees in the blocks of forest that often separated one field from another had been sheared off high above the ground by artillery air bursts. Stone barns that had stood for generations now opened to the sky, their roofs collapsed and blackened by direct artillery strikes.

It was a land that had been gutted by war, its energy drained by endless destruction. As the 442nd approached Epinal, on the Moselle River, foothills rose from the farming country. Here, the ridges became more pronounced and farm fields more compact, as the Vosges Mountains began to dominate the landscape. On October 15 the 442nd detrained and reentered combat, joining the campaign to capture two key railroad towns, Bruyères and Belmont, on the drive toward the German border.

Men in the 442nd again demonstrated remarkable bravery in a new kind of war. Italy's expansive terrain had given way to dense and darkened French forests. Combat bordered on hand-to-hand among the trees. Mud and relentless rain made trench foot a potential enemy. Suffocating cloud cover was another, preventing air support when the 442nd needed it most. Yet time and time again, the 442nd achieved its objectives, often on the backs of individual bravery.

The day after Bruyères fell, Hajiro stood sentry duty on an embankment when the ground around him exploded with sniper fire. Rather than dive for cover, Hajiro intentionally drew more enemy fire to his exposed position so others could spot the Germans' location. Hajiro managed to shoot 2 snipers and enabled the unit on his right to eliminate the rest of the German threat. Someone in Hajiro's unit marveled at his bravery and later jotted down a few notes, describing his feat. A few days later, Hajiro and another soldier had dug in to protect their platoon's right flank. They heard German voices. They waited as the voices approached. Hajiro took a deep, calming breath before he ambushed the 18-man enemy patrol. He killed 2, wounded another, and took 15 prisoners, nearly single-handedly.

After nine days of combat and the recent ridge attack, the 442nd had looked forward to several days' rest. The regiment had lost one-third of its fighting strength since arriving near Bruyères. One company in the 100th Battalion had only 15 men left, compared to an authorized strength of approximately 180. Its commander and all its platoon leaders had been killed or wounded. On October 24 the 442nd needed to regroup, resupply, and maybe enjoy a hot shower in nearby Laval.

A FEW MILES TO THE EAST, MARTIN HIGGINS AND THE REST OF the 1/141 climbed out of their foxholes on the morning of October 24. Bone-weary men stretched as the forest lightened. Most had tried to sleep in shallow craters scraped between roots and rocks. They had dozed in wet uniforms, made stiff by caked mud and minor wounds. An invisible enemy waited, perhaps within shouting distance. The lead scouts in all three companies would have to separate innocent forest features from enemy positions. A gray boulder barely visible through the trees ahead might conceal a sniper. A shallow ravine would be good cover for a machine-gun team. A nearly invisible game trail may be laced with land-mine tripwires. They would know with certainty when they stood, fully exposed, and advanced toward their enemy's crosshairs.

Colonel Oran Stovall, commanding officer of the 36th Division's 111th Engineer Battalion, had already scouted the planned route of advance and didn't like what he had found. The narrow ridge posed significant logistical problems for those units that would be following the 1st Battalion. "I took Lieutenant Beahler and an infantry patrol of four men to make recon[noiter] of the area," Stovall wrote later. "I started with one man on the trail in front of me, one on either flank and Beahler and one man in the rear as getaway men. The underbrush became so thick the flankers could not keep up so I pulled them into

the road." Although Dahlquist had told him, "There are no 'bosch'
[Germans] up there," Stovall's patrol came under long-range enemy
artillery fire. Surely, there had to be at least some German spotters in
the forest. "I then reported to the General [Dahlquist] . . . that the
attack could be supported if nothing larger than a light tank company
was involved."[12]

Companies B and C took the lead, with Company A trailing by
about five hundred yards. Again the forest seemed too quiet. More
than 250 men crept forward, from tree to tree, scanning the forest
ahead for unnatural or inconsistent movements, shapes, colors, and
lines, knowing that almost nothing in nature is truly horizontal or
vertical. Sight lines changed with every soft step and by the slightest
crouch. The dense underbrush forced squads onto game trails and
nearly invisible paths. They advanced, slowly, and found only enemy
litter. "The trail was littered with all sorts of German equipment—
guns, helmets, gas masks, packs—that they [had] discarded on the
way," recalled Sergeant Bill Hull. "We didn't know the Germans
were as strong as they were because all that discarded equipment gave
our battalion commander the wrong idea about their strength."[13]

At one point during the advance, enemy fire confused the 1st Battalion. It appeared someone in street clothes was firing at the advancing units. Were French civilians firing at the Americans? Frantic radio
traffic to regimental headquarters indicated that it appeared members
of the French Resistance were attacking the 1st Battalion. The French
Resistance, called the FFI (Forces Françaises de l'Intérieur), was critical to Allied operations as they pushed through France in 1944. FFI
members wore civilian clothes and carried their own weapons in guer-
rilla campaigns against the Germans. It didn't make sense that the FFI
was now attacking the Allies. Division headquarters responded, specu-
lating the enemy fire may be coming from French civilians who supported the Germans. Or perhaps it was from Germans wearing civilian
clothes. Regardless, all three companies of the 1/141 were taking serious enemy fire toward the end of the long ridge, miles from the nearest reinforcements.

By midday they had advanced nearly another mile and had passed Col de la Croisette, a critical crossroads of trails with the main logging road. It would have been a perfect place for the Germans to ambush the Americans. About eight hours later, Companies A and C were nearing the end of the ridge that overlooked the valley below. Company B was a short distance behind. Incredibly, they had advanced nearly six miles from the point where they had left the Belmont valley and had climbed up on the ridge. There had been some German resistance, but in a little more than twenty-four hours they had nearly reached an objective that had looked ominously distant on the briefing map.

But then the forest exploded with enemy fire. Men fell as Company A's Higgins and Company C's Kimble yelled orders over the sounds of gunfire to fall back as Huberth's Company B caught up.

By this time Dahlquist had arrived at regimental headquarters, several miles to the west. He had told regimental command not to worry about counterattacks by Germans approaching the ridge from the northeast. He had the 3rd Infantry Regiment in place to prevent that. But Higgins's, Kimble's, and Huberth's men were taking fire from multiple directions. Lieutenant Colonel Bird ordered light tanks forward. Within minutes Bird's command post shuddered as German artillery began pounding his location. Not only were the three companies on the point taking serious fire, but now the battalion's command post more than a mile to the rear was under attack. Bird asked Dahlquist for more tanks as the fighting intensified.

Dahlquist had planned for the 1/141 to dig in for the night at 1700 hours. But the Germans' attack unraveled the general's plans. Radio communications had been sporadic during the surprise attack. He didn't know how many casualties the three companies had suffered. Regimental and division headquarters would have to wait for a radioman at the far end of the ridge to report how many men had been killed, whether any were missing, and how many men lay wounded on litters or the ground.

Tanks had been brought forward, but the forest was so dense that they provided little support. Largely for the same reason, American artillery could do little to suppress enemy fire where the 1/141 had been ambushed. Engineers were repairing and strengthening the eroded logging road so reinforcements and supplies could be brought forward, but that was going to take some time. Dahlquist's tactical options were limited. A single battalion had advanced too far and too fast in a dense old-growth forest that gave every advantage to the defenders, some of whom had been dug in for weeks, waiting.

At about 1615 radio traffic ceased for perhaps two hours, as the three companies dug in for the night. It was a perfect time for the Germans to launch a concentrated attack. An enemy force moved into the forest along a trail to the northeast. They attacked Huberth's and Kimble's companies near Hill 645. Higgins's Company A moved forward to join the fight. While the 3rd Infantry Regiment may have protected the 1st Battalion's northern flank, the enemy had launched the attack from the valley to the south. At about the same time, German artillery pounded the 1st Battalion's command post, several miles to the west. Now Dahlquist faced the prospect of the 1st Battalion being decimated. As the forest darkened, the enemy had herded the 1/141 onto a single hilltop, and its artillery had forced the 1/141's command post to retreat farther away from Higgins's, Huberth's, and Kimble's men. Dahlquist needed a situation report from the far end of the ridge.

Meanwhile, Higgins, Kimble, and Huberth gathered their forces on a relatively sparsely wooded hilltop. One of their first priorities was to create an aid station in the relatively flat forest that offered no natural cover other than trees. A crater would have to be dug, large enough for several men, to give medics and the wounded some semblance of protection from enemy fire and the elements. A night's brutal cold could prove deadly to the wounded. Perhaps the wounded could be evacuated in the dark? Three teams of litter bearers were sent in the general direction of where the battalion's command post had been. They were attacked and returned to the three companies' position, along with the wounded they carried.

The battalion's next priority was resupply. A day's fighting had depleted ammo, and soldiers generally didn't carry much more than a day's worth of food. Called K rations, they consisted mostly of canned food, biscuits, dried coffee, and cigarettes.

Another small patrol was dispatched, in search of a potential supply route that might have escaped the Germans' notice. They met enemy resistance almost immediately and returned. Was the 1/141 fully cut off? Higgins sent a third patrol to be sure. When two men stepped on land mines, the remainder returned. Resupply routes were blocked, and the number of wounded men was mounting by the hour. Higgins knew the three companies were trapped near the far end of the ridge.

The situation was dire. The surrounded battalion had no immediate prospect of retreat, and the position of any potential reinforcements was unknown. They had been isolated on a hill with the enemy on three sides, pinning them against a steep drop-off. Battalion and division commands knew their location, so they weren't lost in a literal sense. But they stood a very good chance of being lost as casualties or perhaps as prisoners of war. If the 1/141 could not be relieved quickly, Dahlquist would have to mount a rescue mission if he was to avoid losing an entire battalion in the dash toward Germany.

That night the men of the 1/141 sat, lay, or crouched in a relatively thinly wooded area on the ridge that overlooked the German-held valley to the south. Higgins had already lost ten men who had been killed by the enemy. Germany artillery during the coming night would kill three more.

Not far away was a primitive crossing known as Le Trapin des Saules. In local slang it meant "Trap of the Willows." According to a German soldier who had been captured, the Germans knew the Americans' battle plan. The advance along a narrow ridge had been an ideal opportunity to trap any American unit by lying in wait and then closing in behind it. The trap had been executed perfectly by the Germans. They now had a battalion in their grip.

Higgins's men who weren't wounded were exhausted. Their final message that night to division command summed up their plight: "No rations, no water, no communications with battalion headquarters, four litter cases."[14]

The Germans had allowed them to advance too far in front of the rest of the 36th Division. Then at dusk they had closed in behind 275 American soldiers and cut them off from headquarters and re-supply. Higgins, Huberth, and Kimble could only speculate when the next enemy attack would come.

CHAPTER 2

BACK TO THE FRONT

A SINGLE CANDLE FLICKERED IN THE HORSE STALL OF A BARN NEAR the Bruyères cemetery. The cold air smelled of wet straw and horse manure as ten men held crumpled papers close to their faces. The letters carried them away from the persistent rain to another world. To a place where mothers worried. For some, to a place where wives tended their children. And where the water was hot and where beds held clean sheets. Sergeant John Kashiki read his, eager for news from Mary, his wife of less than two years.

Kashiki was a member of the 442nd's cannon company. As a young man he had run the family farm in Holtville in the desert east of San Diego after his father had fallen ill. He was a student at the University of California–Davis studying agronomy and economics when he and his family were sent to a relocation center in Arizona. He had volunteered for the 442nd in 1943 after he married Mary. She was pregnant with their second child when he shipped overseas. When Mary's thirty letters were handed to him in Bruyères on October 25, he wondered if his daughter, Judi, now had a brother or sister. Mary numbered her daily letters so he could read them in order. The first one reported no birth, quite yet.

Hundreds of other 442nd soldiers also eagerly absorbed their news from home. Nearly all of the 442nd's units had been placed in reserve to rest in the area surrounding Bruyères and Belmont. A primitive shuttle system had been established to transport handfuls of men back to another nearby town, Laval, for a precious hot shower and clean clothes. Laval was safer than the 442nd's service (supply) area near Bruyères, which was getting shelled by German artillery. Blackout conditions were in effect, so Kashiki and nine others huddled around the candle, even though they were supposed to be dispersed when within range of the enemy. News from home easily trumped army regulations.

Bruyères had been liberated by the Americans seven days earlier. The town of three thousand residents had suffered through German occupation since June 22, 1940, and then near-constant artillery fire and house-to-house combat as the Americans approached in October. Bruyères is located on a broad plateau at sixteen hundred feet in elevation directly in the path of the American 36th Division's assault through the Vosges. Four of seven heavily wooded hills at the town's edge had seen fierce and costly fighting as the Americans and Germans alternated control of each. Shrapnel gashes from grenades, mortars, and artillery on light poles, churches, schools, and the town hall bore witness to its strategic value as a railroad center and gateway into the Vosges. The two main thoroughfares, rues Grande and J. Ferry, were littered with roofs blasted off homes and buildings turned to rubble by direct hits. None of that mattered to those lucky enough to have letters from home handed to them in the war zone, even though some may have been written more than a month earlier.

Tattered troop transports, supply trucks, and jeeps rolled into Bruyères, Belmont, and the surrounding farms with replacement troops for all three battalions resting there. The new faces reminded battle-weary veterans of buddies who had died only a few days earlier. While some of the losses had been strangers, far more difficult to accept were the grisly deaths of friends. Some wondered if they could possibly forge the same level of trust with the newcomers who had yet to see a German sniper draw a bead on them or who had not yet survived a blizzard of shrapnel. Some men thought back to how suddenly death had come.

About a week earlier George Sakato had been chatting with Yohei Sagami. They talked about what they would do when they got home. What they would eat and who they would see. Only a few months earlier, Sakato had left his family in Poston, Arizona, for basic training, where he was a poor marcher and a worse shooter. His family had avoided internment by moving to Arizona and staying with a farming family. They slept on the family's back porch, picked cantaloupe in the blistering Arizona summer sun, and plowed farm fields at night. Although Sakato had lost thirty-five pounds as a farmworker, it was better than internment. He had earned a little extra money by sneaking cases of bootlegged liquor into the nearby Poston internment camp.

Sakato and Sagami ended their conversation when their unit moved out and soon engaged the enemy. Only minutes into the fighting, Sakato had heard the "vroom" of an incoming shell for only a second before it exploded yards away, knocking him off his feet. Stunned, he looked around. Sagami was lying facedown. Sakato turned him over. Blood pulsed out of Sagami's neck. "Medic!" Sakato pressed his hand against the side of Sagami's throat to avoid choking his friend. A medic slid to a stop next to Sagami. He tore open bandages as Sagami's blood tapped against Sakato's palm and then trickled through his dirt-encrusted fingers onto the ground. Sagami died where he fell.* It had been Sakato's first day in battle.

Replacements arrived from the rear and looked for their unit's commanding officer. The sheer numbers of men new to combat drove home just how many soldiers had been lost in the preceding days of the campaigns to capture Bruyères, Belmont, and Biffontaine. The 100th had lost 21 killed in action, 122 were wounded, and 18 had been captured. The number of newcomers, however, fell short of

---

* Like thousands of other Japanese American soldiers, Sagami's family was forcibly relocated to an internment camp in Idaho. Government death-notification letters to his father and brother, both living in the camp, offered no details of how Yohei died. A half century later, Sakato became close friends with the Sagami family.

returning the 442nd's combat units to full strength. The 442nd would have to enter combat without nearly enough men necessary to face the enemy that was waiting for them.

The only good news was that the beleaguered 442nd would be given a few days to recover and assimilate their replacements. That was especially vital because the losses suffered in the region had included some men who commanded extraordinary respect and trust among the men in foxholes. Some were officers who had led daring and dangerous assaults in Italy and then again in France. The loss of those men represented not just a loss in manpower but also a loss in leadership and morale. One was a Korean, Young Oak Kim.

Young Oak Kim had joined the 100th Battalion at Camp Shelby, Mississippi, in early 1943 after graduating from officer candidate school. He had been raised in a family whose alcoholic father, an illegal immigrant to the United States in 1906, had hated the Japanese for occupying Korea. Kim was a quiet, hardworking boy in a family on the brink of poverty and one that endured frequent anti-Korean discrimination in Los Angeles. He had enlisted in 1941 at the age of twenty-five, shortly before his father died of liver cancer. Kim had started military life as a mechanic before his leadership skills and photographic memory made him a candidate to become an officer.

At Camp Shelby his orders were to train Japanese American recruits for combat as the 100th Battalion. He had been offered a transfer to another outfit, given the historic and deep-seated animosity between the Koreans and Japanese, but he refused. He inherited an unfit, poorly disciplined unit in which Japanese Americans from Hawaii thought their counterparts from the States were too Americanized. Meanwhile, the Stateside Japanese Americans openly taunted the Hawaiians over their pidgin English. At first his recruits called him *yeobo*. In English it meant "darling," so to use it with a superior officer was an intentional insult.

The living conditions at Camp Shelby had been primitive at best. Young men new to the army slept in quarters made of moldy plywood and damp tarpaper. Swamp life sickened many who missed their rice diet and gagged at the sight of beef liver or tongue. Many made peanut-butter–and-jelly sandwiches and a piece of fruit as their standard meal. The training was worse. Four- and five-mile marches through swamps teeming with mosquitoes, chiggers, leeches, and wood ticks sapped the strength and stamina of the slightly built Nisei.* Suffocating humidity threatened to choke exhausted soldiers wearing full combat gear that weighed as much as seventy-five pounds. Infantrymen often carried two hundred rounds of ammunition, enough for one day's fighting. Other gear included K rations for one day, a first-aid kit, a trenching tool, a full canteen, a mess kit, a blanket, and personal items such as a toothbrush, razor, and soap powder. Letters from home were wedged into a helmet's lining, while diaries and cameras were forbidden for fear of their falling into the enemy's hands. Under Kim's tutelage, they had learned how to properly pack gear that could weigh nearly half as much as they did.

After landing at Salerno, Italy, Kim and the 100th Battalion had entered combat for the first time against the Germans' Tenth Army on September 29, 1943. On his first day in battle, Kim had refused an order to send his troops directly into enemy positions. He suggested alternative routes less deadly and more effective. But it was the 100th's first firefight. Japanese Americans could not be seen as cowardly, so his men convinced Kim they should advance into enemy fire as ordered. The word spread. Kim had his men's interest at heart.

In the following months, he became known as "Samurai Kim" for his courage in the Italian campaign. On one patrol he encountered four enemy machine-gun nests, each time intentionally taking fire so the Germans could be spotted and counterattacked. He earned the

---

*A Nisei is a Japanese American born in the United States whose parents (Issei) are immigrants from Japan.

Silver Star that day. On another, he followed a German night patrol on his belly approximately eight hundred yards back to its camp in German-held territory. He hid, waited until sunrise, took two Germans prisoner, and crawled back under barbed wire and between enemy listening posts to his unit's position with his prisoners without being seen. That day he earned the Distinguished Service Cross.

Kim's courage, serenity under fire, innate battlefield intelligence, and idiosyncrasies became widely recognized. He risked a fifty-dollar fine for wearing a knit cap instead of a helmet, so he could "think straight." He disdained foxholes. If it was his fate to die, he would accept it where he stood or slept. He also had the odd habit of unnecessarily skipping meals.

Kim's hand had been severely mangled by a sniper on October 22 in the assault to take Biffontaine. Kim thought it a worthless mission, because it had taken his men off a ridge to capture a town of debatable value. It was the same ridge that the 1/141 would be ordered to secure the following day. That night 100th Battalion chaplain Israel Yost encouraged him to fight, as significant blood loss and shock gripped Kim.

He made it through the night. The next morning Lieutenant Jimmie Kanaya, other medics, and nearly forty German prisoners of war formed a litter team to carry Kim and ten other wounded men to a field hospital away from enemy fire. Kanaya, a former mechanic from Pontiac, Michigan, had received a battlefield commission after earning a Silver Star in his first week in combat in Italy three months earlier. The medic had crawled into intense enemy fire to treat nine badly wounded men for more than two hours. A week later he had earned a Bronze Star for walking up a road into enemy fire to find and treat a soldier who had been shot and then rolled down an embankment.

"Let's hang back," Kanaya told some of the other medics. He didn't like the idea of a long line of stretchers, carried by Germans and guarded by Americans, stretching more than one hundred yards, crossing enemy territory on its way to an American field hospital. "We'll be the last ones through. Let them go first and see what happens."[1]

As they crested a hill, a German patrol of about thirty-five men spotted them. An intense standoff resulted, as each side ordered the other to surrender. But the Americans were outnumbered and out-gunned. In the initial confusion, Kim and another medic slipped into nearby bushes. Kanaya stayed with the remaining wounded. As Kim made his way west toward an American field hospital, German sol-diers led Kanaya and the rest of the American prisoners east toward a prisoner-of-war camp.

Now all three battalions of the 442nd had to set aside the loss of veterans like Kim and Kanaya, men who had led them into combat and men they knew would be at their side if they fell wounded. Ru-mors of Germany surrendering by Christmas now seemed no more than idle hope, given the enemy's stiffening resistance in the Vosges. If the Germans were fighting as hard across Europe as they were in the Vosges, a brutal war of attrition might last forever. But at least the 442nd could rest and recover from the price it had paid in recent days.

———— ◦)◦ ————

ABOUT SIX MILES AWAY ON OCTOBER 25, THE PREDAWN CLOUDS that cloaked the forest lightened slightly at Col des Huttes, a stretch of forest about fifteen hundred yards from the end of the ridge. After assigning lookouts, all three companies of the 1/141 had dug in late the previous night. They had yet to reach their objective, and the fighting the day before indicated they may have advanced far into enemy positions designed to entrap rather than delay and fall back. *How could they be sure?*

Higgins's Company A got to its feet and moved back along the trail they had used the day before. They needed to make sure the trail was clear for reinforcements and supplies. Perhaps they could make it nine hundred yards back to Col de la Croisette, the junction of several logging roads. Meanwhile, Huberth and Kimble led Companies B and C farther east. They were taking a chance, splitting the 1/141 into two groups nearly a mile apart. But their two objectives overruled caution. They had to protect their rear and also reach their objective at the end of the ridge.

Company A had barely gotten under way when once again enemy fire ripped into it. Exhausted soldiers dived to the ground, crouched behind trees, and returned fire. Dozens of trees had been cut to fall across the logging road, and they had probably been mined by the Germans during the night. One of Higgins's men was killed and another wounded before he pulled them back toward Companies B and C, ultimately consolidating the battalion in the same area where it had spent the night.

They were trapped. Germans had closed in behind them to the west the night before and built at least one roadblock. The enemy was dug in to the north, and the forest precariously dropped off to the south to the valley that still held German infantry units, tanks, and artillery. The 1st Battalion led by five lieutenants had been advancing and fighting on the trail for a little more than twenty-four hours. They had advanced approximately six miles before entering the German net. Now their casualties were mounting, as the Germans had trapped them on a small rise in the forest. The enemy roadblock would stop any easy reinforcement or resupply attempt from the west. When the battalion's radioman contacted headquarters, he was assured that a "friendly force" would be coming. But that didn't matter to the lieutenants who found themselves in charge. Decisions had to be made. Quickly.

The senior men in the group gathered: Higgins, Huberth, Kimble, First Lieutenant Gordon Nelson of the weapons company, and Second Lieutenant Erwin Blonder, forward artillery observer. Although junior to the other four lieutenants, Higgins was elected to make the command decisions, with Huberth second in command. Higgins would be responsible for this beleaguered, understrength battalion that had already suffered major losses. Higgins was the only Company A officer left from when it had come ashore in France two months earlier.

Higgins and Huberth made an unusual pair. Higgins had been a tempestuous Irish kid living in a clearly defined New Jersey ethnic neighborhood. Huberth was the son of a well-to-do German commercial and residential real estate manager for the Hearst Corporation raising a family in Scarsdale, New York. Huberth had traveled to South America and France. In Huberth's household, the family always ate together, and attending an Episcopal church was mandatory. Higgins had attended neighborhood schools, while Huberth had been sent to a private school with a stable nearby. He cleaned stalls and groomed and exercised horses before attending college as a social science and history major. Huberth had grown to admire Higgins's Irish sense of humor, calm demeanor, and steel nerves under fire. Both had developed a deep respect for each other as well as self-confidence.

Higgins placed decisiveness as the most important quality of a leader. "You tell the men to do something. You don't stand there looking puzzled. You can lead a company one of two ways. You can lead them or push them from the rear. I led and Harry Huberth led," Higgins recalled years later. That self-confidence had been instilled in Higgins by his parents throughout his boyhood. Huberth had witnessed Higgins's confidence and "steel nerves" as his immense respect for Higgins developed under enemy fire. "You don't bond with a man until after you've looked at him. It happens because you see what he is made of. He is not afraid. He will stand up for you. You know you can trust him. That comes from actual experience under fire," said Huberth after the war.[2]

Higgins knew he had to establish a defensible position for his men. He set a .30-caliber machine gun at each end and at various points along a 350-yard oval perimeter. The easternmost was manned by Sergeant Jack Wilson and the other by Staff Sergeant Bruce Estes. Harold Buchheim was assigned a third light machine-gun post, and a fourth was positioned to guard what appeared to be the only nearby water source. Higgins placed the bulk of his men in a belt of foxholes to protect against enemy advances from the west, north, and east. The precipitous drop-off on the south required fewer foxholes to defend. Higgins didn't have a large-enough force to secure the water hole. He and Huberth would have to devise a plan to send patrols to get water if their men's supplies ran low.*

Higgins had an array of firepower at his disposal: 81mm mortars, heavy automatic rifles, M1 rifles, .30-caliber carbine rifles, six light machine guns, and bazookas distributed among the three companies and a weapons platoon. A few months earlier, Higgins had developed a particular appreciation for the weapons platoon. He had bucked standard army doctrine by moving his weapons platoon from the rear to the front, in order to lay down suppressing fire to protect the rest of the unit when it first met the enemy. His weapons platoon was now positioned to play a similar role when the inevitable German attack came. But Higgins couldn't predict the Germans' available firepower. Additional enemy reinforcements may have arrived during the night.

His men were huddled together in an area the size of a few football fields, and they were stationary targets for German artillery. Higgins needed every advantage he could manufacture. He established an observation post in front of each company with sound-powered telephones linked to Higgins's command post. He also established listening posts about one hundred yards in front of each of the platoons he had positioned along the perimeter. The posts were hardwired back to his foxhole command post, giving him 360-degree sound-surveillance capability. The listening posts would track and report German movements for Higgins so he could request American artillery strikes onto their positions. While the 1/141 was outnumbered and short on firepower, at least it would not be surprised when the inevitable attack came.

Meanwhile, his men pulled folding shovels and knives out of backpacks to chip and scrape as deep into the muddy forest floor as

---

* Experts question whether a muddy water hole on the crest today is the same as the one Higgins's men used in 1944. Today's bog is too close to American foxholes to be considered outside Higgins's perimeter. It's more likely there was another water hole more distant in the forest at that time.

possible. Slit trenches afforded minimal protection, so if they could somehow dig deeper foxholes on both sides of the logging road that bisected their position, they might elude deadly shrapnel. Sometimes massive roots or boulders stopped them cold, forcing them to shift a few feet to one side or the other and then resume digging. Breaks came only when they flopped onto their bellies when a new round of enemy artillery arrived.

To the east the 36th Division and 141st Regimental headquarters had mobilized efforts to relieve the trapped battalion. A bombing mission was planned for 0900. The targets were south and east of the surrounded battalion, along routes enemy reinforcements likely would take if the Germans planned to press their advantage against Higgins's troops. Shortly thereafter, several American units would be sent to the edge of the forest north and south of the surrounded battalion to prevent enemy troops from entering the forest from the valleys below. Dahlquist couldn't let the Germans bring more troops into the battle. When the bombers approached the drop zone at 0830, they would receive the latest reports on the location of American troops advancing toward the 1st Battalion to make sure they didn't bomb the relief units.

About the time Company A returned to the other two companies, it became apparent that the relief would not reach the companies' position anytime soon. Enemy machine-gun nests had blocked the advance of both the 2nd and the 3rd Battalions of the 141st. The 2nd Battalion reported that it was taking direct artillery hits. "It [is] believed that the enemy has an observation post along the trail as a great deal of artillery was falling in the sector," summarized an after-action report. Supply units had also been halted by the Germans more than one thousand yards from Higgins's men. Some units remained more than two thousand yards from the stranded men.

At midmorning the commanding officer of the 141st, Colonel Carl Lundquist, delivered a bleak report to the 36th Division's chief of staff, Colonel Charles Owens. Both the 2nd and the 3rd/141 were taking heavy fire. A German force of company strength had pinned down a unit of the 3rd Battalion, comprising mostly replacement soldiers, led by Technical Sergeant Charles Coolidge. He had the nerve to demand the Germans surrender. They opened fire in response and pinned Coolidge's unit to a cluster of trees in the forest.

The Americans brought four light and four medium tanks forward, but the Germans were pounding the American armor and other vehicles as they moved up the trail toward the battle. Owens told Lundquist to bring up the remaining seven tanks in reserve. Already the heavy and armored vehicles were destroying the one marginal logging road, just as Colonel Stovall had predicted. Two battalions, a tank company, supply units, and heavy road-building equipment committed to the rescue mission overwhelmed the primitive roads leading to Higgins's men. They bounced from one muddy rut to another on the logging road as they avoided the litter jeeps that were ferrying wounded men back to field hospitals.

Lundquist had been in command of the regiment in combat for less than a month when confronted with the potential loss of an entire battalion that morning. Like Dahlquist, the forty-year-old Michigan native with jet-black hair and a matching pencil-thin mustache had been a planner. He had spent the previous year as the chief of the Plans Division, G-3 in the European Theater of Operations. He had planned combat missions. Now, for the first time, he held operational combat responsibility. His most immediate decisions could determine the fate of the stranded men and whether he could demonstrate to his superior officers that he could effectively lead men in combat.

But Lundquist couldn't deploy all his tactical combat and support units if he couldn't get them where they were needed. A timber-and-gravel road capable of supporting a constant stream of multiton vehicles would have to be constructed on top of the forest-floor muck if the division's heavy assets were to join the battle. Two rocky sections of the forest were spotted, converted into gravel pits, and heavy equipment moved in to dig them up. American personnel arrived at sawmills near Bruyères and Belmont and appropriated their inventories of plank boards. Vehicles labored up the rutted roads, weighed down by stacks of planks strapped to their hoods, roofs, and beds. Crews with saws inventoried the stands of timber alongside the primitive main road and began cutting down hundreds of relatively young trees, most with trunks twelve to eighteen inches in diameter. As sections of the road inevitably would fail under the endless traffic, they would have to be rebuilt immediately with stockpiled gravel and precut timber.

On the front line, progress by the remaining battalions of the 141st was agonizingly slow and in some cases nonexistent. The 2nd and 3rd Battalions reported stiff enemy resistance throughout the day, and by midafternoon it had already become clear that more manpower and firepower would be necessary to reach the trapped battalion.

At 1450 the 2/442 was officially attached to the 141st, as Lundquist finalized plans for a renewed assault at 1600. He now had three combat battalions under his command to reach the 1/141st. He also wanted his tanks to attempt a breakthrough in the dense forest, loaded with supplies for the surrounded troops. Lundquist hoped the addition of the 2/442 and tanks would push the Germans back. But if the tanks couldn't blast a path to the 1st Battalion, Company L would take the point in the infantry's push toward Higgins's men. Each man in the company carried an extra two bandoliers of ammunition and an additional canteen full of water for the stranded battalion. It was unclear how Company L could accomplish that, given the minimal ground that had been gained after several hours' fighting. The 1st Battalion would soon be critically low on food, drinkable water, medical supplies, and ammunition. The Americans needed to reach them quickly, by any means possible.

———◦———

LIEUTENANT GENERAL ALEXANDER PATCH'S JEEP WOVE THROUGH the exhausted soldiers of the 442nd on the winding streets of Belmont. Some looked like they had aged years in the past week. Those on their feet trudged—almost shuffled from exhaustion—up the slop-ing streets, kicking dislodged bricks and stone chunks aside. Many sat shoulder-to-shoulder against scarred buildings, their legs splayed across the sidewalk, a cigarette hanging precariously from the corners of their mouths. Rifles leaned gun-barrel up on the brick buildings. A few men lay on their backs on cobblestone streets, their feet rolled outward, their bedrolls pressed against the curb as a temporary pillow. Mutt Sakumoto and others played poker and chain-smoked.

Patch was brokenhearted as he considered sending the 442nd back into battle sooner than expected. Only a few days earlier, on October 22, his only son, Captain Alexander Patch III, had been killed in an assault against entrenched German positions. The general knew that he was about to send dozens, maybe hundreds, of men to the same fate.

When Generals Patch and Dahlquist walked into the 442nd's command post, Colonel Charles Pence, commanding officer of the 442nd, braced for new orders. At fifty years of age, he was literally considered "the old man" by a regiment whose average age was less than half that. Pence had commanded the 442nd from its inception. Pence had served in China on an army mission about ten years earlier when Manchuria had been occupied by the Japanese. His superior officers considered him an expert on Far East cultures. One historian noted that Pence had spent more time in Asia than nearly all of the Nisei he commanded.

Pence had attended Depauw University in Indiana, where the 140-pounder had been the captain of the football team and senior class president. A natural athlete, nicknamed "Six Pence," he had also played basketball and baseball before leaving college a year early to fight in World War I. He had been wounded in Europe. He still looked like a football player, with a dimpled square jaw, crewcut, and furrowed brow that deepened when his men didn't measure up to his standards.

His executive officer, Virgil Miller, had joined him in June 1943. Miller was quicker to smile and more engaging, and he favored a bright-colored ascot. They were an effective leadership tandem, as neither tolerated discrimination, expected the Nisei to perform like any other soldier, and had their men's welfare at heart.

Pence and Miller had crafted innovative ways to build unity between the Hawaiian-born and U.S.-born recruits and volunteers. In basic training at Camp Shelby, the Hawaiian-born soldiers had a hard time understanding why young men on the mainland had volunteered for the 442nd from internment camps. Pence and Miller arranged a field trip for the men during basic training to a nearby internment camp in Arkansas to build a common bond between the two Nisei groups.

Interned families had saved a week's rations so they could host a proper party for their uniformed visitors. Guards armed with rifles watched from their guard towers. After the Hawaiians of the 100th saw the conditions in which mainland Japanese American families lived, they returned to Camp Shelby in a bus that was eerily quiet. What they thought would be a liberty lark had instead sobered them. A newfound respect developed for the Nisei from the mainland who had volunteered potentially to die for the same country that had incarcerated their families.

Some, including future U.S. senator Daniel Inouye, were humbled. "Would I have volunteered from that camp?" he wondered years later.[3] Another Hawaiian recruit was equally humbled in a letter he wrote to his family: "These guys [mainland Japanese Americans] have been pushed around too much and they feel that no one give a dam [*sic*] for them. Have they anywhere to go after the war? Have they any faith in democracy and tolerance? These fellers' spirit is broken. They might be smart, but their guiding principle is to look out for themselves."[4]

But by late 1943, Pence and Miller had begun to mold a unique fighting force within the army. Army censors reviewed more than thirty-five thousand letters written by Japanese American recruits and found relatively few complaints. Pence and Miller had overcome issues between the Hawaiian-born and mainlanders, as described by one recruit: "The mainland boys is [*sic*] very much different from us. There [*sic*] looks are more like the boys who has [*sic*] just come from Japan. And lots of the Hawaii boys don't like them. But I'm just keeping cool headed and wait until better understanding. Besides that, they are many half-bread [breed]."[5]

At least the Hawaiians and mainlanders had a common enemy: the South. They made that clear in their letters. "Mississippi is just about the lousiest place we could have been stationed. We hope that soon we could be transferred . . . away from the deep (and dark) south, where the broiling sun is interspersed with thunderstorms, where chiggers and wood ticks make mincemeat out of our Hawaiian suntanned flesh, where the people still fight the Civil War and where the southern belle is just a myth."[6]

PENCE KNEW THE DAY WAS NOT GOING WELL FOR THE TRAPPED 1st Battalion and those attempting to reach it. There were only about four hours of daylight left, probably less given the heavy cloud cover and persistent rain. Although his men were exhausted, he had already been told to prepare one of his battalions for immediate reengagement and to be prepared to order the other two battalions back into battle. It would be up to company commanders and platoon leaders to somehow maintain the troops' morale when the veterans knew what would lie ahead and the replacement troops would only imagine what it would be like to confront the enemy intent on killing them.

And he got the word from Dahlquist—order the 2nd Battalion of the 442nd to move out before dark. Its mission was to destroy German positions on the north side of the ridge and protect the left flank of the other units trying to rescue Higgins's men. The mistake of allowing the 1/141 to advance so far without protection on its flanks would not be repeated this time. Pence was also told to notify the 100th and 3rd Battalions to prepare for deployment into enemy territory on a moment's notice. But for now, the 2/442 alone would enter the combat zone. The rest-and-recuperation period for the 442nd had officially evaporated in a single briefing.

"We are ordered back to the front again." Mutt Sakumoto couldn't believe what his acting platoon sergeant, Takahashi Senzaki, had just said. It couldn't be true. The Hawaii native had been born on a sugar plantation. He had lived in farmworker camps with plantation workers imported from Japan. His father was something of a mystery. When Mutt was young, his father had left the family to fight for Japan in the 1930s. He later returned and shared nothing of his experience. The middle child of seven youngsters, Mutt knew only poverty. He walked a mile to school barefoot and didn't wear shoes until they were required in the seventh grade.

One of the smallest men in the outfit (friends said his height was anywhere between four feet ten and five feet four), he had fished on weekends as a boy and read the box scores of baseball games between sugar-plantation teams. One day his brother noticed a player was called "Mutt" and decided that was a perfect name for Matsuji. Mutt liked to imitate the great samurai Miyamoto Musashi with swords shaped by pounding soft Hawaiian wood.

He had been a prankster as a boy and smoked his first cigarette with friends in high school. Soon he was sneaking his father's Bull Durham tobacco and cigarette-making machine to make unfiltered cigarettes. "I smoked, smoked, smoked. I liked the taste of cigarettes. Oh boy, it was good."[7] At one point he was suspended from school for smoking.

Sakumoto's Company I had taken a brutal beating in the campaign to liberate Bruyères and Belmont. But the Hawaii native now had to gear up for reengagement. Soldiers began gathering their equipment, filling canteens, inventorying ammunition, and in many cases wondering why the 442nd was mobilizing. They didn't know that other units of the 36th Division had failed to advance very far toward Higgins's position. But they did know that the 36th Division had other regiments it could assign to this relief mission, if the first day's attempt ultimately proved fruitless. Not nearly enough replacements had yet arrived to offset the men the 442nd had lost. Some of the veterans were still looking forward to their first hot shower in more than a week. So why was the entire 442nd mobilizing again so soon and so quickly? *What happened to having at least a few days in reserve?*

No one knew at the time that the Americans closest to Higgins's men were not part of the relief mission but prisoners of war. Jimmie Kanaya and the others who had been captured two days earlier were marched to within a few hundred yards of Higgins's position on their way to a German camp. "I could hear them [the surrounded men] talking and somebody fired a round and I could hear them cursing," he recalled later. "This German noncom that had taken my wrist-watch when he first captured us, came running to me and gave my wristwatch back to me because he thought we were going to be get recaptured, you know, by our own side."[8] But an hour later the American prisoners reached the German line, and all hope of escape evaporated.*

Small bands of aggressive Germans had stopped the American soldiers' advance cold throughout most of the day. Near sunset Lundquist had moved some companies forward for the final breakthrough assault. Tanks were supposed to accompany them under the cover of noise created by friendly artillery fire. But for reasons of a "lack of coordination," the tanks had remained in place.[9] The final assault petered out as a result.

At 2115 Higgins informed Lundquist by radio that a patrol he had dispatched earlier in the day had discovered the Germans' roadblock and that he had suffered two casualties. Higgins's message was

---

* Several were taken to Stalag VII-A, near the Austrian border. More than twenty thousand POWs were housed there until the Allies liberated them six months later, in April 1945. A staple of their diet was a black bread that was more than one-third sawdust, leaves, and straw.

clear: the 1/141 did not have the strength to break through the German line back along the same logging road it had used earlier.

But Lundquist told Higgins to "have Company A send out strong patrol to knock out roadblock so tks [tanks] can get through with supplies; use a company if necessary. Company A to report when this is accomplished."[10] If Higgins sent an entire company on the mission, he would have risked about one-third of his men.

Lundquist didn't explain to Higgins why he was ordering an attack, even though Higgins had told Lundquist he was understrength. Perhaps Lundquist didn't believe Higgins. Or maybe Lundquist thought he knew better. Lundquist may have concluded that his remaining 141st battalions were not capable of reaching the 1/141 without significant support by Higgins's men from the rear. Or maybe Lundquist was simply passing along orders from Dahlquist.

Regardless, Higgins faced an impossible decision. Sending a company-strength force to the rear would seriously weaken his position. *What if the Germans spotted dozens of men leaving the perimeter and disappearing into the forest? Would they immediately launch an attack against the remaining men? Will I have enough firepower to repel them?* Worse, Lundquist wanted Higgins's patrol to loop around the roadblock and attack it from the west. That meant the patrol first would have to flank the roadblock to get to the other side. Higgins had already discovered he could not flank the roadblock from the north. That had proved costly earlier in the day. He would have to send his men south. They would slide down off the ridge and move west along the edge of the valley held by the Germans. Then they would have to climb back up onto the ridge to attack the west side of the roadblock.

Higgins couldn't know the Germans' strength along that route, even though that area had been bombed earlier in the day. He did know his men would be climbing down and then up an extremely steep forest slope, slick with mud and moss. They would be soaked to the skin from the constant rain, exhausted from two nights in slit trenches, and dangerously low on ammunition. *How many men do I* *send? Under whose command? With what weaponry? What will that leave me inside the perimeter?* The record indicates Higgins sent the combat patrol down the ridge sometime before dawn the next morning.[*]

Although Lundquist had ordered Company A to attempt the flanking move, Higgins had other ideas. He canvassed his men, asking some to make suggestions. He needed to balance the firepower he was sending out with the firepower that would remain within the perimeter. Machine gunner Jack Wilson knew exactly whom he would send, even though he only had seven men left in his weapons platoon. He told Higgins to take his three best men who had grown up in the country and could handle themselves in the woods: the man he shared his foxhole with, Burt McQueen, Tillman Warren, and Robert Camaiani.[11]

By midnight it had become clear the day's final assault to reach the 1/141 had failed and that Dahlquist wanted Higgins to fight his own way out. Knowing the high cost and the likelihood of failure, the breakout patrol prepared to move out.

———◆———

AT THE END OF EVERY DAY'S BATTLE, A SOLDIER WOULD HAVE considered it successful if he had simply survived. When the enemy fired, his entire focus was on surviving—to simply reach the next tree, boulder, or ravine. It was only when the gunfire ceased that a man's horizon expanded. That's when the quiet emboldened reflection, supplanting the survival instinct—when the reality of the day's casualties swamped the noble cause of warfare. That was when discouragement, disillusionment, and depression became the enemies of many men in the 442nd. The break from battle had become an illusion. Now the 2/442 was again mobilizing, as word spread among the men of the 100th and 3rd Battalions that they might be joining

---

[*] The record is unclear on whether forty-eight or fifty-five men were selected for the mission.

the 2nd Battalion far sooner than they had anticipated. They would have to put disgust and depression aside.

Israel Yost, a chaplain with the 100th Battalion, had felt both emotions in the aftermath of taking Biffontaine. "I was furious when I saw the life draining out of the young men in Biffontaine, and at seeing them pushed toward annihilation in the forest," he recalled.[12] The twenty-eight-year-old Lutheran had knelt next to untold numbers of soldiers since he had enlisted two years earlier, leaving his wife, Peggy, behind. She was pregnant with their second child. An intellectual man, Yost had experienced tragic loss early in life when his father, a traveling salesman of farm equipment, had been killed while standing on the side of the road when he was hit by a drunk driver. Now Yost was surrounded by death and loss.

Yost's Pennsylvania Dutch accent had brought ridicule in school and spawned an intense desire to prove himself in the eyes of others. After he was confirmed in the Lutheran Church at the age of fifteen, Yost was inducted into the National Honor Society and skipped his senior year to enroll in a Lutheran-affiliated college. The former language major (Latin, Greek, German, French, and Spanish) had graduated from the seminary in 1940. Four years later he knelt next to medics tending to wounded and dying men every day. Yost conducted services for support personnel in the rear and at forward aid stations for shell-shocked men fresh off the battlefield. He witnessed the barbaric toll that assaults on nameless ridges and numbered hills exacted on young souls in battle. That included Young Oak Kim, who had soured on how General Dahlquist was deploying the 442nd in battle, especially when Kim learned his battalion would assault Biffontaine. This new mobilization reminded him of an earlier mission.

The sun had finally broken through the clouds on October 21 when Kim learned the 100th would attack Biffontaine (where Kim would be wounded) the following day. Kim was irate. Kim's unit would have to drop off an elevated position to attack Germans holed up in buildings and basements. Better to stay on the ridge, bypass Biffontaine, and pressure the retreating Germans from an elevated position.

As Kim debated the plan with Pence over the radio, Kim realized that General Dahlquist was standing next to Pence. Kim knew he wasn't going to win the argument. "I want to state for the record that I am very much against this," said Kim.[13] The only concession Kim exacted was assurance from Pence that other units would advance to maintain American control of the ridge that had already cost dozens of wounded and killed men. Meanwhile, the Germans were sending reinforcements to Biffontaine by bicycle.

That wasn't the first time that Kim had been disgusted by Dahlquist's orders. Two days earlier Kim had been on the radio with Colonel Pence after his unit and others in the 100th Battalion had taken one of four distinct hills that rose at the end of several streets in Bruyères. Each offered a commanding view of the town.* Bruyères could not be liberated without first clearing the hills of Germans. Kim's men had paid a steep price in blood when taking one of them. "Can you do me a favor? Whatever I say, just answer with 'yes, sir,'" Pence asked Kim over the radio. Kim's instinct was to refuse, but he thought better of it and asked if Dahlquist was nearby. He was. Kim realized Pence was relaying an order Pence knew Kim might not accept. "This is an order from the division commander. Retreat from Hill C right now."[14]

The 100th Battalion had finally taken the high ground from the Germans and now was being ordered by Dahlquist to give it back to the enemy. Kim reluctantly agreed, only after talking to his battalion's commanding officer, Lieutenant Colonel Gordon Singles. Later, rumors swept through the front line that there had been confusion over whether Dahlquist's 36th Division or the 3rd Division was responsible for taking Hill C. *Could it be that division politics could cost lives? Could an arbitrary line on a map take the lives of sons, fathers, and husbands?* The 100th retreated off the hill, and the Germans returned without firing a shot. More than one hundred casualties resulted when units from the 3rd Division retook the hill.

---

*The hills were designated 555, A, B, and C.

BATTLE STRATEGIES ASIDE, THE HORRORS CONFRONTED BY soldiers in the foxholes sometimes spawned a fatalistic wish that otherwise would have been inconceivable back home. About six weeks earlier, devout Catholic Martin Higgins had attended Mass. "I prayed to God to be killed and have the war end. I was under the assumption I would be killed. It was the only way I could fight," he recalled after the war.[15] Five years earlier, he had looked forward to his unit being shipped overseas so he could wage war. Now he was surrounded and had accepted his fate.

About fifteen hundred yards away, George Sakato had undergone a similar transformation when it seemed to him that units of the 442nd had been thrown one after another against the enemy, with little apparent regard for the horrific casualties they were taking. Dwindling supplies and mounting casualties fueled anger and frustration. At one point Sakato had flinched at the bottom of a hill when another soldier detonated a land mine above him. He crumbled to the ground on his remaining leg. "Land mines!" someone yelled. Sakato dropped to his knees and crawled up the hill, sticking his knife into the dirt ahead of him, praying it would not *clink* against the side of a buried mine. Mines detonated in the face of some men not far away. *Oh my god,* Sakato thought to himself. *What am I doing here? I volunteered for this?*[16]

Later that day, when Sakato ran out of ammunition with no immediate prospect of resupply, he found a machine gun and ammunition among the dead and bloated German bodies. The infantryman who had been a horrible marksman in boot camp found spraying the enemy left and right was more effective than bracing for the recoil that came from shooting straight ahead. By that point dead enemy soldiers rarely bothered Sakato and others. But as the continuous combat had strung the days and nights together, dead American soldiers splayed across downed trees and straddling ravines disturbed them deeply. *Is this worth it? Why us? Don't they have anyone else?*

MORALE HAD BECOME AN ENEMY ON BOTH SIDES OF THE VOSGES battlefield. "Never before have I led in battle such motley and poorly equipped troops."[17] General Hermann Balck, commanding officer of Army Group G, was hardly satisfied with the fighting strength and discipline of the men in General Friedrich Wiese's Nineteenth Army. Like Wiese, Balck was career army. He had been an infantryman in World War I after enlisting in 1913. The son of a renowned military tactician, he had spent most of World War II on the Eastern Front, where he had established his reputation as a battlefield commander who often defeated larger enemy forces.

For weeks Wiese had been fighting the 36th Division with under-strength regiments, some filled with troops that either were on proba-tion or had health problems. He had lost more than one hundred thousand men since August 15. Wiese was fighting a war on his heels, giving ground grudgingly and looking for every tactical advantage he could find. He had discontinued using forward reconnaissance units as his men retreated toward the Vosges. Wiese had one principal as-set: his officers generally were experienced, well-trained, and dedi-cated professional soldiers. They knew battlefield tactics. They had become hardened to horrific casualty rates. And they shared his passion for not allowing the Allies to reach the German border under any circumstance.

In mid-September Hitler had permitted Wiese to retreat to the Moselle River on the condition that he mount a counterattack when the Americans arrived. But that failed to materialize, as the 36th easily built bridges across the Moselle and pressed ahead toward the Vosges. Wiese instead intended to use the Vosges to his advantage. He likely knew, as Truscott certainly did, that the constant near-freezing rain, fog, and possibly snow would persist for the rest of October.

The bad weather also contributed to the Americans' inability to accurately assess Wiese's fighting strength in the Vosges. In October Seventh Army intelligence could account for only six of nineteen

German fortress battalions and only one of three fortress infantry regiments in the region. The closer the Allies pushed the enemy to the German border, shorter supply and reinforcement lines made it easier for the Germans to conceal their actual fighting strength. Wiese's artillery made effective use of its moderate supply by stationing observers in trees to provide precise targeting information. Advancing American artillery battalions tended to use more shells in the absence of well-established observers. Ammunition shortages had forced Truscott to impose artillery rationing in some sectors of the VI Corps' advance.

At least Wiese could expect the arrival of the 201st and 202nd Mountain Battalions, even though they would be undermanned and poorly equipped in most cases. That would amount to about 2,000 reasonably fresh troops to supplement the depleted 933rd Grenadier Regiment of 350 men and the 198th Fusilier Battalion in the immediate area. His battle plan was simple: Establish squad- and platoon-size strong points throughout the mountains to maintain pressure on the advancing Americans. Fight a war of attrition through attack and counterattack. Rugged hillsides with slopes of nearly 45 percent, a confined battlefield of approximately twenty-five square miles, peaks that reached two thousand feet in elevation, slick trails, and relentless rain were ideal for that strategy.

Higgins had at least an inkling of what he faced. The 1/141 had captured three Germans from the 198th and placed them under guard. They told Higgins their units were severely shorthanded and that they were supported by two light tanks. During the day two additional Germans from the 202nd Mountain Battalion had also been captured.

But as battered as they had become, the Germans held the high ground in most of the forest and had what was later estimated to be 700 troops in the immediate area. This was the enemy force that the Americans faced early on October 26.

THE PLAN WAS FOR THE 2ND AND 3/141 AS WELL AS THE 2/442 to launch their assault at 0730. The 3/141 was to attack Hill 633. George Sakato and others of the 2/442 would use the same trail the 1/141 had taken and take a strategic hill to the north.

If the 2/442 reached Higgins's men, they would not immediately be brought to the rear. Presumably resupplied upon their relief, the 1/141 would keep fighting—and proceed north along the ridge: "If contact was made with the 1st Battalion by the 2nd Battalion, the 1st Battalion was to press on to the heights just north of La Houssière while the 2nd Battalion protected the right flank along the edge of the woods."[18] Clearly, headquarters did not yet consider this solely a rescue mission. Higgins's men were simply to be reached, resupplied, and sent on to their original objective. Battle plans were to be followed precisely, and timetables had to be met.

It was an ambitious plan, given the fact that no significant air reconnaissance of the area had been conducted. The Americans had a poor idea of the enemy's strength. Much of the strategy rested on reports from a handful of German prisoners, some of them newcomers, who had been captured. It amounted to little more than a "follow me and fight" battle plan.[19] Even more ominously, Lundquist's written assessment of his troops late on October 25 reflected the beating they already had taken: "Combat efficient: Poor—limited by combat fatigue, weather and terrain difficulties and approximately a 50% reduction in rifle company strength on position."[20]

Higgins's troops were running low on supplies, the relief force had suffered significant numbers of casualties and been halted by the Germans, and Dahlquist had ordered an exhausted 442nd back into battle. Mounting desperation soaked the battlefield as night fell and the rain persisted.

CHAPTER 3

FIRE FOR EFFECT

"On your feet!" A few men in 2/442 stirred at the predawn roust by platoon leaders and company officers. Others remained motionless, some under freshly issued rain gear, buying every extra second of dry comfort possible. Stirring would confirm what they hoped had just been a bad dream: that it was time to get up, find the enemy again, kill or be killed. But within minutes hundreds were on their feet in the predawn darkness of October 26. Gun barrels were cold and the backpack canvas was damp as they assembled their gear. Packs needed to be reloaded, a day's ration double-checked, and ammunition counted before hiking up into the Vosges Mountains, still shrouded in heavy predawn clouds.

The battalion's mission called for assembly in the darkest and coldest hours that always came just before dawn and then advancing long before sunrise out of the Belmont area and up onto the ridge. They would be following Higgins's trail to an assembly area about three tension-filled miles from where they would first climb onto the ridge. Long before the sun rose, Technical Sergeant Rocky Matayoshi in Company G and others who served as scouts moved toward the front of their units. Platoons of riflemen and weapons squads prepared to head up the logging road before the forest lightened.

They headed out, slightly bent forward at the waist, with their backs rolled forward under the weight of gear that might determine whether they would survive the day's fighting. Some hauled a radio that weighed as much as thirty pounds. Rather than a pistol, most radiomen preferred a Thompson machine gun and eight magazines of ammunition. Rations, a canteen, a few personal belongings in a pack, and a bedroll added up to nearly fifty pounds on the back of the men who rarely weighed more than 150 pounds. Some radiomen looped their pack's strap over a tree branch before climbing a hill with their radio and then retrieved their pack when their unit paused.

As they climbed up the ridge, each man focused on the middle of the back of the soldier immediately in front of him. The darkness was so suffocating that some soldiers tied white fabric or a glow-in-the-dark watch on their packs so the man three feet behind could see him. Others reached out and grabbed the pack of the man ahead of them, creating a human daisy chain. Each had to trust the man in front and mimic his stride, hoping he'd find tree roots or half-exposed rocks that could serve as stepping-stones as he climbed. If one man slipped and fell on the steep, mud-slick trail, he could knock the legs out from under several others below him, as if a bowling ball had found its mark among the human pins. Only the scouts at the head of each advance had a dim view of the forest ahead.

The 442nd's scouts often worked in pairs, followed by the riflemen and then those carrying the heavier weapons, such as mortars and BARs. Sunrise dimmed by thick clouds revealed the ridge ahead. They couldn't be sure the western end of the ridge had been cleared of every German, even though the 1/141 had moved through it a few days earlier. Matayoshi knew that if he failed to spot the enemy, his entire unit might be exposed. A single enemy soldier with a radio could bring a storm of artillery onto them in seconds. It was his job to find the enemy first and then use hand signals to pass the word back to his unit as it crept from tree to tree.

Their advance unfolded in gut-wrenching slow motion. Progress was measured in increments of twenty yards. Some men could hear their hearts pounding, and many were not aware their breathing had drawn thin. Others less physically fit breathed heavily during the climb. An observant enemy soldier knew to watch for the puff of a misty breath. Although the forest floor was saturated, even a single bone-dry twig could reveal the presence of the Americans. Flat-footed walking dispersed a soldier's weight to create a more reliably silent advance. Scouts paused for a minute or longer behind trees or boulders every few yards, scanning, sensing. Frozen in position, sometimes a scout could sense movement up ahead, seconds before he could see anything or anyone he could identify.

George Sakato and others used forest sounds as sentries. A forest typically quiets when soldiers slowly advance from tree to boulder to gully. On occasion the warning cry of a marmot, red squirrel, bullfinch, or jay revealed a German machine-gun nest or betrayed a stealthy advance by a 2nd Battalion squad. One 442nd veteran likened patrol to Boy Scout camp in the woods. There was a lot of crouching, watching, and listening. But no Boy Scout was prepared for gunfire eruptions, mortar explosions, and the battle cries of men.

The 2nd Battalion advanced in a northeasterly direction toward a relatively flat junction of three logging trails and then planned to swing left and advance toward the Germans on their right flank. They would be moving through the 3/141 and taking the point on the Americans' left flank in a region of the forest known to be targeted by German artillery. The 2nd Battalion's advance would prevent German reinforcements from entering the battle from the north and east. But as the sun rose and vision improved, small-arms fire brought the advance to a halt. Clearly, the Germans had yet to be cleared off the western portion of the ridge.

ABOUT THREE MILES AWAY, HIGGINS'S MEN WOKE UP AND scanned the forest for signs of a German attack as they resumed digging in. If a man wasn't watching for or fighting the enemy, he had better be protecting himself against the next enemy attack. A helmet, trenching knife, folding shovel, and even a penknife made digging exceedingly slow for some, while others kept watch for the enemy. After each thin scoop of boggy forest dirt, groundwater seeped into the deepening holes. Somehow foxholes large enough for two men took shape. Two adjacent holes that were particularly large—perhaps to be used as an aid station and command post—were located in the center of Higgins's position. Some men began cutting stout branches to build a roof over their crater. Once in place, dirt, pine needles, cantaloupe-size rocks, and mud were layered on top to create a roof capable of withstanding a blizzard of metal and wood shrapnel from tree bursts. Crawling into a dark hole, hoping to sleep in a filthy uniform, and trying to ignore the bone-chilling groundwater didn't seem so bad if a soldier knew his roof would protect him from iron shards the size of a man's palm and swarms of ten-inch wooden daggers that sounded like angry bees during an artillery attack.

It was impossible for Higgins to determine how many enemy soldiers had surrounded his men, what kind of heavy weapons they had at their disposal, or if reinforcements were arriving sooner or later by the hour. (The 442nd's headquarters staff estimated there were at least two hundred Germans between Higgins and the relief force.) Despite his lack of intelligence on enemy strength, Higgins knew he could lessen the odds of the enemy overrunning his men.

His men had experienced how difficult and deadly it was to attack uphill. But now they held the high ground—a high point on the ridge. The Germans would have to attack uphill against Higgins's defenders. If the 1/141 could somehow be kept supplied, Higgins was confident his men could hold out until relieved. And if the Germans gave Higgins's men enough time to establish dug-in positions, it would be even more difficult to attack the 1/141. An entrenched force in fortified foxholes enjoys a three-to-one advantage in manpower over an attacking force. Digging in would essentially triple the combat effectiveness of Higgins's men.

Higgins could also take away the element of surprise by posting lookouts, who scanned the dense forest for enemy movement. For the first time since August 15, the enemy would have to come to the 1/141 instead of the reverse.

Higgins made other tactical decisions to both protect and repel. He ordered mortarman Bruce Estes to bury his mortar and ammunition. The vast stands of black and stone pines trees that rose more than one hundred feet over their position created an impossibly dense canopy that made mortar warfare impossible. Unable to use it themselves, burying it might prevent it from falling into German hands. Free of his mortar assignment, Estes was sent to man a machine-gun post.

Higgins placed his heavy machine-gun positions for maximum range and spread. Twenty-year-old Jack Wilson was responsible for one of the two World War I–era .30-caliber heavy machine guns on the eastern end of the perimeter. The nearly one-hundred-pound tripod-mounted weapon fired up to six hundred rounds per minute and had a maximum effective range of six-tenths of a mile. But he had set it on "single shot," partly to save ammunition and also to avoid revealing his position. Wilson had fought with the 141st through some of Italy's toughest campaigns and might have been one of its luckiest soldiers. Shrapnel had once grazed his lip and embedded itself in his backpack. A machine-gun round had creased a finger and broken his shovel's handle. A water can attached to a jeep next to his leg had been shot away by enemy fire. And only a few days earlier, his rifle had been shattered, the binoculars on his hip had taken a direct hit of shrapnel, and he had been knocked unconscious during a German tank attack. He had opted to stay with his unit rather than report to an aid station. His head still ached and his ears rang as he and Burt McQueen set up their machine-gun station.

Not far away on the perimeter, an Irish kid who had grown up around Amsterdam Avenue in New York City peered into the forest from his foxhole, looking as far as the mist would allow. Edward Guy carried a rifle and memories of growing up in a poor family of ten children in a five-room house. His mostly unemployed father had provided as best he could as a dishwasher and by carrying signs on the street, but it was a family at loose ends. Guy had dropped out of school after he tired of playing hooky and risking the wrath of his mother, who favored whacks with a shoe as corporal punishment.

Only two years earlier, he had been working in a pharmacy in Newburgh, a town of about thirteen hundred residents perched on the Ohio River in southwestern Indiana. He had received his draft notice when he was working as an apprentice engineer in an Evansville boatyard, building navy landing craft, called LSTs. He opted for the army rather than taking a chance in the navy. He didn't have much confidence in the navy's LSTs after seeing how they were constructed.

He had met Higgins when Guy arrived as a replacement the year before. Higgins had impressed Guy right away as "a tough little guy. A regular guy. Honest, fair, and wouldn't [order his men] to do anything he wouldn't do. A lot of officers aren't like that. He demanded discipline," Guy recalled after the war.[1] Now Higgins had assigned him to protect the trapped men within the perimeter.

But the deadliest enemy facing the 1/141 was the most basic: a lack of food and water. Most men had carried only a day's ration and a canteen of water. The food supply was soon exhausted, and a few slightly orange chanterelle mushrooms scavenged among the pine needles were nutritious but woefully inadequate. A communications sergeant, James Comstock had lived on a farm in Pennsylvania and knew how to find them. Boiling the few he scavenged in his canteen's water produced little more than a thin broth. He had earned a battlefield commission to become a sergeant four months earlier in Italy and had been eager for his parents and girlfriend to learn of his promotion. He was nineteen years old. Meanwhile, the two French guides, Henri Grandjean and Pierre Poirat, showed others how to scavenge for other edible mushrooms and pointed out which wood should be used to heat water because it produced minimal smoke.

There was a marginal supply of water a short distance away outside the perimeter. Some men thought it was a seeping spring. Others saw it more as algae-covered groundwater in a crater. Nevertheless, the Americans craved that water supply—the safest way to collect water was to send a night patrol crawling to the mud hole, some men carrying the canteens and others sweeping the forest with their rifles and machine guns, safeties off. Although the Germans had placed a sniper near the water hole, Higgins ordered his men not to shoot any Germans there. He didn't want decomposing bodies contaminating his only water supply.

The supply of water-disinfecting Halazone tables lasted only one day. Higgins and the other lieutenants could only imagine how their exhausted, starving soldiers' stomachs might react to contaminated water if help didn't arrive soon.

Mortarman Estes, though, had found a temporary solution in the bottom of his foxhole. He had grown up on a family farm in Georgia. The youngest child in the family, he had taken care of his mother and family while siblings raised cotton, corn, cattle, pigs, and mules. Along the way he had developed some self-reliance skills. He carried a small gas stove in combat. As long as his fuel supply lasted, he mixed lemon powder with the brown water and boiled it. A metal cup of steaming gritty water held between two aching hands in a constant misty rain provided a few seconds' relief for those lucky enough to share the bounty. Higgins later marveled at the variety of equipment his men carried in battle as well as their ingenuity.

But Estes couldn't be distracted from watching for Germans in the morning. Higgins's men had noticed a pattern was emerging—the Germans seemed to favor an early-morning probing attack on the Americans. Some men called it "time for breakfast," in a bizarre universe defined by hunger, thirst, and uncertainty.

———◦———

By now the rescue cast had grown to include thousands of men, from riflemen to truck drivers to artillery crews. At Dahlquist's division headquarters, there were intelligence, operations, and logistics units each focusing on their aspect of the mission. Dahlquist's chief of staff, Colonel Charles Owens, was the liaison between

Dahlquist and the 141st's commander, Colonel Carl Lundquist. Lundquist also had intelligence, operations, and logistics officers under his command. Although the 442nd's 2nd Battalion had been assigned to Lundquist, the 442nd's commanding officer, Colonel Charles Pence, monitored radio messages and the situation on the battlefield. He needed to maintain overall situational awareness in the event the impulsive Dahlquist called the 442nd's remaining 100th and 3rd Battalions out of reserve with little notice.

Dahlquist had the entire 442nd, 142nd, 143rd, and two battalions of the 141st at his disposal. So far, units of the 142nd and 143rd had made minimal progress trying to reach the 1/141. He also commanded 131st Field Artillery Battalion and 111th Engineer Combat Battalion. Tank units had been brought forward to engage the enemy, and air support was also available if the skies cleared.

But no military mission could be successful if it could not be reliably supplied with ammunition, food, medical supplies, weapons, and replacement troops. The 141st's logistics officer radioed the 36th Division's engineer battalion that the heavy vehicles and light tanks were destroying the muddy paths used by supply trucks. As the ruts deepened, some vehicles bounced off the road, while others high-centered when their undercarriages dragged through the mud. Thirty truckloads of gravel were dispatched to the front, just as Dahlquist arrived at the regiment's command post at 0850 for a briefing by the regimental operations officer. It was a brutal report.

The 2/442 was already stuck in place, unable to cross a trail. Sakato and others were several hundred yards from their objective, Hill 617. If the 2nd Battalion could capture it, the high ground would protect the left flank of the rescue mission. But the direct approach up a draw on the southwest side made the 2nd Battalion an easy target for the Germans.

Sakato and others were pinned down by an unknown number of enemy infantry supported by least five machine-gun nests. The Germans held Hill 617 and had placed dozens of guns in broad foxholes facing down the draw where the Americans were approaching. To

Sakato, the enemy seemed nearly invisible. The Germans were experts at camouflage. They had mounded the dirt they had excavated by hand onto the backside of their foxholes to camouflage their silhouettes when they fired at the advancing Americans. Two companies of the 3/141 had also been halted by enemy fire. Although the 131st Field Artillery Battalion was firing on enemy positions, a mud-soaked stalemate had developed. It was only midmorning.

About one hour later, the new commanding officer of VI Corps who had replaced blunt and driven Truscott, Major General Edward Brooks, appeared at the command post. A World War I veteran, the square-jawed Brooks was an imposing figure. His superiors thought so highly of Brooks that he had skipped the rank of colonel when they promoted him to brigadier general in 1941. He had led troops in some of Europe's toughest battles and had helped pioneer self-propelled guns. Now a single trapped battalion threatened to throw a tightly coordinated VI Corps advance off balance. Dahlquist's 36th Division was supposed to stay abreast of the 3rd Division in the advance toward St. Die. If too many assets of the 36th were shifted to a rescue mission, the 36th's advance would be slowed, creating a gap between the 36th and 3rd that could become an open invitation for a German counterattack. Even though Wiese's German units were generally short of men, Brooks could not allow that to happen. So the commander of the VI Corps had to devote his time and attention to reaching a single battalion that could be lost to the enemy.

His orders on arrival were as precise as they were unquestioned. Direct the 2/442 to fight due east across Hill 617 toward the surrounded battalion. There would be no flanking attempts by the 2nd. Further, Colonel Lundquist was to send his tanks directly forward toward any German roadblocks they encountered and blast a clear path. Reports from the field indicated there were as many as three enemy roadblocks in place, plus an untold number of strongpoints. Many would be heavily mined. Finally, send the remaining infantry of the 141st around both sides of the first roadblock. Brooks wanted an all-out assault.

Following Brooks's orders and sensing his urgency, Dahlquist lambasted Lundquist. Dahlquist reminded Lundquist that he had four battalions at his disposal but "still are not doing anything." According to Dahlquist, the 2/442 was to operate on its own. Dahlquist pointedly asked, "Can't you use artillery on the enemy?" It was on only the last point that Lundquist stood up to the general. He told Dahlquist the Americans were so close to the enemy that they would suffer casualties from friendly artillery fire. Dahlquist didn't buy it. At 1108 he ordered, "Artillery fire on enemy in front of the 2nd Battalion. Have artillery fire over target first; then adjust by sound; forward observer with 2nd Battalion should be able to do this."[2]

Dahlquist had set aside his responsibility as the 36th Division's organizational leader to become the operational leader of the 141st Infantry Regiment, issuing tactical orders that usurped Lundquist's authority. Dahlquist, a general with three months' combat experience, had taken control from Lundquist, a man with one month's combat experience. One prewar planner was taking over for another, commanding troops on the front line. Dahlquist's chief of staff, Colonel Owens, had been Dahlquist's top aide for only fourteen days. Dahlquist and Owens collectively had less than five months' combat experience. Many men under Dahlquist's command suspected the imperious general was intent on becoming the first senior officer to enter Germany. Dahlquist, they said, would not tolerate an extended delay to rescue a single battalion in his advance toward the Rhine River.

He also expected Higgins to fight his way out of his predicament. At 0835 Higgins's only radio operator, Erwin Blonder, had received a bewildering message. Higgins was to launch a major attack against the Germans from the rear and break through the roadblock that held his battalion prisoner. No matter how bloodied Higgins's unit had become, his men were to leave their foxholes and attack the Germans from the rear. Whether they had enough ammunition or what they were to do with the wounded men on stretchers apparently did not concern the anxious division commander.

For his part, Higgins couldn't accurately assess the combat strength of the enemy, know the enemy's strongpoints, or anticipate where enemy troops in reserve might be stationed. He would be attacking blind and would be leading a depleted unit hobbled by debilitating hunger and more than twenty wounded.

Radioman Erwin Blonder was the link between the surrounded battalion and thousands of men fighting to reach it. Tall and lanky, Blonder had grown up in the Cleveland, Ohio, area, the son of a prosperous wallpaper and paint business owner. A thoughtful and introspective youngster, he had played the piano, met his future wife when he was in high school, and been an average student before attending the University of Arizona and Ohio State University. Very patriotic and interested in world history, he had volunteered one month before graduation.

As a forward artillery observer with the only working radio, it was Blonder's job to keep Higgins advised as infantrymen, tank crews, mortar squads, artillery batteries, road builders, supply personnel, truck drivers, medics, mine diffusers, and others planned, reacted, and mobilized. Most of the radio traffic for nearly two days had consisted of variations of "Hang on. Sizable force coming your way."

Blonder's radio was crucial because Higgins's field telephone was useless. Communications Sergeant James Comstock had strung telephone wire as Higgins's force had advanced. But a German artillery barrage had cut the line the first night. Comstock and another man had left Higgins's position almost immediately as the others dug in. They sneaked through the forest in search of the break in the seven-strand line. As they backtracked they ran the one-eighth-inch-thick wire through their hands in the darkness, feeling for a break in the black tar-covered line. When they found it, Comstock quickly repaired the break. But then they were nearly captured when "German soldiers came up the path [so close that] we were able to identify them as German soldiers by looking up toward the sky and seeing the dips in their helmets. We lay still until they passed us. . . . [T]hey were so close I could have reached out and tripped them, but I think I was too scared to move."[3] The two Americans returned to their battalion. But the telephone was still out of commission. There must have been other breaks. Throughout their battalion's ordeal, the telephone line was never repaired.

Blonder's SCR-300 field radio had become standard issue to army units just a few months earlier. Ultimately, fifty thousand "300s" would be deployed in combat. The thirty-eight-pound low-power backpack radio had proved itself reliable, easy to use, and relatively waterproof. With its antenna extended, its range was approximately three miles, although the weather and nearby peaks sometimes lessened its effective range. Most critically, its battery life was eight to twelve hours. And it was already reaching that limit. Whether Blonder could coax additional power out of his battery might determine the fate of the surrounded battalion. He was receiving and sending as few messages to the regimental command post and others as possible, mostly in code and always brief. He and Higgins could control how many messages they sent, but they were at the mercy of how many messages they received from Colonel Lundquist as well as division and regimental intelligence, operations, logistics, and artillery personnel. Each message drew the battery closer to death.

In the Vosges Mountains, Blonder had found himself on a far more intimate battlefield than anything he had experienced previously. As an artillery observer alongside infantry units in Italy, he had typically seen "Germans moving a thousand yards away from you and [then] you bring artillery fire on them," he had written to his parents three weeks earlier. "You kill a few and wound some. You don't stop to think whether it is right or wrong but know that the more Germans you kill the quicker the war will be won."[4] Now the former Boy Scout licked his cold radio battery to extend its life as he relayed messages between Higgins and various command posts, hoping that the communication would result in enemy killed.

Higgins relied on Blonder to monitor his waning battery power as much as Higgins and the other lieutenants gauged the declining combat strength of the 1/141. Several men had been killed shortly after being surrounded. German artillery fire wounded others. They had suffered additional casualties on earlier probing attacks and patrols. The severely wounded needed stretchers in order to be moved. A number of trench-foot cases were developing.

Higgins had already sent a major breakout force the night before to flank the enemy's roadblock and attack it from the front. He calculated that the forty-eight-man breakout patrol he had dispatched represented half his firepower. How many men could he now spare on Dahlquist's orders for another assault on the roadblock and still retain a passable fighting force against the next German attack? So far, the attacks on his men had been measured, but Higgins couldn't know if an all-out assault on his position was imminent. What types of weapons could he spare? Which weapons would be more effective in his defensive position? Who had the most ammunition? Who was critically short? Which of his men were the toughest? The most reliable?

The previous night's breakout patrol was led by Second Lieutenant James Gilman of Company C and Sergeant Harold Kripisch of Higgins's Company A. Moving slowly, eyes scanning the forest ahead, the patrol had inched across and down the slope on primitive game trails toward the valley. They approached some land mines they had uncovered the day before. They had already been reset by the Germans. But now, if they could navigate their way down off the ridge to the south and reach Harime, a cluster of farmhouses at the edge of the valley, a trail there would lead them back up to the front of the roadblock. About one thousand yards from Higgins's position, the breakout patrol spotted more land mines. They were planted in the soil and nestled along narrow paths where dense vegetation forced advancing soldiers into a single predictable line.

When a member of the patrol tripped one of the mines a few minutes later, the blast rocked the forest. Germans quickly appeared uphill of the patrol, pinning it against another minefield. Enemy fire shredded troops and tree trunks. The Americans flopped into the mud or dove toward the nearest cover. The firefight blistered the forest and echoed across the valley. Gilman and Kripisch yelled over the cacophony, ordering small units to make flanking attempts and to search for a tactical advantage in the dense stands of timber. Men fell wounded, gasping and crying out in agony.

Meanwhile, Higgins sent another patrol of an unspecified number of men back on the logging road. It met an estimated force of about fifty Germans only about four hundred yards from Higgins's perimeter. They were defending a major roadblock. It now appeared the Germans had constructed at least two major roadblocks, one at Col de la Croisette and the other at Col des Huttes.

At 1337 Higgins asked for artillery support. He also updated his casualty total to twenty-eight injured men. That left him with fewer than two hundred men inside his perimeter, with one patrol near the new roadblock nearly a third of a mile away and the breakout patrol on the southern slope whose exact position and status were unknown.

Only three minutes later, Lundquist issued new orders to Higgins, presumably dictated by Dahlquist: "Move troops through to Point 30, contacting our king [Company K] three hundred yards SE Point 30."[5] That location was approximately two miles away! It was inconceivable that either patrol Higgins had already dispatched, much less the remaining combat troops and injured men within his perimeter, could fight their way through the Germans that far away, not with dehydrated and hungry troops critically low on ammunition.

Higgins refused. He radioed a reply an hour later, stating he could not move his men one-third of a mile by sunset, much less two miles through enemy territory. Higgins asked for permission to remain in place until the following morning. He also needed to know the fate of the breakout patrol dispatched the night before.

Higgins's depleted force apparently didn't matter to those in charge of the rescue mission. A few minutes later, Lundquist told Higgins another major attack by the other battalions of the 141st would be launched at 1600. It would be preceded by ten minutes of heavy artillery fire by two battalions, each gun firing fifteen rounds.

Further, Higgins was to continue his attempt to break through entrenched German positions at Point 9 and to fight his way to Point 30.* Lundquist also ordered Higgins to acknowledge he had received the order.

———◉———

COLONEL WALTER ROLIN'S 933RD GRENADIER REGIMENT WAS among those units that stood between the rescuers and Higgins's men. His was a crippled German fighting force. He had lost more than 2,000 men in the two months since the 36th Division had come ashore near Marseille. With only about 350 combat troops, the veteran Prussian combat officer drew on his experience that dated back to World War I, where he had earned First and Second Class Iron Crosses. While his regiment had been fed generally unfit replacements in recent weeks, Rolin was typical of the battled-hardened senior officers that Dahlquist, Owens, and Lundquist faced. He knew how to bleed an enemy.

On an intimate battlefield such as a mountain ridge, his MG-42 machine guns were priceless assets. They had an effective range of four-tenths of a mile and could fire eighteen hundred rounds per minute. At twenty-five pounds, they were as mobile as they were lethal and perfect for a rubbled battlefield of foxholes, stacks of logs, and ravines. A handful of MG-42s, strategically placed, had pinned down most of the 2/442 nearly all day.

The Germans called them "Hitler's bone saw." To GIs, they were the "buzz saw" that sounded like a zipper when firing. Before attacking it, Sakato and others usually waited until a 42's barrel overheated or its crew ran out of ammunition, or they waited until an American tank arrived. On Hill 617, there were few options in the face of the "buzz saw."

---

* While locations on the battlefield were generally numerical coordinates, a few in this battle were designed as "points," such as Point 8, Point 9, or Point 30.

Rolin was fighting what military strategists call a delaying action: slow the American advance, and make it pay for each step forward. German doctrine called for constant contact with the enemy in such circumstances. Never give the enemy a chance to regroup. At each strongpoint, establish multiple machine-gun positions, support with heavy mortars or self-propelled guns if possible, and liberally plant land mines.

It seemed to the 2/442 that German S-mines were buried everywhere. Steel cylinders six inches tall and about four inches wide, they were positioned in irregular patterns in roadbeds and alongside roads as well as on game trails and logging paths. Each was fitted with either a pressure-plate igniter or a trip wire. Sakato and his men knew that when they stepped on an S-mine, they had only about a half-second to hit the dirt face first. The mine shot three to five feet into the air and detonated, sending 360 steel balls or rods or scrap metal in every direction. Its lethal range was 60 feet, but even a soldier 460 feet away could suffer injuries from a single S-mine. Sometimes an S-mine caused "sympathetic detonations" of others nearby. The French called them "silent soldiers."

Another type of antipersonnel mine, the Schu-mine, was equally dreaded. The small six-inch-square wood box concealed a detonator and a piece of TNT. It was nearly impossible to locate with metal detectors and tended to cut the lower legs off soldiers rather than kill them.

Rolin relied heavily on these strategically placed mines. They were relatively easy to install and significantly extended the line of defense from south to north across the ridge that his beleaguered men had been ordered to defend. It was the 2nd Battalion's assault on Hill 617 that demonstrated how lethal mines could be to the newcomers on the battlefield.

Veterans like George Sakato and Mitsunori Masunaga had learned to spot a thin wire stretched across a game trail that was connected to an explosive device under a bush. Under leaden skies and constant rain, trip wires were nearly invisible. When one was discovered, it required enormous discipline not to dive for cover when someone whispered "Mines!" A soldier could easily dive onto an unseen trip wire or detonator a few yards away. In a split second, a half dozen men could be killed or wounded. One or more medics would be necessary to treat them, and more men might be taken off the line to carry the wounded on stretchers back to an aid station. A single mine could nearly destroy a squad. Instead, newcomers to the 2nd Battalion were told to freeze when a mine was spotted and wait for a combat veteran to either disable it or find a path to safety.

"BATTERY RUN. FIRE FOR EFFECT."[6] WHEN THE GERMANS PINNED down the 2nd Battalion with ground fire, mortars, and mines, Sakato, Matayoshi, other infantrymen, and medics looked to their artillery to break the deadly stalemate. Forward artillery observers from the 522nd Field Artillery Battalion batteries were attached to each of the 442nd's battalions and fought alongside infantrymen. They notified their artillery battery when support was needed and "walked it" onto the enemy. Artillery support had been valuable in Italy, but in the Vosges more intimate combat made it less effective. Yet throughout the day both sides fired artillery at very steep angles to drop the shells onto precise targets on the congested battlefield.

Nelson Akagi was one of the observers attached to the 442nd's ground troops. He had grown up in a relatively prosperous farming family in Lindsay, California. His father, Jack, made sure each teenager had a small plot of farmland for which he was responsible. The family's prize possession was a forty-acre hillside plot. All the youngsters in the family had worked from dawn to dusk in the summer to clear it of rocks and make it arable. In early 1942 they had lost all their possessions—farmland, planted crops, equipment, trucks, a pool hall operated by one of the boys, and home—when they were forced to evacuate to an internment camp in Idaho. Akagi figured the farmland and its tree crops were worth close to thirty thousand dollars; the family sold it for two thousand. A few months after arriving in Idaho, Akagi volunteered for the 442nd. He was nineteen years old. Two years later, the farmer was crawling from bush to tree, looking for enemy positions a few yards ahead.

Under ideal conditions, the 2/442 typically had four-man forward-observer teams. One man was a spotter, another ran telephone wire back to headquarters, a third operated the phone, and the fourth, an officer, decided when to ask for artillery support. On occasion a lone forward observer accompanying a patrol used a radio to send instructions to his artillery battery. When an enemy position in the Vosges was spotted, a single artillery shot from a 105mm howitzer was requested.

If the first shot missed the Germans on Hill 617, a "Battery adjust" call was made with corrections, such as "Right 100 [yards]." If the next shot was on target, "Battery run. Fire for effect" called for three or four more shots, within sixty seconds, on the hapless enemy position. Kats Miho, a gunner corporal with the 522nd Field Artillery Battalion battery assigned to Sakato's company, was one of those men who translated forward-observer reports into precise fire by the battalion's howitzers.

He was part of a five-man team at each gun firing in support of the 2nd Battalion. The crew's job was twofold: harass the Germans surrounding the stranded battalion and support George Sakato's Company E and the rest of 2/442. As the 2nd Battalion advanced, artillery crews had to adjust their range to stay a few dozen yards in front of the infantry. Then at night the crews fired just outside the perimeter of where the battalion had dug in. The youngest of eight children, Miho had grown up in Kahului, a Hawaiian port town that shipped sugar and pineapples to the mainland. As the son of a bookkeeper and store manager, his boyhood had been filled with swimming, fishing, crabbing, playing marbles, and glimpses of the outside world during Boy Scout outings.

"Artillery had to guard the perimeters of the infantry at night. About the only time that we got . . . emotionally involved was the

Lost Battalion. We knew that we had to be extra, extra careful. We were firing maybe fifty yards in front of the boys, our own boys, fifty, twenty-five yards in front," he said later.[7] Throughout the day on the twenty-sixth, Miho's battery had fired on precise targets less than two hundred feet in front of Sakato.

Not only did the artillery have to be deadly accurate, but it also had to be perfectly timed to be effective. Other men in Miho's battery had to know the precise amount of time each shell required to reach its target and then set the timing fuse on each shell so that it exploded about seventy-five feet above the ground. "This was our forte in the 522," recalled Miho, proud that his crew's accuracy and timing precision rained shrapnel on enemy positions in front of the 2nd Battalion. When forward artillery observers and their artillery batteries two miles distant worked in perfect unison under enemy fire, "We could drop it right into a foxhole," forward observer Akagi boasted after the war.[8]

Artillery accuracy aside, the 2nd Battalion firefights taking place across clearings only twenty-five or fifty yards wide made artillery fire extremely dangerous. By early afternoon the 2nd had advanced a mere two hundred yards, the equivalent of a single city block. The rescue mission was quickly proving to be an unequal battle between enemy machine guns and small-arms fire.

Replacement troops haunted Kelly Kuwayama, Sakato's medic, that day. He had come from an affluent New York family in which all the children had gone to college and whose parents had allowed a daughter to marry a Caucasian. He had graduated Princeton University with a degree in politics, economics, and history before being drafted. Through a quirk of transfers, he had become a medic without completing all the required medic-training courses. Combat in Italy had taught him to pay particular attention to the 2nd Battalion's replacements.

"I would shake the hands of the guys coming in knowing that by the next day I might be picking them up dead. They were replacing our men who had been hit that day. I knew these guys were scared.

They were also very anxious not to let the unit down. When you're advancing on the line, the guy in the front is going to get picked off. They were so anxious . . . to be the first to go and [then] would be the first to get killed," he recalled after the war. "When I looked at them and their eyeballs didn't move, I knew they were dead. That was tough."[9]

Mines and enemy ground fire might be evaded, but it was impossible to escape German artillery. The approaches to Hill 617 forced most of the 2nd Battalion onto well-known paths. The Germans had been preparing defensive positions for weeks in the Vosges and knew precisely where paths of advance were located near Hill 617. That greatly increased the accuracy of their mortars and artillery. "Anytime the [Germans] felt there was movement, they would start lobbing those [mortar] shells or they would call in the 88s [artillery]. And they would pound the heck out of where we were. So we had to lay low. Otherwise, you know, we'd get killed," scout Matayoshi recalled.[10]

Sakato and the others had learned to ignore the spooky whistling sound created by enemy artillery fire. If a soldier could hear a whistling sound, the shell was far-enough away that it posed no threat. "Wooom, wheeee," they told newcomers, was the sound of enemy artillery passing by. At most, they said, you could hear a brief "swish" for a split second before the first incoming artillery shell exploded on your position, never enough time to dive into a foxhole or ravine.

Another member of Company G, Kenji Ego, saw exactly what a well-targeted enemy mortar shell could do. His unit dug temporary foxholes, simply called "holes" by soldiers, when their advance had stalled. The foxholes were little more than trenches frantically dug before the enemy's mortars and artillery began pulverizing their position. A German mortar shell landed on one of Ego's friends during an attack. "But none of us could leave our holes. After it stopped, we ran to the hole. There was smoke drifting up. I looked in the hole and the first thing I saw was his helmet. He was giving his last death rattle. I couldn't help him," Ego remembered decades later.[11]

As darkness settled on the forest, the commanding officer of the 2/442, Lieutenant Colonel James Hanley Jr., had endured a brutal day. The son of a prominent judge who was also a battalion commander in a federalized National Guard unit, Hanley had accompanied his father as "mascot" when it searched for Pancho Villa in Mexico. He was eight years old. By the time the battalion was recalled, Hanley had decided to become a lawyer and serve in the military. He had earned his law degree from the University of Chicago in 1931. Hanley started his career as a justice of the peace, was elected state's attorney, and then became an assistant attorney general of North Dakota by 1941.

At one point during the day's fighting, Hanley had moved the 2/442's command post forward to a point where he planned to send two companies on a flanking maneuver against the enemy. But when he discovered an accompanying communications platoon had taken a spool of telephone wire with them but had not laid it out as they advanced, he had to hand off command of the two companies to another officer, who led them on the counterattack mission. Unexpected enemy resistance and inconsistent communication and coordination had stymied the 442nd's first day's attempt to reach the 1/141.

Hanley's men had advanced only a few hundred yards that were littered with empty ammo belts and medical supplies. Throughout the day, when men had called "Medic!" Kuwayama ran to them. Months of battle experience had taught him how to assess and triage. He knew that enemy bullets and shrapnel powerful enough to enter and exit a man's chest or torso were more deadly. Those soldiers usually were not in a great deal of pain, and some sensed their death was near. They often laid still and were silent. Kuwayama likely gave those men morphine but could not do anything about internal bleeding. He could say little more than "We're going to take care of you," the one thing every wounded soldier that day wanted to hear.[12]

Wounded soldiers who rolled over onto their stomachs and curled up probably had wounds slight enough that they remained alert and instinctively positioned themselves to protect their stomachs and genitals. They tended to be more aware of their wounds, could be vocal, and certainly were scared. It was up to the medics to maintain calm in a forest of chaos.

"I'm going to lose my leg, aren't I?" a soldier might ask. Part of a medic's job in battle was to maintain hope. "No, you're not going to lose it. You're going to be all right." Then Kuwayama and others had dragged those men on a poncho or carried them on a litter to a safer location, perhaps to a primitive aid station. Many aid stations were simply a collection of medical supplies in a gully or on the back side of a hill, presumably out of the direct line of enemy fire. Those aid stations had largely remained in place throughout the day, given the lack of meaningful advance by Hanley's men.

The other battalions of the 141st had made minimal progress as well. A substantial German force remained entrenched between them and the 1/141. Despite repeated orders from Lundquist, Higgins had no real ability to fight his way toward friendly forces. At 1840 he radioed Lundquist, "No rations for three days, seven new casualties. Where is our patrol which moved this day in order to meet mission force? Need ammo before attack possible."[13] Higgins's men weren't going anywhere, and he was using precious battery power to make that clear to his superior officer. Cold was about to join the Germans as the 1/141's enemy.

———◆———

MEANWHILE, AT DIVISION HEADQUARTERS, DAHLQUIST WAS realizing the late-afternoon assault had not developed into the breakthrough he sought. The reports from the battlefield had been as disheartening for Lundquist as they likely were infuriating to Dahlquist. Sakato's Company E had not moved in hours, and two of the platoons had suffered nine casualties. Every platoon leader and noncommissioned officer had been killed or wounded. The company could muster only ten men per patrol. The survivors were pinned down by enemy machine gunners. Company F had dug in for the night, estimating at least one hundred enemy soldiers were a few yards away. Some Germans wore camouflaged and hooded uniforms, indicating they were well trained and probably battle tested.

The 3/141 reported that it had dug in for the night in front of at least two German companies of one hundred men each. Eight enemy machine gun emplacements had been spotted before nightfall, making the prospect of the next morning's assault hellacious at best. The battalion had lost two of its three tanks. A messenger from the 3rd Battalion had reached Lundquist's headquarters and requested multiple litter-bearer squads to follow him back to where wounded men lay in the mud.

Two battalions of the 141st had failed to reach the 1st Battalion the day before. Now the disappointing progress of three frontline battalions on the 26th had made it increasingly clear that the surrounded men would have to be resupplied directly if they were going to survive until friendly forces reached them. The mission to relieve the 1/141st could soon become a rescue mission.

The options for resupplying Higgins's men were limited. Ground resupply was out of the question, as the combat engineers could not build a fresh-cut log road on top of the muddy logging road any closer to Higgins than the infantry could advance. And the engineers were suffering casualties from enemy artillery as they painstakingly converted the muddy route into a wooden surface that could support heavy vehicles.

It was a tedious and dangerous process. First the road and nearby woods had to be swept for mines. Then earthmovers moved forward to clear the sodden roadway and scrape a relatively uniform roadbed, despite the thick mud. The equipment was loud, smoky, and relatively stationary. Each dozer was an ideal target for enemy artillery. During a German artillery attack, some men in the road-building crew dove for cover. Others opted to stand upright, against a tree trunk, and hope they became a smaller target for the relentless tree bursts several yards above their heads.

The main supply road began to take shape, as gravel was dumped into the mud and compressed and then wood planks laid down. If the roadbed was still deemed unstable, tree trunks were laid end to end on both sides of the road. Then hundreds of logs were laid crosswise, side by side on top. The third layer was tree trunks again laid end to end on both sides of the new road. They were secured with six-inch posts pounded into the ground every thirteen feet. The wood rails helped keep vehicles from sliding off the makeshift road. Mud and brush were packed in between the parallel rails to marginally smooth the crosswise tree-trunk road surface. It required hundreds of tree trunks six to eighteen inches in diameter to build a road of any significant distance. Given the rippled surface of the road from the side-by-side logs, they were called corduroy roads.

Much of the work took place at night and in the rain, when combat troops rested and there was less vehicular traffic. Some engineer squads patrolled just-built stretches of road to clear them of trees uprooted by enemy artillery.

Another way to reach the 1/141 immediately was to fire specialized 105mm and 155mm artillery shells (designed to carry propaganda materials) into the surrounded battalion's position. Shells would be filled with vitamin-enriched D rations, sulfadiazine tablets for the wounded, and Halazone purification tablets. Although the shells would not explode into a torrent of deadly shrapnel, they had to land close enough for Higgins's men to retrieve them, but so not close as to score direct hits on the 1/141's foxholes. Assuming no one was killed by this friendly fire, the capacity of the shells greatly limited the amount of supplies that could be delivered to more than two hundred men.

A third option was to drop supplies in auxiliary tanks equipped with parachutes from aircraft flying through the rain just above the treetops. Utilized earlier in the war with mixed results, certainly the tanks' larger size could deliver significantly more supplies than those delivered by artillery shells. But it would require twelve hours to ready the aircraft with the requested supply list, the specific drop location, and the estimated time for the drop. Additionally, as the aircraft approached the 1/141's position, the pilots would have to fly below the clouds, evade German fire, and have only a few seconds to spot the markers laid out by Higgins's men in the forest. Once the tanks were released, they would help the Germans determine Higgins's position.*

Higgins was told to expect an airdrop at 0800 the following morning, even though the forecast called for another day of low clouds and heavy mist. The pilots were told to be on call and that the go–no go decision would be made at the last minute. If the weather and enemy allowed the flight to proceed, Higgins could expect two days' supply of K rations and water, medical supplies, one case of .45 ammunition, one case of carbine ammunition, two cases of machine-gun ammunition, four cases of M1 rifle ammunition, twelve batteries for Higgins's radiomen, and a handful of field telephones. Of course, friendly artillery fire would have to be suspended minutes before the supply aircraft reached the 1/141.

Dahlquist, however, wasn't ready to give up on the day's rescue. If the 141st and the 2/442 couldn't break through in the late afternoon, once again he wanted Higgins and his cabal of young lieutenants to mount their own attack. As night fell he ordered Lundquist to have Higgins move "out in open ground across to Biffontaine." Lundquist knew better. "This plan has already been discussed but don't believe it is good due to litter cases," Lundquist radioed Dahlquist. The general answered with a vague order: "I do not order you to leave wounded but the battalion must be gotten out tonight."[14]

Lundquist was standing in the radio cross fire between Dahlquist and Higgins. His superior officer expected a rescue by Lundquist's battalions and the 2/442 within a few hours, but the rescue units had taken horrific casualties and were dug in for the night. Higgins was

---

*Contemporary accounts in 1944 described the parachutes as red and yellow. French residents recall seeing white parachutes attached to the tanks. They say the parachutes were only about twenty inches in diameter.

telling Lundquist his men were starving, increasing numbers lay wounded, and his ammunition was dwindling. Higgins also pointed out that he had about half as many combat effectives after sending out his forty-eight-man patrol at least fifteen hours earlier. And now Dahlquist wanted Higgins to mount a dash off the ridge and down the slope to Biffontaine? At night?

As Dahlquist's order was never implemented and no one could predict when relief units would reach the surrounded battalion, re-supply by air became the top priority. At 2010 Blonder relayed a message to Lundquist, telling him the stranded soldiers would construct a white arrow (using paper maps and all the light-colored cloth the troops could muster) in a clearing near the stranded men. When the supply aircraft approached, they would release yellow smoke, if possible. Blonder's message made it clear how risky the air-supply mission would be to the surrounded men. "Request rations, ammo, [unintelligible], medical supplies so that enemy will not observe and inform enemy of our position." Although the 1/141 was pinned down in a confined area, apparently the exact deployment of the soldiers wasn't readily discernible to the Germans. Blonder also asked, "Have you heard from our [breakout] patrol?" Lundquist had not. All he could do now was oversee the details of the airdrop, now scheduled for late morning the following day.[15]

———— ✦ ————

Company I rifleman Lawrence Ishikawa didn't get to finish his hand of poker after supper in his temporary Bruyères barrack. He had showered for the first time in days and then enjoyed a tray full of hot food. He and others had received new gear and clothing, including underwear, socks, wool trousers, field shirts, and a jacket, although their winter gear had not yet arrived. Shaving for the first time in nine days was a treat that had capped off the first day of much-needed recuperation. Ishikawa had survived continual combat for more than a week and had seen dozens of men wounded or killed. Now Company I was standing down for several days' rest before going back onto the line. But shortly before midnight, the prospect of rest and recuperation disappeared. Ishikawa and his buddies were told that in a few hours, Company I would be reengaging the enemy. They would have less than one night's good sleep before predawn assembly. Platoon sergeants reported to company commanders to get the lowdown.

"Okay, get ready because you're going back on line." Not far from Ishikawa, Company K radioman Jim Tazoi didn't believe what he had heard. Less than two days earlier, the bloodied men of the 3/442 had been granted rest and recuperation following the Bruyères and Biffontaine assaults. *My gosh,* he thought to himself, *you said we were going to be in the rest area for two or three days. But here you've kicked us out already, telling us to go back on line.*[16]

Not only would the 3rd Battalion jump off before dawn the following day, but the 100th Battalion would also be alongside. Al Takahashi had taken a precious shower, put on clean clothes, and shaved for the first time in more than a week. "So we shaved and that night that damn stupid general, he got his battalion lost . . . and he says 'Hey, we have to go rescue them,'" he recalled.[17] Takahashi and others were flabbergasted that Dahlquist wasn't calling on other regiments in the 36th Division to launch a rescue mission. Yet Takahashi and the others likely didn't know that the other two battalions of the 141st had failed for two days to reach Higgins's men.

Sleep was impossible for much of the 442nd's 100th and 3rd Battalions that night. At 0300 on October 27, company officers and platoon leaders rousted their men and ordered them to gather their cold and damp gear at about the same time. The 442nd would attack the enemy at 1000. The 100th and 3rd Battalions had to be on the front line well in advance of that, and they faced a long, brutal climb up into the mountains immediately after leaving their temporary barracks.

When the remainder of the 442nd attacked at midmorning, it would have the option of asking for full support from the 141st. If that circumstance developed, the 141st would make a frontal assault if the 442nd believed it could flank the enemy. The infantry would be accompanied by forward observers from the 131st Field Artillery and 522nd Field Artillery Battalions.

———◆———

MEANWHILE, A GROUP OF PILOTS WAS CALLED INTO A QUONSET hut at an American air base near Dole, about one hundred miles away. They were part of the 405th Fighter Squadron, 371st Fighter Group, 70th Air Wing, U.S. Ninth Air Force. Eliel Archilla, John Leonard, Paul Tetrick, Robert Booth, Milton Seale, Robert Dixon, Robert Gamble, Arthur Holderness, and Leon Hopper were among them. Some had been with the fighter group when it was one of the first squadrons to fly into Europe during the Normandy invasion on reconnaissance missions.

They were told a battalion of soldiers from Texas was surrounded in the mountains to the north. They were stranded on a single ridge in a twenty-eight-hundred-square-mile forest spanning ninety miles from Strasbourg to the north, nearly to the Swiss border. They had run out of food and needed resupply by air, delivered over enemy territory. The briefing officer asked for volunteers. Everyone raised his hand. None had flown a resupply mission before.

They knew the weather was bad and that the cloud ceiling was at only two hundred feet. They would have to fly nearly at treetop level. Most thought their chances of success were only about fifty-fifty. But before they could fly their risky mission, a lot of work had to be completed. Ground crews initially thought they could attach canvas bags to the underside of aircraft wings that could be released over Higgins's position. But the bags ripped apart on practice takeoffs. They'd have to use auxiliary fuel tanks. The crews worked through the night, cutting small access doors in the tanks so they could be filled with supplies. They would be ready when the weather cleared in the morning.

The plan of the mission was straightforward. Leonard, Tetrick, Booth, and Seale would make the first drop attempt, designated "Flight Green." They would be looking "below the deck" (under the cloud cover) and peering through a dense forest to spot the arrow. Normally, they flew their four aircraft single file. But on this mission they would fly in pairs on the last leg of the mission, wingtip nearly to wingtip, to create a wider search area when they approached the reported location of the surrounded men. Archilla and the others would fly on a subsequent resupply mission.

John Leonard would take the lead on the first attempt. The son of an army colonel, he had attended various schools in Massachusetts, Idaho, Minnesota, and Florida before graduating West Point in 1942. For nearly two years, he had been flying as a bomber escort over France and Holland. Others in the rescue flight had less experience. Robert Booth had arrived in Europe in late 1943. He had always been fascinated with flying. After high school he delivered milk to help support his family and then volunteered for the army air corps in 1942. During training he flew over his nearby hometown and buzzed the house where his girlfriend's mother lived. He had a little more than a year's combat flight experience when he volunteered for the mercy mission.

The mission's aircraft was to be the P-47D Thunderbolt. Nicknamed "the Jug," the Thunderbolt was a stout fighter, designed for "dive-and-attack" tactics. It could reach a speed of 550 miles per hour in a dive. Its eight heavy machine guns across a forty-foot wingspan were deadly against the enemy's infantry. Each plane would be rigged with two 150-gallon wing tanks filled with supplies. Crude ten-inch-square cargo-loading doors had been cut into each one. The pilots would have to fly low to spot Higgins's arrow, form up at a higher altitude, and then drop the tanks rigged with parachutes through the clouds. The mission plan appeared as dangerous as it looked improbable.

LUNDQUIST'S WRITTEN SUMMARY OF THE STATE OF AFFAIRS AT midnight on October 26 was as bleak as the constant rain and fog that had draped the rescue mission. "Combat efficiency: poor. Limited by combat fatigue, weather and terrain difficulties and approximately a 50% reduction in rifle company strength on position." He couldn't tell that to Higgins, however. He sent a very different message to him in the final radio transmission that night: "Strong friendly force coming."[18]

This time it would be the entire 442nd leading the way. Its soldiers had received the ammunition, equipment, and some of the rest they desperately needed.

CHAPTER 4

COMBAT EFFICIENCY: POOR

THE PATH LOOKED FAMILIAR TO ARTHUR CUNNINGHAM AS HE approached Higgins's position early on October 27. He and five others had sneaked through the forest for hours after a long, cold night. Somehow they had avoided the German troops who surrounded the 1/141 and then got the American lookouts' attention before entering Higgins's perimeter. They were exhausted. Their report, sobering. The attempt to flank the Germans and attack the roadblock from the front had failed. "Five men from combat patrol returned with one prisoner. Remaining men of patrol captured in ambush," Higgins forwarded to headquarters.[1]

There no longer was any hope that the 1/141 could break out on its own. Its fighting force had been substantially weakened by the loss of more than forty men. Higgins didn't know exactly how many had been captured, how many were wounded or left for dead, sprawled across boulders and downed tree trunks. Regimental headquarters now knew Higgins was down to about two hundred combat troops, after accounting for the wounded and killed over the past four days.

A country boy from Virginia, Arthur Cunningham had carried a heavy automatic rifle and pockets full of ammunition on the ill-fated breakout patrol. A year earlier he had been hunting rabbit, squirrel, and quail near the north fork of the Holston River in western Virginia. Part Cherokee, he had quit school in the ninth grade and worked on the family farm, raising tobacco, corn, and vegetables that were canned for the winter. He fished the Holston with a cane pole or slammed a sixteen-pound sledgehammer onto rocks to stun fish to the surface. Anything to help feed the family.

More than twenty-four hours earlier, he and his patrol had advanced slowly down the ridge in a southwesterly direction away from Higgins's position, knowing the forest was filled with Germans. The path funneled the patrol into the heart of the enemy's position opposite a minefield. As the patrol entered an open area near the foot of the ridge, a mine exploded and the Germans opened deafening fire. Some men fell dead; others dove for cover. It was hopeless. The firing ceased when an American raised something white, perhaps a map or piece of fabric. A white flag. Most of Higgins's patrol gave up. Not Cunningham. "I went crawlin' on up the mountainside and there was a big old high rock and an old pine tree growed up by it. I went on up 'round the mountainside and I heard somethin' come thrashin' through the woods behind me. So I got up into an old pine and hid, to where I could look out. And it was four other Americans. We started back. . . . I could hear someone a-walkin' and when [a German] walked up, I dropped my Browning [rifle] down on his side and he throwed his hands up."[2]

Cunningham and four others had escaped the ambush. The six men, including the German prisoner, had hidden under a rocky ledge most of the day and endured an American artillery barrage most of the night. They never introduced themselves to each other. When they reached the 1/141, Cunningham reported to Higgins. "Captain, I brought you a prisoner." "He ain't no prisoner of mine, he's yours," said Higgins. "You take him and take care of him."[3]

The prisoner told Higgins there were about 150 Germans in the area where Higgins knew the thrust of the rescue mission was directed. Higgins told Blonder to forward that intelligence to regimental command. Meanwhile, Cunningham, Kripisch, Private Robert Camaiani, Private Tillman Warren, and Private Burt McQueen returned to their foxholes. The German prisoner became Cunningham's unwelcome foxhole buddy.

A single patrol had cost Higgins nearly 50 men. At least 10 of them had arrived as replacements on October 18. They had barely enough time to report to their units and collect their gear before heading out on the doomed mission. Now, with only a few days' combat experience, the wounded American prisoners were being taken to a German aid station. The others were on their way to a prison camp near Moosburg, in southern Bavaria. Several were shot by a German sergeant on the way, Private Joe Hilty of Company A recalled after the war. It's not known exactly how many of Higgins's men reached Stalag VII-A alive.

Lieutenant Colonels Gordon Singles and Alfred Pursall were fiercely loyal to their men. They were about to lead the 100th and 3rd Battalions, respectively, back into battle, where the enemy held every advantage. Singles had taken command of the 100th at Camp Shelby. The third-generation West Point graduate had no combat experience until Italy. Wavy hair and a fresh face gave him a youthful appearance that perhaps led him to rely heavily on his officers. He encouraged their input and developed close and informal relationships with several. He had relied on Young Oak Kim almost as a chief of staff. Kim's loss a few days earlier had been devastating. The 100th's mounting casualties weighed heavily on the thirty-eight-year-old Philadelphia native, who was married and had a ten-year-old son.

On the day before his thirty-ninth birthday that morning, Pursall towered above his men. Most soldiers estimated him to be at least six feet five, with shoulders to match. The opposite of Singles, Pursall's wireless glasses and size gave him the appearance of an older stern schoolteacher. But he looked down on his men only figuratively. The Missouri native's command style was similar to Singles's, often asking battalion headquarters' enlisted men, like messenger Rudy Tokiwa and radioman Ernest Uno, for their opinions. That approach had stunned them when he had taken command in Italy a few months earlier.

Oh my God, they're sending us a gray-haired old man. What in the hell's he gonna do for us? Tokiwa first thought. But when Pursall nearly beat Tokiwa into a foxhole during an enemy artillery attack in Italy, Tokiwa began to change his mind.

"I hear they call you 'Punch Drunk,'" Pursall had said to Tokiwa by way of introduction.

"Yeah, I guess they do."

"But they tell me you're the smartest man in the group."

"No, I'm the dumbest one. I wouldn't be here if I was smart."

"Well, show me how to be dumb. Let's go up there [to the front]."[4]

Pursall was as fearless as he was unflappable. On one occasion, he and Uno were moving toward the fighting when one of them tripped a land mine. They had no time to even hold their breath as the mine flew up into the air, and they heard *pak* before it fell to the ground. A dud.

The fearless Pursall laughed. "Boy we got a narrow one there," he said, before continuing his advance. "That's the kind of guy he was. Fearless," Uno recalled later.[5]

Before dawn the 100th and 3rd Battalions began their climb into the forest and into clouds that nearly touched the ground. Visibility ended at the man in front or alongside. Only the muted rustle of canvas revealed their presence as they walked, two battalions abreast. They had six hours to get up onto the ridge and then advance nearly two miles to be in place to attack later in the morning. Tension mounted as they neared the Germans.

On the far left, the 2nd was up ahead, but not far, given the previous day's brutal fighting with the Germans. The 100th would advance on the right, along the southern side of the ridge. The 3rd was in the center, with Companies I and K at the point, atop the narrow ridge. The battalions' route of advance was in a southeasterly direction toward the 1/141. It would concentrate some units into strings of ants on paths along the sole logging road, making them obvious and predictable targets. Others would have to fight their way through the forest, a tree at a time.

Company I's Hajiro, Ishikawa, Sakumoto, and others looked to the only man in the battalion taller than Pursall, their company commander, Captain Joseph Byrne. He was another Caucasian officer they deeply respected, in part because he took a personal interest in his men. When he had been assigned to a post in Hawaii, he learned how to pronounce Japanese names. Technical Sergeant Jim Yamashita marveled at how Byrne could hear a new Japanese name once and always pronounce it correctly thereafter. Everyone else seemed to place the accent on the wrong syllable. Few Caucasian officers extended such common courtesies. Yamashita, once a popular student who was student body president when growing up in a Mormon community, appreciated Byrne's respect for the Japanese Americans under this command.

Byrne had sold furniture after graduating high school in Elmira, New York. He was inducted into the army in 1940. He had been assigned to the 442nd after graduating officer candidate school. When Company I entered combat for the first time in Italy, the troops had been flabbergasted by this tall, lanky Caucasian officer fighting alongside them, crouching behind the same boulders, shouting orders, and advancing shoulder-to-shoulder.

As the hour of attack approached, the forest surrounding the 2nd and 3rd Battalions shuddered when the planned artillery attack began, pinning them in place. Every fifteen seconds an artillery shell exploded in the tree canopy or slammed into the damp ground. The command post to the west, a farmhouse shared by the 442nd and 141st, took enemy fire as well. It was American artillery fire, falling short of its target—not an uncommon occurrence in combat. The ability to target the enemy from two miles away, without being able to see the target in foul weather, was as much art as it was science.

As word reached the batteries to cease fire, General John Dahlquist arrived at the command post for a situation report. All three 442nd battalions were committed to the mission, and all available tanks in the sector were assigned in support of the 442nd. The success of the relief mission would be entirely up to the 442nd. The remaining battalions of the 141st would remain in place and be ready to attack, just in case they were needed.

At 1053 the assault began. The Germans fired back almost immediately. Men fell wounded. Nearby buddies yelled for medics such as Jim Okubo to save them.

When he volunteered for the military, Company K radioman Jim Tazoi's mother had told him, "Die if you need to, because you're going to war, but do not bring shame to your country or your family."[6] He had been raised on a family farm and was an excellent baseball player. He had left Utah State University in his sophomore year to enlist in the army. Five months' fighting had taught him to trust his instincts, day after day.

At one point when he approached a small gully,

> I just happened to look down and there in that trench was a German soldier. He looked right at me and—I don't know if he had a gun or not—maybe ten seconds before that he could have been firing at us. But he was hoping that I wouldn't notice him, but when I looked down and saw him, I raised my gun and he let out a squeal that I still remember. I had presence of mind enough that I didn't want to shoot him in the face so I put about four or five rounds into his chest hoping that I could kill him right away.[7]

Down on the side of the ridge where the 100th slowly advanced, the instincts of another farm boy, Al Takahashi, were equally sharp. He had grown up in central California and tried to join the air corps but was rejected, so he volunteered for the army. As he trained for combat, his family was given two weeks' notice to liquidate their leased farm before internment. As a replacement in the 100th going into France, battle had hardened him in the previous two weeks.

When you see an enemy, you fire. And then it became just like when you were a kid. You're playing cowboys and Indians, you're shooting. Well, it just got to the point where you got to shoot first before they shoot you. . . . You don't even think about anything else, just get him.[8]

———◦———

As weapons fire filled the woods and the rescue battalions' advance quickly slowed, others looked up into the mist and listened hard for the hint of an aircraft's engine. At 1050 Higgins radioed the command post, asking when he could expect the airdrop. The reply was succinct and vague: "Not yet."

Not far away, unrelenting light rain over the past twelve hours had soaked the twenty-five-foot arrow lying on the forest floor. Various men had contributed what they could to cobble together the makeshift beacon for the morning's airdrop. Each had decided what was critical to his ability to fight the Germans and what might make the difference in getting food, ammunition, and medical supplies for those lying on litters, their wounds stiffening in the cold. Despite the bone-chilling cold, parka liners helped make their arrow. T-shirts had been torn into strips, not missed by soldiers already sore from the cold.

———◦———

At dawn on the twenty-seventh, the news had been bad. Nearly all of France was "socked in." The 9th U.S. Air Force's operations were grounded with one exception. The two scheduled resupply flights to the lost battalion, however, were told to proceed. Flight Green launched at 1045. Given the low altitude and mountainous terrain, the four aircraft flew the early part of the mission in a string, one behind each other, as they snaked through valleys, looked for checkpoints, and avoided enemy fire. They followed railroad tracks that ended at Biffontaine at the base of the ridge. Leonard had the lead, with Booth last in line.

As they neared the Vosges foothills, flight leader Captain Gavin Robertson ordered the four to pull up through the overcast near Fougerolles and assemble in formation for the final leg to the target. Each pilot increased throttle, got his nose up, and disappeared into the clouds. As Higgins and his men listened for the approach of their airborne saviors, only three emerged from the clouds. Booth was missing. He didn't answer radio calls. Leonard couldn't wait.

The remaining three continued to the point where they hoped to see Higgins's arrow below. The plan was to approach as close to the ground as possible and then bank hard just as the tanks were released. In a sense, the pilots would try to skip the tanks into the forest, much like a flat rock on a pond. The tanks would approach at an angle until their parachutes caught air and slowed the tanks' speed into a vertical descent.

But the cloud cover was so thick they could see nothing as they circled, hoping for a break in the clouds. At 1115 it was obvious the mission would have to be scrubbed. Flight Green turned for home, its precious cargo still attached to its wings. They had been led to the target by an L-4 observation plane flown by Captain Mayhew Foster. He threw a few boxes of supplies out his door and down into the cloud cover before leaving the area.

The three remaining Thunderbolt pilots dropped down through the clouds and again flew just above the trees on their way back to base. They flew so low that one of Leonard's wings hit a tree and suffered moderate damage, but not enough to keep him from landing safely at Dole. About the time they landed, Higgins was told at noon the resupply mission had been a failure and that the aircraft had returned to base. It would return if there was a break in the clouds. Attached to the message was the standard assurance that a friendly force was heading Higgins's way. It had been nearly seventy-two hours since the lost battalion had been cut off. Much-needed supplies were still at Dole.

Without them, Higgins's men would have to cope with their hunger, and some would suffer more with developing trench foot or infections. Radioman Blonder's feet, in rancid, unchanged socks, no longer were just cold and stiff. Pain had replaced the stiffness. He could barely walk as trench foot took hold. The initial burning and swelling in his feet hadn't seemed so bad. But then the pain intensified as the swelling increased and the bottom of the feet turned dark blue. If it got worse, the toes could begin to seep like a bad burn. The pain would become excruciating. More began to suffer the same initial pain in their feet, with no relief in sight.

The wounded were in worse shape. A few bandages remained, but the painkiller supply had been exhausted. Blonder worried the enemy would hear the cries of men with seeping wounds. Meanwhile, Lundquist had authorized Higgins to begin burying his dead. Shallow graves were dug after a brief moment of hushed reflection. Their locations were recorded for the grave-registration units to someday retrieve the bodies.

<hr />

WHILE THE 1/141 HAD WAITED FOR THE AIRDROP, A GERMAN patrol accompanied by a tank probed the perimeter but had inflicted minimal damage. Higgins had arranged his men to maximize fields of crossing fire. The ranks of the wounded were mounting, but it appeared the Germans weren't yet prepared to mount an all-out assault on the surrounded men. Only exploratory attacks from different directions had taken place so far. There may have been several reasons for that.

Commanding officers of German battalions, regiments, and armies in the area were almost unanimously appalled at the quality and numbers of their troops. In most cases, the condition of their equipment was substandard, and many lacked critical supplies. The officers' frustration was clearly evident in their written reports. When General Hermann Balck had taken command of Army Group G and assumed responsibility for much of the Vosges fighting, he was mortified at what he found at his disposal, given the führer's demand that the Germans turn retreat into victory in the Vosges.

"We urgently need mountain troops," he wrote General Alfred Jodl. "Flatland troops are not suited to fight in the Vosges Mountains and are not properly equipped in comparison to the enemy's mountain troops. . . . [T]he Nineteenth Army are [*sic*] pitiful in both materiel and personnel. Never before have I led such thrown-together and poorly trained troops."[9]

His plea for more men led to only an additional five thousand inadequately trained men in October. General Wiese would have to shuttle units between firefights in the Vosges because there were not enough men to establish a continuous line of defense. That placed a premium on communication across a fluid battlefield as crises and opportunities developed, such as surrounding a battalion of American soldiers. An undated entry in the Nineteenth Army's log at the time revealed the limits of Wiese's ability to wage war: "Communications between the various fighting units and command posts is problematic. Many of the incorrect or delayed messages can be explained by the difficulty that messengers encounter in the deep ravines of the wooded thickets. By the time a messenger reaches the command post, the situation at the front usually has already changed."[10]

Yet to the men of the 442nd, it seemed every ravine, ridge, and boulder concealed a German soldier. The Germans were waging a brutal, agonizing war of attrition that likely made their combat firepower seen greater than it was. The Germans' objective was to inflict as many American casualties as possible, pause, perhaps fall back a few yards to new concealment, and force the Americans to continue climbing up into murderous fields of carbine, machine-gun, and artillery fire.

The Germans' strategy for Higgins's situation was similar. The enemy infantry was regularly engaging the perimeter and then using artillery to pound the foxholes of those hunkered down. Yet the thick forest worked to Higgins's advantage.* If the Americans couldn't see the Germans, in turn the Germans couldn't be sure of exactly how many men they had surrounded or precisely what firepower the 1/141 had at its disposal. A stalemate had developed, and it would remain until one commanding officer or the other risked the lives of his remaining men to force the issue.

——⊙——

BY EARLY AFTERNOON, THE COMMANDS OF THE 442ND AND 141ST had consolidated at a single command post on the ridge, about fifteen hundred yards from the fighting and more than two and a half miles from Higgins's position. At 1315 Dahlquist arrived. Once again, the situation report on several fronts was not encouraging.

Much like Higgins's men, for four days a company in the 3/141 had been initially pinned down by a superior German force. Technical Sergeant Charles Coolidge's men had held the Germans at bay as the situation developed into a standoff, but now German tanks approached Coolidge's position. Coolidge refused a surrender offer from a German officer riding in a tank. A furious battle of grenades and weapons fire ensued. Coolidge and his men killed or wounded an estimated seventy-five Germans before they were forced to withdraw.†

Dahlquist knew the air resupply mission for Higgins's men had been scuttled. The 100th and 3/442 were to have launched a coordinated assault at 1000, but radio traffic indicated they had yet to make contact with each other after several hours of fighting. Some tanks were running low on fuel, and enemy resistance was proving difficult to predict. Minutes before Dahlquist arrived, one company

---

*One member of the 1/141 likened the forest to a giant's scalp, with huge follicles nearly identical in size every few feet as far as he could see.

†Coolidge was awarded the Medal of Honor for his bravery over the course of the four-day standoff in the Vosges.

of Germans had surrendered, while a few hundred yards away another unit was reported to be digging in to fight the Americans. A 442nd patrol reached one of the German roadblocks and discovered it was not in the location first reported. When such command confusion reigned, it fell to individual soldiers to rise to the occasion and to trust one another under fire.

The 3rd Battalion's Companies I and K were at the forefront of the Americans' assault. They had been ordered to drive a wedge in the middle of the German defense. Company L was slightly to the rear in reserve, and the 100th Battalion was fighting on the right flank. Jim Yamashita and Nobuo Amakawa of Company I faced some of the most deadly fire.

When a man fell wounded in the firefight, Yamashita called for a medic. Sometimes it was obvious to Yamashita the man was already dead. When the fighting intensified, no one could reach the dead soldier. He simply lay there, within sight of his buddies, perfectly still, as shouts, weapons fire, explosions, and ricochets filled the air. As Yamashita, Amakawa, and others slowly advanced, they left bodies where they fell. It was important that someone remember their locations, so the grave-registration crews could find them later when the forest had been cleared of Germans. If the rain turned to snow in the days ahead, a soldier's body could become very difficult to find. In the weeks ahead, a family might be notified a loved one was missing from the day's fighting, assume he had been captured, and then learn perhaps months later that his body had been found where he had been killed that day. Direct artillery hits obliterated some bodies, leaving only a hand or leg hidden among the patches of barren, waist-high blueberry bushes.

Much of the fighting was coordinated at the squad level. Nobuo Amakawa worked one side of the fighting, guarding against a flank attack. When he discovered an enemy machine-gun emplacement only twenty yards away, he yelled to his squad to take cover. He then advanced to within ten yards of the enemy, so brazenly that the Germans abandoned their position. His squad was saved from devastating fire. A few minutes later, a German sniper drew a bead on Amakawa and shot him dead.*

Other young soldiers faced a different threat, an alien creature different from anything they had known as boys. James Oura had grown up poor in Hawaii. Both parents had worked on a sugar plantation, and the family raised chickens and rabbits and fished in order to put food on the table. He had volunteered without his parents' permission shortly after his eighteenth birthday. He had never left the Hawaiian Islands. Now, half a world away, Oura spotted what many infantrymen feared most: a German tank sat hidden in the trees, its turret turned toward the Japanese Americans. Despite their bulk, stationary enemy tanks sometimes were difficult to spot through the dense forest. Their first deadly shot revealed their position.

"Bazooka!" Rifleman Oura crouched as his bazooka man crawled forward, stopped, and took aim. There were only a few places on a German Mark IV tank that were vulnerable to an American bazooka. One was the engine. A single shot started a fire in the engine compartment. Panic and fumes swamped the crew. Seconds later, the tank's top hatch swung open, releasing smoke and men. It was an awkward and agonizingly slow escape for the Germans as they fled a burning fire into direct gunfire. Each man had to stand upright on an interior step, his upper body exposed to Oura, before he could swing his legs free of the tank. One man at a time. Each an easy target. Perhaps too easy.

When Oura watched a wounded German struggle to climb out and then fall to the ground, Oura raised his rifle. He paused. *Would you like to be picked off like that?* he asked himself. It was the first time he realized that his conscience could surface in combat. He decided not to shoot that German. Oura wondered if he would again freeze in battle in the months ahead. But it happened only once. He didn't hesitate to shoot the enemy after that. Shrapnel had shredded too many friends. Too many young replacements had been shot dead in their first few hours of combat.

---

*Amakawa was posthumously awarded the Silver Star five months later.

War had also hardened Al Takahashi, a few hundred yards to the south, where the 100th was trying to connect with the 3rd Battalion. Like many others, he had developed a kind of scar tissue that separated conscience from reality and the threat of immediate death. "It just got to the point where you got to shoot first before they shoot you. That's the only thing you had in mind because, you figure, if you don't shoot, he's gonna get you, and you'd be dead. We're just pushing through, and we're really pushing, so that's part of war. And after they start shooting at you, you forget all about shooting at the other guy."[11]

Another soldier in the 36th Division recalled why men in war developed a callousness that was inconceivable to civilians. "In war you learn everything fast; you have to. At first you assume that death is for others and it won't come to you. Later, you realize that everyone will 'get it' if he is there long enough. There is no time for grief, for mourning, or for wasted emotion of any kind. I resolved never to really look at a dead body. They were 'noticed' hundreds of times, but never really 'seen.' In twenty-one months in Italy, France, Germany, and Austria I never saw anyone shed a tear."[12]

———— ◈ ————

BY MIDAFTERNOON COMPANY K'S JAMES OURA, JIM OKUBO, AND Jim Tazoi were exhausted. Along with the 100th Battalion, the 3rd Battalion had jumped off long before dawn, climbed onto the ridge, and fought Germans for hundreds of yards, slowly pushing them back and then having to fall back. They had scaled mossy rocks, climbed over tangled webs of downed tree trunks, and slogged through boggy mud. But the 1/141 remained more than one and a half miles to the east. To the north, the 2nd Battalion had fought all day at the base of Hill 617 but gained almost no ground. Only the casualties mounted. The primitive logging road had become clogged with two-way traffic, as jeeps ferried the wounded off the ridge and down to a field hospital in the valley.

As the fighting continued, the most seriously wounded were tri-
aged by forward medics like Okubo before they were extricated from
one battle to another kind of war. It was a war that medics fought at
collecting stations, a wounded man's first stop on the way to a hospital. Convenience and efficiency dictated the location of most of the
stations. A few hundred yards behind the fighting, a stand of trees
alongside the logging road that had become a quagmire was designated an aid station. Medics waited for a field telephone or radio
message that patients were inbound from the front. Everything was
soaked—medics, the wounded, and the bandages that Okubo and
other medics had applied on the battlefield. "I never felt so damn
mad at weather than at that time, because there was nothing we could
do about it. The rain just made everything impossible to do, but
worst of all the casualties had rain in their faces. We couldn't strip
them to take care of their wounds adequately and it beat down on
their faces and added to the cold and the misery," medic Minoru Masuda later wrote to his wife.[13]

Not far away, other aid stations were carved out of the forest floor
by ammunition-and-pioneer platoons assigned to dig, carry, and construct just about anything needed in combat.* Now they were digging
dugouts in the forest as the fighting intensified. A dugout was little
more than a man-made crater in the mud, about eight feet wide and
fifteen feet long, just large enough for two litters and a medic or two,
about three feet below ground level. Once it was dug, logs were cut
and laid over the top, leaving an entrance at one end. Then the medics
took over. They used one or two shelter halves to shield the entrance
before crawling into the three-foot-high cave to treat two wounded
men. A candle or two provided the only light. Gaping wounds were
marginally cleaned, and junks of barely attached flesh were secured. A
kind word was passed to a wounded man desperate for any assurance
in the dim, damp light that he would make it back to a hospital, where

---

*Ammunition-and-pioneer platoons consisted of a pool of men available for a
variety of manual tasks.

the cots were clean and dry and bright lights hung over surgeons' heads. Artillery boomed far off in the distance, adding to the gloom both wounded and medics endured.

Medic Kelly Kuwayama, near Hill 617, had treated and sent more casualties to aid stations than he could count. As usual, it was the replacement troops that now outnumbered the remaining battle veterans who suffered the most. Kuwayama had raced to several who had fallen in the field of fire. He knew that some had been desperate enough to earn the respect of the veterans that they had taken unnecessary risks in battle. Kuwayama had treated those still alive but couldn't save others who had arrived only the day before.

Lieutenant Colonel James Hanley had to get his 2nd Battalion moving. After nearly two days of fighting, it had not captured Hill 617. The Germans still held the high ground and likely outnumbered Hanley's force. The former state's attorney general who had once chased Pancho Villa in Mexico with his father's reserve unit had to change his strategy. He decided to split his battalion, leading Sakato, Kuwayama, and the rest of Companies E and F on a flanking move to the north. He ordered Matayoshi and the rest of Company G to spread out in front of the Germans to give the impression of full battalion strength. Would the Germans fall for it, enabling Hanley to attack from two directions? Hanley would find out the next morning.

Then the Germans counterattacked at the heart of the 442nd's advance, attacking the 3rd Battalion's Companies K and I north of the logging road. It came at midafternoon and only a few minutes after Colonel Pursall had waved off artillery support. The battlefield had become so intimate, so blended, that it was impossible to target enemy positions without jeopardizing American troops. The fighting had compressed into sight lines of perhaps seventy-five yards and firefights of less than fifty yards. German Mark IV tanks blasted 3rd Battalion positions. On the Americans' side, the 3rd Battalion had been reinforced with a tank battalion company and a mortar company. The 100th had received a company each from a tank battalion, tank destroyer battalion, and chemical weapons (mortar) battalion.

Moss, dirt, rocks, and chunks of wood, mixed with the metal shrapnel, slammed into the foxholes where Okubo, Oura, and Ichiyama crouched. Tanks, mortars, and artillery on both sides pounded almost the same location. The ground shuddered, trees exploded, and men cried out in pain as shrapnel split the air in every direction.

Private Matsuichi Yogi balanced a bazooka on his shoulder as enemy fire intensified. Yogi had a decision to make. He could take advantage of available cover and not have a good shot at an enemy tank. Or he could step out into the open, risk getting shot, and get a good angle on one of the tanks attacking the Americans' position. As enemy fire frothed the air around him, Yogi stood and fired. A second later, the enemy tank groaned to a stop. Smoke appeared, and its hatch flipped open. As far as Yogi was concerned, the tank was dead. He looked for more enemy targets. He fired again, killing a German firing a bazooka. Then Yogi picked up a rifle, spotted another enemy bazooka man, shot, and killed that German, too. His decisions and extraordinary nerve and marksmanship helped thwart a German counterattack. Company K held firm.

Meanwhile, confusion between the front line and the rear command posts surfaced as a new enemy. Radio traffic between Hanley and 442nd artillery crews dissolved into a debate. At one point, an artillery officer radioed Hanley's battalion headquarters to explain that his unit's firing had been ordered by Colonel Hanley and his forward artillery observer. He insisted his artillery crew would not fire without a specific request from the front line. Hanley's radioman didn't buy it, as Hanley and his forward observer stood near the radio. "They are both here and say they didn't call for it."[14] The last thing Hanley needed was friendly artillery on top of his men.

Meanwhile, good communication between foxholes and a command post was as essential as a direct hit on the enemy as the Americans' advance ground to a standstill. Communication, or lack of it, could shift the tide of the day's assault in an instant. Messengers assigned to each battalion raced on foot between the 442's regimental, battalion, and company command posts. They avoided enemy fire and navigated slick moss, sucking mud, crazily stacked logs, rocks, creeks, and enemy mines. They had to know where company command posts were at the edge of enemy fire and then return to Singles's, Hanley's, and Pursall's positions.

Radios, of course, were far more effective when circumstances allowed. Company I's Shuji Taketomo led a four-man radio communications crew. They carried the same 300 radio that Blonder was using, miles ahead in the forest. The son of a prosperous agricultural businessman made sure his unit laid telephone wire through the trees as his company advanced. He had to remember frequently changing codes in order keep his reports secure. On some days, additional rations might be called "moonlight," or a company commander would be called "Sunray."

Radio crews in the 100th Battalion had an additional advantage. The Hawaii Japanese Americans used pidgin English. Their distinctive lexicon—they called it "Nihongo"—had once been derided by the American-born Japanese Americans. But it was indecipherable in battle. An order to get the troops moving would be "hele on" in pidgin. To investigate would be "spark." Destroy became "all buss up," and alarm became "fo real." That gave Singles additional security when he sent reports to Pence on what his 100th Battalion was facing throughout the day.

The German counterattack threatened to split the rescue mission in two. If the Germans could drive a wedge within the rescue force, it would be easier to stop. Intense enemy fire and mounting casualties forced the 3/442 to withdraw several hundred yards along the logging road, giving back a significant portion of the ground it had gained in nearly a day's fighting. Pursall now needed to confirm the position of the 100th relative to his 3rd Battalion. When he sent a platoon out to contact the 100th, he learned the 100th was more than one thousand yards away. Pursall had no way of knowing whether the Germans had spotted the gap as night fell in the forest.

The entire 442nd had now been committed to the mission, but after a full day's fighting the Germans had held firm. Only a few hundred yards had been ceded to the Americans, and a bloody toll had been extracted from them. The 2nd Battalion was stalled in place, and it was unclear whether the 3rd and 100th could sustain a coordinated attack into the gap between them. That would have to be resolved through the night if the 442nd was to resume its assault the following morning.

———◦———

A FEW FEET FROM HIS FOXHOLE AND MORE THAN A MILE FROM the Japanese Americans trying to reach him, Eason Bond stared at a thicket of trees only a few yards away. The nineteen-year-old had grown up near Thomaston, Georgia, a company town of about six thousand residents at the start of the war. The B. F. Goodrich cotton mill had dominated life there. His father had worked in the mill before buying a small farm outside of town. As a boy he favored pranks such as putting a bag of rocks on a sidewalk where passersby were sure to kick them. He and some of his seven brothers and sisters went to church on Sundays, mostly to play with friends before and after church services. He had no plans in life and not much education. Bond was "plowin' a mule" in cotton, corn, and sugar-cane fields in the sweltering Georgia summer heat for one dollar a day when he was drafted in 1943.

Now, for the third consecutive day, he stared at a small stretch of forest directly in front of what he called his "trench." Unlike others in the 1/141, he didn't spend every free minute deepening what could have become his foxhole. He favored a trench, the shelter a soldier typically dug at sunset, knowing it would be his shelter only until dawn. Eason had quit digging when his trench was shoulder width, long enough for his six-foot frame and about two feet deep. *Good 'nough,* he figured. The Georgia native preferred to sleep on bare dirt next to his trench, close enough that he could roll into it when enemy fire arrived.

Sleep had become only a fond memory for Bond, Estes, Comstock, Cunningham, and the others. Most had been in near-constant combat since the 36th had stormed ashore in mid-August. They had learned how to rest—not really sleep—on the ground, in trenches, and in the rain. Newcomers had learned to cope with a single hot meal every few days when it was too dangerous for cooks to drive up to the front line. Exhaustion had taken root in every man, a constant companion that drained energy, resolve, and hope.

There were no shifts of on-duty and off-duty when a man was surrounded by Germans. Bond and the others took catnaps through the day and night, trusting the men on either side of them to keep a sharp lookout. For three days Bond had kept watch and not seen a single German. *What the hell are they waiting for?* he asked himself. Bond and the rest had a lot of time to think. They might wonder about loved ones back home. Or imagine how it would be if this was the forest where they would die. When they fell, would they feel the wet forest floor a split second before they died? Would their family freeze at the knock on the door, fearing a telegram waited on the other side? They couldn't tell if the echo of machine guns far off in the distance was a sign of relief or disaster.

Bond was part of Company C, commanded by Lieutenant Joseph Kimble. Most of his men didn't think much of Kimble, some calling him "a smart ass who thought he was too good looking." Instead, Bond looked to his section sergeant, C. J. Barby, and the four or five men he had bonded with on the battlefield for camaraderie and support. Like many, Bond's family was his platoon. He knew most by name, but recognized the rest of the men in his company only well enough to nod a greeting. Now Bond's war had shrunk to a single trench and the forest directly in front of it.

Bond scanned the dirt near his trench. *There it is.* Two days earlier, he had finished his C ration, battlefield food in a can that was despised by most soldiers. He had tossed the rock-hard crackers on the ground. They were nearly inedible unless soaked in water or coffee. Some men joked that their shelf life would probably last until World War III. But by now the hunger in his gut had become an ever-present ache. It had become a deep pain that never lessened and now felt as if it were spreading throughout his body.

While most soldiers found K rations passably edible, most despised C rations. But after two days without food, Bond found the dirty crackers, now swollen by the rain, and ate them. Who knew when the men of the 1/141 would see any kind of food again?

———— ⚜ ————

SOME MEN IN THE 1/141 KNEW THE 442ND HAD BEEN COMMITTED to reaching them. Many had heard about the 442nd in Italy, as its reputation for extraordinary courage had spread among the troops via the grapevine, in articles in the military's *Stars and Stripes*, and in newspapers at home. "I'll bet the 442 is the first to get to us. I'd give $1,000 to see a Jap come through these woods," Blonder told Lieutenant Gordon Nelson. "Yea, and I'll bet you're the first man in the American Army [who] ever said he wanted to see that," replied Nelson.[15]

By midday it was clear to Dahlquist that the 1/141 may not be reached for a third day. At 1400 he told Lundquist that in three hours, American 105mm and 155mm artillery shells filled with medical supplies would be targeted on the 1/141. Lundquist passed the plan on to Higgins a few minutes later. Higgins had to know it was a daring and potentially deadly plan. More than two hundred men would be crouching or lying in perhaps one hundred foxholes, some of them uncovered.

Dahlquist's plan called for seventy shells packed with medical supplies to be fired at Higgins's men, based on coordinates provided by

Blonder.* Artillery crews wrapped medical supplies, water-purification tablets, and D rations (vitamin-laden chocolate bars) in a thin cloth before inserting the bundle into the base of each shell.

The shells would carry enough explosive to break apart in the forest's canopy, spilling the supplies onto the ground. It was a risky ploy. Jack Wilson and his machine-gun assistant, Burt McQueen, had been building a foxhole roof of stout logs, so they were in good shape. But men like Eason Bond, who had nothing more than an open-air trench, would be at extreme risk. If any of those shells scored a direct hit on a foxhole, Higgins's medics would have more casualties—and possibly dead soldiers—on their hands. The 1/141 would have only about thirty minutes' final warning before they were to endure the friendly artillery fire.

Adding to the danger, the attempt would take place only about thirty minutes before "official" sunset. However, darkness crept into the dense forests of the Vosges Mountains much earlier. The artillery would be hitting Higgins's position through the clouds at nightfall. Somehow Higgins's artillery observers would have to spot where the initial shells landed and then have Blonder radio corrections in course and distance in the fading light. The observers and artillery crews would have to be very accurate, very fast.

Meanwhile, back at Dole, at least a dozen P-47 crews waited for the call announcing a second attempt to bomb the 1/141 with food before dark. They had been waiting all afternoon after the earlier flight had returned to base. The aircraft had been refueled, and pilots had been asked if they had any issues with the aircraft. The supply tanks remained attached to the wings. They waited as the light faded first in the east and then watched the cloud cover darken across France.

But nightfall had sabotaged everything. Although it's not clear how many shells were fired at the 1/141, at 1825 Blonder radioed the 141st's operations officer, saying, "Cannot continue [artillery] adjust-

---

*Some division documents indicate that as many as one hundred shells were packed with supplies.

ment for supplies; will continue in the morning." It had become too dark to adjust artillery and too dark for aircraft to spot the location arrow. With desperate hope, Blonder continued, "Will aircraft be used in the morning? Give pos[ition] of friendly troops. Morale high."[16] Another day had ended with no resupply.

A message two hours later made it clear how desperate the 1/141 had become, and it tempered the "morale high" message sent earlier: "Need halizone [*sic*]. Men weak. 9 litter cases. 53 MIA [missing in action] from patrol.* (Whereabouts of) 1st and 2nd platoons of Company A not known. 4 killed."[17]

THE 100TH AND 3RD BATTALIONS HAD ADVANCED ONLY A FEW hundred yards and been bloodied. Various historical reports indicate the Americans took between forty-three and seventy prisoners, including a battalion adjutant. For the first time, the Germans had focused their poorly trained, inadequately supplied, and significantly depleted battalions on stopping the 442nd rather than attacking the 1/141. Lawrence Ishikawa in Company I never forgot that night in battle and how close he was to the enemy. "We could hear the German soldiers. You know some of these German soldiers were probably not even graduated from high school. Young kids! In the night you could hear them saying, calling for their mother, crying for their mother, so that . . . I guess they knew the next day was going to be a battle, battle royal."[18]

Lundquist may have anticipated the same for the following day, but it must have been clear to him that he was being pushed out of the action and onto the bench. Dahlquist was now making tactical

---

*Earlier, Higgins had reported he had sent a forty-eight-man patrol on the attempt to flank the Germans' roadblock. Fifty-three men missing in action may have included the portions of other patrols he had sent to probe the Germans' positions.

decisions, and near the end of the day Lundquist's 141st had been temporarily attached to Colonel Charles Pence's 442nd. In the span of about twenty-four hours, impulsive Dahlquist had moved from attaching a battalion of the 442nd to the 141st to attaching the entire 141st to the 442nd, "for the time being."

In what could become Lundquist's last daily summary report, at midnight he acknowledged the 141st's combat efficiency was "poor," due to fatigue, terrain, "and approximately a 60% reduction in rifle company strength on position."[19]

He made no mention that Higgins's men had now been stranded more than three days after jumping off on their patrol with only one day's worth of supplies. And he couldn't know how much longer Blonder could nurse his radio's batteries in order to stay in contact with battalion headquarters.

CHAPTER 5

KEEP THEM COMING

RELENTLESS COLD HAD STIFFENED GEORGE SAKATO AND THE REST of the 2/442 on the second night of their rescue mission. It was a far cry from the brutal Arizona summers when he had picked cantaloupes as his family evaded the internment camps. It had insidiously sapped their energy and left a dull ache that was as impossible to ignore as a hangover. Knees had tightened overnight, and bruises had taken root in bones. Shoulders had grown raw under the strain of thirty or forty pounds of gear strapped to the backs of some men.

The cold threatened to erode the inner strength that each man needed to face a third day of fighting and the resolve to press ahead into enemy fire as buddies fell around them. Worse, cold never lost in combat. The Vosges cold before dawn on October 28 was as omnipresent as the Germans. It was just as invisible, invasive, and deadly.

A few hundred yards to the south, Barney Hajiro and the 3/442's Companies I and K woke to enemy artillery pounding the forest floor and shattering the trees above their trenches. Most had lain in their trenches all night for fear of the tree bursts. Some had used their helmets as a urinal and then poured it out at arm's length away from the trench. Modesty could become lethal on the battlefield. If their canteens were low on water, they didn't bother rinsing their helmet. Personal hygiene had become a luxury.

The day before, medic Jim Okubo had dragged bleeding men to safety behind splintered trees and into muddy craters. The wounded were always relieved to see the medic known for his friendly, engaging manner. He had patched them with wet bandages and left them for stretcher bearers who carried them back to aid stations in ravines, carved out of saturated hillsides, and in timber so dense no sunlight reached the ground. Then he had dug in for the night, almost in view of the Germans.

When Company K cautiously got to its feet that morning, the men knew there would be no element of surprise. Company K advanced less than one hundred yards when gunfire erupted. Within minutes soldiers on both sides were firing from the hip as the two forces blended into a cacophony of gunfire, ricochets, and explosions.

"Medic!"

Okubo ran toward the plea and dropped down into the mud. His corpsman training surfaced in staccato: *Where is he hit? Any of them life-threatening? Breathing okay? Sounds pretty good. No chest wounds. I need the supplies on my left hip. Damn mud. Find the safety pins and get that belly wound closed a bit. Do I have any more dressings? There. Get one on that gash. That one, too. How many more dressings do I have? Put a sulfa tablet in his mouth.*

"You'll be okay," said the easygoing medic.

Another cry for help, much too far ahead of Company K's covering fire. *Now what?* Okubo began crawling on his belly through the mud and over tree trunks that vibrated from enemy gunfire. He kept crawling. Directly toward enemy machine guns. Mud danced around him as mortar shrapnel barely missed. He crawled 150 yards until he reached the wounded man, only 40 yards from the enemy. Okubo shimmied to the enemy side of the wounded soldier to shield him from gunfire.

Once he had applied basic battle dressings, Okubo faced an even more horrifying prospect. There was no one to carry the wounded man back to where Company K could protect him. There was only one way to do that. Okubo picked him up and carried the wounded soldier, who probably weighed 150 pounds, across the battlefield. Okubo carried him across the equivalent of one and a half football fields while ignoring his burning lungs, aching legs, and flying shrapnel as two German grenades barely missed him. Miraculously, Okubo made it, laid the soldier down, and looked around. There were more men to be saved.

Through the smoke and mist, the Americans could see another roadblock on the trail ahead. The interlaced stacks of logs held snipers, riflemen, and machine-gun emplacements. Their cross fire seemed insurmountable. Another member of Company K, Sergeant Gordon Yamashiro, decided to take a chance. He set up his squad to cover him, and then Yamashiro advanced alone. Fifty, 75, then 100 yards, killing a sniper and then three more in a machine-gun nest. But another nest remained deadly. Yamashiro pressed ahead, believing his men would cover him. As bullets whipped through the air, he killed two more Germans in the second machine-gun foxhole. A few minutes later, a remaining German sniper spotted Yamashiro and took careful aim. The former carpenter in Hawaii fell dead onto the forest floor, only two days after celebrating his twenty-third birthday near Belmont.[*]

———◆———

IT BEGAN AS A FAINT, FAR-OFF RUMBLE ABOUT TWO HOURS AFTER daybreak. Unidentifiable at first, it grew into a grinding growl. Approaching aircraft above the clouds. They seemed to be heading straight toward the 1/141 on the ridge's crest. American? German? Bound for the 1/141 or on their way somewhere else? How many? The far-off explosions sounded like antiaircraft fire. So did that mean American aircraft were in the air despite the cloud cover?

---

[*] Yamashiro was posthumously awarded a Silver Star for his heroism at the roadblock.

Eason Bond could only wonder. Martin Higgins and a few others knew they were Americans. If the clouds thinned a little at the right moment, the pilots might spot the twenty-five-foot arrow his men had cobbled together. If so, the 1/141 would be bombed with food, water, ammunition, medical supplies, and batteries.

At about 0915, Wilson, Estes, McQueen, and others spotted them crashing through the forest. Six-foot auxiliary fuel tanks dropped nose down through the clouds and plummeted through the canopy. The Thunderbolts had flown through heavy antiaircraft flak from German artillery batteries at La Houssière at the foot of the ridge and near Vanemont. Their white, yellow, orange, and red silk parachutes only marginally slowed their descent. Some hit the ridge at an angle, bounced, flipped, and then rolled away from the 1/141. Some landed one hundred yards away, down on the south side of the ridge and well inside enemy-held territory. The Americans were re-supplying the Germans.

Cunningham and two others left their foxholes and chased some of the Germans who began collecting supplies from tanks that had broken apart on impact. They opened fire to force the Germans back into the forest. But it was too late. The enemy had already collected most of the supplies meant for Cunningham and the others. Cunningham could find only three untouched C rations. The three men collected them and returned to the 1/141's perimeter. Frustration and anger mixed with hunger as sounds of the aircraft drifted away into nothing. The forest fell silent as they canvassed a few handfuls of graham crackers, canned meat, biscuits, bouillon, fruit bars, chewing gum, cigarettes, toilet paper, and sugar tablets. Enough for one man.

For the second time, resupply by air had failed. Although Higgins radioed at 0959 that "our pals did all right last time, get this word to them in a hurry," subsequent radio traffic indicated that the 1/141 could see many of the auxiliary tanks, but they were too far down the hill in enemy territory from the 1/141's position. While the 131st's artillery's liaison officer reported no tanks reached the 1/141, division operations staff believed at least some of the medical supplies had been secured by Higgins's men. Meanwhile, they were already planning a series of subsequent drops, this time by pairs of aircraft that would be aided by a spotter aircraft.

Eason Bond was elated. *They're gonna try again*, he thought to himself. It had been a brutal four days, surrounded by the enemy, waiting, wondering, and fearing an all-out attack. Would unit discipline ward off the enemy when the assault finally came? Would everyone stay at his post and follow orders? Basic training had recast the individual survival instinct into a group survival instinct. Few men, though, were prepared for four days of hunger, almost no sleep, and the relentless threat of attack.

At one point, Bond had thought maybe he could find a way out of this mess. Maybe he could find a soft spot in the Germans' position and identify a route that reinforcements and supply personnel could exploit. Without telling anyone, he had gotten to his feet and started walking away from Higgins's position, beyond the listening outposts, and into the forest. Fifty, one hundred, almost two hundred yards into German territory. Germans had to be all around him. Waiting? Why? *What the hell am I doing out here?* Bond stopped and then returned to his foxhole. Whether his one-man breakout attempt had been a heroic deed for the greater good or simply one man's desperate escape attempt, Bond couldn't be sure. But there would be no more such decisions. Bond knew resupply was on the way. He would stand his post for as long as it took for the Americans to rescue him. If they failed, the Germans would probably kill him, either next to his slit trench or in a prison camp.

———◆———

"ON THE WAY!" SUSUMO ITO, A FORWARD OBSERVER FROM THE 522nd Field Artillery Battalion now on the front line, grew more frustrated as the fighting intensified along the 442nd's position late in the morning. It seemed the deafening artillery was coming from every direction and detonating closer and closer to the 442nd's frontline battalions. The 522nd's gun-battery personnel radioed "On the way!" to let him know it had fired. Based on where the shell landed, his job was to reply with range-and-direction adjustments. Given the cloud cover and the dense forest, sometimes he couldn't see where a shell landed. Under these conditions, he was blind, sending instructions based only what he heard in battle.

But other American and German units were firing their artillery simultaneously. Which shell detonation came from which gun battery? American or German? Had the most recent explosion come from a shell fired from his battery, or had it come from another battery? Was Ito adjusting the firing range of the wrong battery?

By 1030 the 3rd and 100th Battalions had hit heavy resistance. Tanks were called forward to support the 100th, but they were of little use. Ito was trying to put artillery onto the enemy positions, but the distance between the Germans and his guns was so short that his batteries had to shoot nearly straight up and then "drop" the shells on the enemy's position. That created a very narrow margin of error and a significant number of wasted shells.

A few hundred yards away, Sergeant Jack Wakamatsu's frustration focused on his feet. Trench foot was becoming a serious problem for the 442nd. Men trapped in waterlogged slit trenches all night didn't dare take off their shoes to change into dry socks, if they had them. The last thing anyone wanted was to confront an enemy attack in bare feet. So their boots stayed on their soaked feet. For many, a burning sensation was developing. Soon the swelling would begin. After a few days, wicked pain would erupt as toes swelled and the bottom of their feet turned blue. In some areas of the forest, the 442nd's advance slowed because walking brought excruciating pain. Some men, like Wakamatsu, were running a serious risk of skin blisters, ulcers, and ultimately amputation if they didn't get medical attention soon.

As a near stalemate developed, some squads advanced a few yards only when a single soldier chose to step out from behind a tree and into enemy fire, only when something deep within him compelled action that might otherwise be impossible to justify and compassion overruled intellect. Several Company K soldiers lay in the open, broken and bleeding. Some were perfectly still and perhaps dead. Others tried to keep from squirming, desperate not to draw the attention of enemy machine gunners and riflemen. There were more wounded than Okubo and a handful of other medics could treat.

Kenji Takubo and his company were already pinned down by enemy fire. But wounded brothers could not be left alone in the field of fire. Takubo left his protected position and crawled fifty yards to a wounded man. Somehow he wrestled him onto his back and crawled thirty yards through ricochets and near misses to a slightly more protected position where a litter team could reach the wounded soldier. Private Takubo moved on, encouraging his squad forward. A few hours later he fell dead in a blizzard of tree-burst shards.*

As the casualties mounted and the 442nd's advance stalled, Dahlquist grew furious with the 442nd's Colonel Pence. Pence had told Dahlquist that he was holding one of his units in reserve, waiting for support from the remainder of the 141st. Dahlquist didn't buy it. "I don't want a holding attack. That's the trouble. Get the men out of there crawling and get the Krauts out of their holes. . . . I want you to go up to Company C and see if they are in foxholes. If they are, get them out and fix a boundary."[1] An hour earlier, the 2/442's Lieutenant Colonel James Hanley had received similarly daunting orders by radio:

"CG [Dahlquist] wants you to put on attack."

"It is not going to be any good."

"I know it [but] the General wants it."[2]

———◦◦◦———

WHAT WILL WE DO IF THE GERMANS REALLY HIT US WITH everything *they've got? They know they've got us cut off. No resupply. Casualties. But they sit out there in the forest. Waiting for what? Will*

---

*Takubo was posthumously awarded a Silver Star for his heroism.

their goddamn artillery open up on us first? Will they bring up some
tanks? Chew us up with their machine guns?

Lieutenant Huberth couldn't be sure. He and Higgins had talked
about it. They had developed various strategies for when the major
assault finally came. At dawn? In the middle of the night? Every plan
would depend on the resolve of those on lookout, men crouched
behind their machine guns, and others who always kept their rifle
within reach.

For Eason Bond, the only real question was how hard could or
should the 1/141 put up a fight. Surely, they couldn't survive on all-
out attack. *Do we fight to the last man? Is getting captured better than*
death in this godforsaken forest? Maybe my odds would be better in a
German POW camp? Bond had pondered such questions in his foxhole for days. Of course, there were no easy answers, particularly in
the aftermath of three failed resupply attempts.

These were questions that required a man to make hard choices between following orders and obeying the survival instinct. Bond suspected others within the perimeter had to be pondering the same.
Most soldiers confronted four great fears in combat: failing their fellow
soldiers, running out of ammunition, being left on the battlefield
wounded, and having to choose between near-certain capture or death.

For some men, like rifleman Al Tortolano, surrendering to the
Germans was never an option. When he wasn't assisting medics, he
was a runner carrying messages between foxholes. One of three boys
in a close-knit Italian family in Massachusetts, he had grown up in an
era of ethnically centric neighborhoods that were clearly defined and
rarely crossed. His family had given him clear marching orders when
he and both brothers entered the service two years earlier: "Just be the
best man you can. Do what you're told. You're no better than the
next person and the next person is no better than you."[3] So he had
figured he and the rest of the battalion would fight to the last man.
Tortolano wondered how his family would take the news of his death.

But Bond believed the men of the 1/141 would likely allow themselves to be captured if confronted with an overwhelming German

attack. There was simply no way they could stave off the enemy. Why die when capture offered a whisper's hope of surviving? Mortarmen like Estes had buried their weapons and ammo and been reassigned to other posts. Bond and others couldn't be sure if that was because the dense forest rendered mortars ineffective. Maybe the lieutenants wanted to make sure the Germans would not collect a bounty of weapons and ammunition when the 1/141 was taken prisoner. Regardless, burying one's firepower was never an omen of victory.

Huberth harbored similar thoughts. But being second in command brought a responsibility that changed a man's view of the world when facing an uncertain fate. "Something told us that we never thought we were going to be captured. . . . Even though there wasn't a defeatist attitude, it was a day-to-day attitude because we couldn't anticipate when we would get out of there. We kept on expecting the Germans to come in and clobber the hell out of us, and we knew we couldn't stand up because we didn't have enough ammunition. We were fairly weak, too."[4] Given the results of the attempts to resupply Higgins's men so far, it was likely the lost battalion would be growing weaker in the days ahead.

But several knew another resupply attempt was imminent. As Dahlquist was urging the 442nd to mount an all-out attack, more Thunderbolts took off from the 405th Fighter Squadron base. The pilots knew they would face foul weather and antiaircraft fire and then would search for a nearly invisible target. Major John Leonard led them. The squadron leader was respected for his willingness to fly both the routine and the more dangerous missions. This time two Thunderbolts at a time would drop supplies on the 1/141. Five passes would be made on a route now predictable from the earlier missions. Leonard and the other pilots knew German artillery was primed and aimed.

At noon over the ridge the pilots looked down at a thick, gray carpet of clouds. The arrow had disappeared. There was no point in resupplying the Germans again if Leonard's pilots couldn't draw a bead on Higgins's position. They turned for home, the supply tanks still attached to their wings. Ten minutes later, faint shadows appeared on the ridge. "Weather is clear now, please do something," Higgins radioed headquarters.[5]

It was too late for Leonard's squadron to return to the ridge. As the aircraft approached the city of Epinal and entered a valley flying only 300 above the ground, tracers shot up from the valley. Leonard had no time to react as .50-caliber bullets ripped through his plane. The fire was inevitable. Leonard chose to stay with his aircraft, flying it toward the countryside past Epinal. His wingman, Milton Seale, knew his commanding officer was in trouble as flames spread and smoke thickened. "It's a little warm in here," Leonard told Seale in what Seale remembered as a southern drawl. "I think I'll bail out."[6]

Although Seale thought Leonard had gone down with his plane, Leonard ejected at the last second after turning his aircraft upside down. He escaped serious injury despite ejecting only about 250 feet off the ground. The squadron later learned that an American mobile antiaircraft crew had shot Leonard down, thinking he was a German aircraft. Stories after the war spread that Leonard located the crew and held a "spirited discussion" about proper aircraft identification procedures.

Gloom settled over Higgins's men as the cloud cover swept away the hint of sunshine that had tantalizingly appeared. Yet the forest never grew completely silent after Leonard's squadron had headed away from the drop zone. Lieutenant Edward Hayes arrived over the 1/141 less than an hour later with three other aircraft carrying auxiliary tanks for Higgins's men. It was the third attempt of the day, the fourth in less than twenty-four hours, and like the others they had flown through German flak to get there. Hayes looked down on the ridge. Nothing. Only the thick, gray fleece of a blanket of clouds. The drop zone once again was socked in.

Hayes and the other pilots had only one option. Reports later in the day indicated they used radar to make blind drops on the 1/141. Tanks away, they disappeared into the clouds. Coming in from the south, the tanks hit the south side of the ridge. They never reached Wilson, Estes, and the others. Hayes and the other pilots had released the auxiliary tanks perhaps a few seconds too early. Even at a relatively slow speed, flying abnormally low gave the pilots almost no margin of error. Germans gathered around most of the tanks, rolled a few over to expose the access doors, and pulled out food, water, ammunition, and medical supplies for their wounded. Much of it was taken a few hundred yards down into the valley, where German units had commandeered farmhouses and hamlets. Another failure.

COLONEL PENCE'S BATTLE PLAN FOR THE DAY HAD BEEN SHREDDED. Dahlquist had ordered Pence to the front, and he moved between the three battalions' command posts, piecing together battle reports. Pence concluded his men had advanced less than four hundred yards. The Germans' roadblocks were deadly when combined with the German artillery that thundered into the forest when his men's advance stalled. All three battalions were suffering significant casualties, far more than the day before. Ultimately, seventeen 442nd soldiers would be killed on this day, with dozens more wounded. More than half would be members of 3rd Battalion. Medic Jim Okubo likely shared Pence's exhaustion when Pence uncharacteristically admitted to an enlisted soldier that he was "really tired."[7]

As he approached Lieutenant Colonel Gordon Singles's position, shrapnel from a German artillery shell slammed into his jeep, most of it missing Pence by inches. One man in the jeep was killed, another wounded seriously, and Pence suffered a leg wound. When the 442nd command sent another jeep to collect Pence and take him to an aid station, the regiment lost one of the two commanding officers the men had known since Camp Shelby. He had led them through Italy and up France to Germany's doorstep. He would lead them no more in this campaign.

Three days into the rescue mission, the 442nd's executive officer, Lieutenant Colonel Virgil Miller, took command. Miller had tried to drop out of school to join the army and fight in World War I. But his father refused until Miller turned eighteen. Miller's eighteenth birthday was November 11, 1918, the date the Armistice was signed and World War I ended.

His men knew the Puerto Rico native well. He had served in Puerto Rico's 65th Infantry Regiment before transfer to the 21st Infantry Brigade in Hawaii, where Miller had developed a personal affinity for the Nisei that he carried to Camp Shelby in June 1943. Miller, a Caucasian, had been a crucial bridge between the Hawaiian- and mainland-born Nisei in basic training. He had also learned that threatening a wayward Nisei with traditional military discipline, such as work details or demotion, was ineffective. Instead, the threat of writing a letter to a recruit's parents informing them of their son's offense proved to be remarkably effective. A son could not bring shame to his family, regardless of the circumstance. He must honor his family name by being a good soldier.

Miller also knew what to expect from Dahlquist, including operational orders for the 442nd down to the platoon level. The forty-three-year-old would experience the same micromanaging command of Dahlquist as every other regimental commander had endured.

Almost at the same time that enemy fire forced a change in the 442nd's regimental command, Dahlquist had had enough of Colonel Lundquist as his commanding officer of the 141st. He was convinced Lundquist wasn't aggressive enough in the scant three weeks he had been in command and no longer accepted Lundquist's explanations for his men's lack of progress. Dahlquist fired Lundquist and replaced him with his division's chief of staff, Colonel Charles Owens. Dahlquist immediately ordered the 3/141 "to crawl and run forward; that is the only way to get enemy to move back. Battalion CO [Owens] and company commanders to get up front and drive companies forward."[8] Owens had been Dahlquist's top aide for only sixteen days when he was tapped to become the 141st's fourth commanding officer in just two and a half months. Higgins and the others had been handed a new regimental commanding officer every eighteen days since landing in France.

Meanwhile, Singles assembled his 100th Battalion's company commanders for a midafternoon brief. He was appalled that only two lieutenants and two sergeants stood before him. He had lost nearly all of his frontline officers and his battalion operations officer, Lieutenant James Boodry. A short time earlier, Boodry and Company C commander Bill Pye had stood together studying a map. Boodry was one of those Caucasian officers who had earned the respect of the Nisei. He exuded an aura of almost brazen invincibility. Somehow, he seemed happy even during the most horrific battles. "You'd think he was watching his football team winning by a tremendous margin when [in reality the lives of his men were] hanging in the balance, and the whole battle was hanging in the balance," recalled another officer.[9]

Suddenly, a tree exploded overhead. Shrapnel slammed into Boodry's skull, killing him instantly. Pye suffered superficial wounds but stayed with his men. A second enemy shell found him later, shredding his leg and bringing his fighting to a bloody end.

As Singles looked at the handful of men before him, a signal officer approached and looked at the collegial commanding officer who relied heavily on his subordinates. He told Singles that Dahlquist was on the field telephone and wanted to talk to him. Singles had two choices. He could take the call and risk telling Dahlquist exactly what Singles thought of him or insubordinately refuse to talk to his commanding officer in the middle of battle. In front of his men, he pulled the thin black wire out of the phone. The message was clear to both Dahlquist and Singles's men: *Stay out of our way. We have objectives to meet and a mission to be accomplished.*

———◉———

GEORGE SAKATO AND KELLY KUWAYAMA WONDERED WHY THE 2/442's Companies E and F were moving through units of the 141st on the extreme northern flank of the rescue mission. *Why isn't the rest of the 141st taking the point to rescue their own guys?* A soldier in a foxhole and a medic climbing over mossy boulders could only speculate.

At midafternoon Lieutenant Colonel Hanley was positioning the companies to ambush the Germans on Hill 617 from the north. He had to clear the hill if his battalion was to protect the 442nd's left flank. The ambush was to be part of a renewed 442nd frontal attack at 1445. Kenji Ego and the rest of Company G, directly in front of the Germans, were a diversion and were paying a heavy price in casualties simply to hold the Germans' attention.

So were others. Company K's Jim Okubo had treated more wounded men by repeatedly running from sheltered positions into a blizzard of noise. Tree bursts pounded eardrums, automatic weapons spewed a staccato cough of death, shrapnel screamed through the air, bullets slammed into logs, squad leaders yelled, and men cried out as they writhed in the mud. At one point, a roadblock and enemy machine-gun fire pinned them to gullies and the back sides of trees until their artillery destroyed it, only one hundred yards in front of them. A short time later, the 100th endured a concentrated enemy artillery attack. By then the heavy clouds had again closed in on the forest, casting a dreary pall over the battlefield.

Scraping replaced the staccato sound of gunfire late in the afternoon, as another cold night loomed and a few snowflakes fluttered onto the battlefield. Some soldiers commandeered foxholes dug by Germans perhaps the day before or weeks earlier. Others started digging, preferably behind a tree for added protection from snipers. Some soldiers still had their shovels, others used a trenching knife, and few had only their hands and helmet.

Forward artillery observer Ed Ichiyama could only wonder how Isamu Minatodani and Goro Matsumoto were doing somewhere on the ridge. Ichiyama, Minatodani, Matsumoto, and Tetsuo Ito had quit their jobs in a Honolulu shipyard, and the group of close friends volunteered on the same day less than two years earlier. Matsumoto and Minatodani had been assigned to Company

I, which had been taking a beating. Tetsuo Ito had joined Company G and been killed three months earlier in Italy. Now it had been Ichiyama's turn to accompany frontline troops into battle on this mission and pass along requests for artillery support. Like many others, he drew from childhood lessons to cope with the realities of the battlefield.

Young Japanese American boys had often been taught *kachikan,* Japanese group values deeply ingrained by family elders who may have been born in Japan. Now, in the middle of a war, those values became a wellspring of strength when a rifleman, scout, or machine gunner settled into his slit trench for the night and looked up at the blackened forest canopy. Some swallowed their growing hatred of Dahlquist with *shikataga nai* (acceptance with resignation). Kikuyo Fujitomo had taught her sons *kuni no tame ni* (for the sake of our country) before her son Kunio had joined the 100th and his younger brother Hikoso later volunteered for the 442nd. Some parents had reminded their sons of *gisei, giri, meiyo, hokori,* and *sekinin* when they had volunteered or been drafted. Sacrifice. Duty. Honor. Pride. Responsibility. Many had admonished their sons *Kamei ni kizu tsukeru bekarazu.* Never bring dishonor to the family name. A value system from another world in a structured culture brought comfort and context when the fighting stopped, the cold night air soaked into a man's body, and certainty grew that tomorrow's dawn would bring more death.

Perhaps some in the 442 drew strength from those values as they speculated whether Dahlquist considered them little more than "cannon fodder." How else could they explain the 442nd being ordered to lead the Higgins mission when the 141st's other battalions were on the sidelines, protecting the 442nd's flanks? Why, many wondered, were horrific casualty rates seemingly acceptable for the 442nd?

JAMES COMSTOCK MIGHT HAVE HAD A HEADACHE AS HE FACED A fifth night in his foxhole and the end of a fourth day of almost no food. Bruce Estes's breath likely had turned sour as his body began to eliminate waste through his lungs. One of the toughest men in the outfit and one who had endured brutal fighting in Italy, Jack Wilson may have been tired, even sluggish. Harry Huberth may have suffered spells of lightheadedness. By now the hunger pains had subsided for most of the men and been replaced by a preoccupation with food. Some dreamed of their favorite meals when they catnapped, while others described their favorite restaurants to the soldiers in the next foxhole. Harry Huberth fantasized over his next breakfast of bacon and eggs. Debating the merits of different breakfasts became a widespread hobby. Some discussed the proper method of making golden-brown waffles. All were common symptoms of extended food deprivation. While four days certainly did not qualify as starvation, the surrounded battalion was enduring an involuntary fast. After more than two months of near-constant combat, their bodies were poorly equipped to function without food and only sips of silty water.

A fifth bone-cold night loomed. Everyone stunk, their body odor becoming sweetly bitter in filthy uniforms. Many men were suffering from trench foot. They couldn't leave the immediate vicinity of their foxhole, and in any event they had no place to go. A few men on water duty prepared to crawl to the muddy bog after dark to fill canteens with the forest's seepage that smelled of a frog pond. *Would the Germans decide that they had waited long enough? Did they know Higgins had lost about one-fourth of his men since he had been cut off? That a weakened battalion was ripe for an all-out assault tonight before the 442nd got any closer?* The 1/141 would be even weaker the following morning if the Germans attacked at dawn. Such prospects lengthened a cold, wet night into eternity. A weak, immobilized, and disoriented soldier could easily lose his inner clock. *Was dawn only an hour away? Two? Three? Will I make it through another night?*

It's unlikely anyone in the 1/141 knew the leading edge of the 442nd remained more than a mile from their position. Higgins knew there was at least one major German roadblock at Col des Huttes that lay in the 442nd's path. He probably didn't know about a second roadblock at Col de la Croisette that would delay the rescuers. Blasting their way through both would cost more lives.

The forest dimmed into a darkened haze of trees and underbrush just before dusk. That's when they heard them, the now familiar growl of approaching aircraft on the other side of the clouds. Another food-drop attempt? Ten aircraft from the 405th were over Higgins's position at 1630. The pilots looked for the slightest break in the clouds. *Where is that goddamn arrow they told us about?*

Suddenly, some of the largest limbs snapped in the canopy above Higgins's men, startling sharp breaks that sounded almost like gunshots. *What the hell? There!* A 150-gallon bullet-shaped auxiliary tank slammed into the ground, a shredded red parachute settling on it a few seconds later. More limbs cracking. Everyone looked up. They were being bombed by Americans! The 405th had found them! In a matter of minutes, a flock of auxiliary tanks pierced the cloud cover. Some plowed straight into the mud. Others caromed off logs and rocks, splitting open. A few parachutes remained high up in the trees after their tanks had broken free on their way toward the foxholes. Other tanks landed farther off in German territory, but no one cared. *They're here!* "Planes successful. Keep them coming," Blonder radioed the 141st's command post.[10]

James Comstock and Peter Bondar knew someone had to get the parachutes and at least one suspended tank out of the trees because they would give the Germans a more precise location of the 1/141. The last thing Higgins wanted was more accurate German artillery. Not when his men finally might have something to eat, his medics would have supplies for the wounded, and Erwin Blonder would have fresh batteries. Once Comstock and Bondar had eaten their first field ration in days, they climbed one hundred feet up the trees under enemy fire to the fluttering parachutes and yanked them to the ground. The parachutes were shredded into small strips as souvenirs. Comstock, the farm boy who could take care of himself in the woods, was awarded the Bronze Star for retrieving them.

It had been a calculated risk, asking to be bombed with auxiliary fuel tanks. Had any hit a soldier, he would have been instantly killed. Several tanks broke apart on impact, their contents flying as shrapnel through the forest. Bond remembered one man being killed by a can of cheese that hit him in the chest. A family's son who had survived the horrors of combat, the loss of mangled friends, miserable weather, and being surrounded had been killed by a can of processed cheese.

Men stayed in their positions, and some returned to deepened fox-holes that now resembled caverns covered with fresh-cut limbs. Some were up to six inches in diameter. Some men had used penknives as primitive saws to cut stout limbs and then gently lowered them to the ground in a blanket. Silence kept the Germans from knowing precise foxhole locations.

The next "attack" by American forces could be even more deadly. Minutes after the 405th's aircraft left the area, American artillery again fired resupply shells at Higgins's position. This time there would be no warning and no parachutes to slow impact. "If they [the shells] hit you, they'd kill you. But we decided to take a chance. We figured, if you don't get hit, you eat. We'd had no food for five days and were desperate," Higgins said later.[11]

Once again, the artillery shells from the 131st Field Artillery Battalion were off target. Cunningham and others heard the first one hit the forest floor, too far away to retrieve, but it didn't matter. It was a smoke shell. "Reduce range by two hundred yards." The next shell burst closer to the 1/141, but still too far away. Another reduction in range. Closer. Finally, after six rounds, a shell landed on the 1/141's position. Nine more quickly followed, mostly filled with D rations. Some slammed into the mud too deep to extract, their timed fuses set a split second too long. Others exploded in the tree canopy, raining chocolate bars onto the 1/141.

As much as he already respected his troops, Higgins was flabbergasted at their discipline when food and supplies finally arrived. "The Joes were as excited as kids at a Christmas party. They'd stayed in their holes while shells and airborne rations were falling and then went out in small armed groups with blankets to bring the stuff to our central distributing point. Hungry as they were, it was actually amazing to see them carrying rations back without so much as nibbling a cracker or a chocolate bar until the food was distributed all around."[12]

After all the supplies were collected, a precise inventory was conducted, so Higgins and the other lieutenants could devise a plan to make them last as long as possible. The intrepid pilots of the 405th had perhaps forged a turning point in the race to reach Higgins's men. If pilots like Eliel Archilla and others could deliver more supplies, the 1/141's odds of hanging on would improve immeasurably. Archilla was typical of many pilots. He had tried to join the navy before his eighteenth birthday and was turned away. When he was old enough, his boyhood love of flying inspired him to volunteer for the air corps.

For the first time in five days, more than two hundred men had a small cache of food. "Aircraft and artillery did wonderful job. Every man thanks every [commanding officer] from bottom of heart," Higgins radioed.[13] Spirits soared within the perimeter. Bond now believed the American army was on its way to relieve the 1/141. Higgins looked across the foxholes. The darkness couldn't hide smiles that reminded him of Christmas morning.

Ingenuity, courage, and devotion to duty by the crews of the 405th Fighter Squadron one hundred miles away had made those smiles possible. The fighter squadron and supporting personnel had delivered two critical loads of cargo to the 1/141: food and hope. Perhaps not enough of either, but at least meaningful contact had been made with Higgins's men. The 405th's feat bought the 1/141st critical time. But now the Germans would be ready for the following day's rescue flights. Young men strapping themselves into cockpits would know the skies above the Vosges foothills would be filled with shrapnel meant for them.

ALTHOUGH HUNGER HAD BEEN BEATEN BACK BY THE AIR AND artillery missions, frustration, inadequate communication, and outright anger ruled a few miles to the west. When Dahlquist was told the 1/141 had secured only some of the shells and tanks delivered to them, his response was blunt: "Tell them to search for the rest of supplies tonight."[14] Reports from the front line continued to anger him.

Telephone lines throughout the forest between units on the front line and the regimental and divisional command posts had been cut, likely by artillery shrapnel. Night had fallen with Dahlquist and his divisional operations, intelligence, and supply officers having only a vague idea of unit location, casualty numbers, and supply status. The latest battlefield report, an hour old, stated that the 100th had progressed a short distance. Company K had been unable to advance and suffered heavy casualties. The 100th and 3rd Battalions were on the edge of a German minefield. Dahlquist called for a situation report from the 141's 2nd Battalion.

"Patrols from E and C Company are out. G contacted patrol from 442," replied the 2/141's radio operator.

"Is that the patrol I had them send out?" asked Dahlquist.

"I think so. They said they had 10 PWs [prisoners of war]."

"The hell they have. Can you get the ground I want?" Once again, Dahlquist was losing his patience. He wanted reports of significant advancement, not speculation from the front line.

"It is rather obscure now."

"Have you contact with F Company, 143rd?"

"No."

"Do you think you can get your people in hand now?" Dahlquist barked.

"Yes sir."[15]

Minutes later, he was in a jeep, left his division's headquarters, and headed for the front line to see for himself. Shortly thereafter, he called back to divisional operations officer Lieutenant Colonel Fred Sladen. Dahlquist was apoplectic after inspecting the front line. "I personally saw the two battalions of the 442nd Infantry advance six hundred to seven hundred yards. Location reports we had were [a] joke. Exact coordinate locations I do not know. I saw Adams' company [143rd Regiment] and it was not where reported. Tell Colonel Adams. I will be here for some time yet."[16] Now Dahlquist was issuing personal frontline status reports to his support personnel, who passed them on to the commanding officers of the other regiments.

Apparently, Dahlquist's report infuriated Colonel Paul DeWitt Adams, commanding officer of the 143rd Infantry Regiment. Adams could not have been more of a polar opposite to Dahlquist. His cold stare and leathery face could melt his subordinates. Those who grew to respect him cautiously called him "Old Stone Face" when out of earshot. He was tough and direct and didn't tolerate nonsense. His approach to combat was as brutal as it could appear to be callous: "The man who creates the most violence in a military situation is the one who will win," he believed.[17]

When Adams learned of Dahlquist's report from the front line, he unloaded on Pence's 442nd operations officer:

F Company did not fight today and I went there and I found that they are not where reported. The General will have to find out where they are even if he has to go up to the front and find out. I had a report that they (141) were never on the nose [point of attack]. I went up there and found that none of the regiment was fighting. If the General doesn't find out the right information, I'll have him busted and the company commanders will have to go up to the front and give the right info.[18]

It was a remarkable public outburst over the radio: the commanding officer of a regiment threatening to have his immediate superior officer, a general who commanded a division, "busted."

Only six days earlier, Lieutenant Colonel Hanley had complained to Pence that it was Adams's 143rd that had refused to support Hanley's 2nd Battalion if a firefight broke out. If unity of command was a multiplier of battlefield strength, as army officers had been taught, the fractured command of the 36th threatened to become as deadly an enemy of Higgins as the Germans. Nerves were frayed and marginal levels of confidence among senior officers were crumbling at various command posts, while Kuwayama, Okubo, and the other medics in slit trenches and aid stations faced an endless stream of bloodstained litters and parades of limping wounded.

When the forest calmed on the front line, men in command posts in the rear worked long into the night, collecting the latest intelligence; resupplying, transporting, and treating the more seriously wounded; assessing situation reports; sorting out inconsistent information; and devising the next day's battle plan. Although Higgins's men had eaten for the first time in days, they were still critically short of other supplies. At 2227 Higgins radioed that he had been able to collect only rations from the airdrops and artillery shells. He still needed medical supplies, batteries, more food, and ammunition. Once again, he added what had become the standard postscript to nightly transmissions: "Hope to see friends tomorrow."

While logistics personnel planned the next day's missions, Dahlquist offered a bribe to the 442nd. He called the 442nd's command post, asking for a situation report, and ordered a flanking attack on the Germans closest to Higgins. The 442nd's signals officer asked for clarification of the objective. Dahlquist left no doubt in the exchange that he was concerned about more than Higgins's plight:

"Drive the Jerries out, rescue 1st Battalion, and drive Jerry south of ridge. Your objective really is that ridge and push out to the south. What about the platoon for tonight?"

"We will send one."

"We want to find out where Jerry flank is. There is a chance they have an undefended area and our 1st Battalion can get out. I want to talk to you before you send out the patrol. You need a good man and if he can get out that 1st Battalion he can have a DSC [Distinguished Service Cross]. You personally interview the man who is going."[19]

The official record isn't clear on how Dahlquist thought Higgins could evacuate his men after Higgins had told him repeatedly that

Many Japanese American business owners faced boycotts and violence in the months following the attack on Pearl Harbor. *Library of Congress*

Internment camps were hastily constructed in some of America's most-desolate terrain in the months following the attack on Pearl Harbor. *Library of Congress*

Thousands of interned families sent sons to war. Here the Yonemitsu family at the Manzanar Relocation Center honors a son fighting in Europe. *War Relocation Authority*

Ansel Adams photographed Corporal Jimmie Shohara when Shohara visited his parents at the Manzanar Relocation Center. Shohara served in the Military Intelligence Service. *Library of Congress*

Japanese American soldiers were filmed at Camp Shelby as part of War Relocation Authority newsreels shown in movie theaters that justified internment of their families. *National Park Service*

The 442nd's troops, particularly the volunteers from Hawaii, generally detested the living conditions at Camp Shelby, Mississippi. *U.S. Army*

Lieutenant Colonel Gordon Singles, commanding officer of the 100th Battalion. *U.S. Army*

Automatic rifleman Barney Hajiro. *U.S. Army*

Medic Jim Okubo

Major General
John Dahlquist,
commanding officer
of the 36th Infantry
Division. *U.S. Army*

General Friedrich Wiese,
commanding officer of the
Germans' Nineteenth Army.

Command
posts were
primitive, cold,
and temporary
in the Vosges
Mountains.
U.S. Army

Steep hillsides were made more dangerous by constant rain, slick rocks, moss, and a dug-in enemy. *U.S. Army*

A fluid battlefield relied on a variety of signs that directed troops to temporary command posts and warned them of enemy mine fields. *U.S. Army*

Unlike combat in Italy, the Vosges forests were so dense that mortars were ineffective so some crews were reassigned as scouts and infantrymen. *U.S. Army*

The ideal foxhole in the Vosges was deep enough to accommodate a roof of logs packed with mud. It protected against shrapnel and effectively concealed a soldier's position. *U.S. Army*

Soldiers slept in hand-dug slit trenches which offered modest protection against enemy shrapnel. *U.S. Army*

The few trails and logging roads in the Vosges often forced the 442nd into positions that were exposed to German artillery. *U.S. Army*

Only one logging road extended the length of the ridge, forcing the 442nd to advance and fight through a treacherous forest. *Photo by author*

Artillery crews relied on forward observers on the front line to direct artillery fire to within fifty yards of 442nd troops. *U.S. Army*

Men wounded in battle were taken to primitive aid stations such as this for life-saving triage before they were transported to a field hospital in the rear. *U.S. Army*

Radioman Erwin Blonder.
U.S. Army

Yohei Sagami was killed the day the 442nd entered combat in France on October 15, 1944. He died in George Sakato's arms. *Courtesy Barbara Berthiaume*

Private Terry Cato was one of thousands of 442nd soldiers who were wounded in combat in only two years' fighting in Italy and France. *U.S. Army*

General Paul DeWitt
Adams, at the time a colonel
and commanding officer
of the 143rd Infantry
Regiment, threatened to
have General Dahlquist
"busted" during the rescue
mission. *U.S. Army*

Medic Jimmie Kanaya
chose to stay with
wounded soldiers and
become a German
prisoner, rather than
escape into the forest.
U.S. Army

In 1948 Saburo Tanamachi and
Fumitake Nagato became the first
two Japanese American soldiers
to be buried at the Arlington
National Cemetery. *U.S. Army*

Robert Allan Booth died while trying to drop supplies to the 1/141 by air. Future missions were successful, days after the surrounded troops had exhausted their food supply. *U.S. Army*

Lieutenant Eliel Archilla led one of the successful resupply missions by air. He had been trained as a glider pilot and had flown P-51 Mustangs earlier in the war. *Courtesy Elliot Archilla*

Major John Leonard was mistakenly shot down by an American anti-aircraft vehicle after trying to drop supplies onto the lost battalion. *Courtesy Michael Higgins*

This photo was taken the day the 442nd reached the 1/141. These men had held off the Germans for a week. *Courtesy Michael Higgins*

Army photographer Lieutenant Harold Valentine captured the exhaustion of men who had been surrounded for a week. *U.S. Army*

Martin Higgins *(left)* is greeted by members of the Signal Corps the day after the 442nd reached his men. *U.S. Army*

The relief was evident on members of the surrounded battalion after Mutt Sakumoto and the 442nd reached them. *U.S. Army*

Exhausted soldiers who had been rescued the day before wait to be driven to the rear. *U.S. Army*

After they were relieved some men of the 1/141 walked off the ridge along the same logging road they had used a week earlier. *U.S. Army*

President Harry Truman saluted the 442nd as part of its seventh Presidential Unit Citation ceremony, earned when it broke through the Germans' Gothic Line in Italy. *U.S. Army*

Captain Martin Higgins received the Silver Star ten months after he had commanded the surrounded battalion in the Vosges Mountains and later escaped as a prisoner of war. *Courtesy Michael Higgins*

Lieutenant Colonel Alfred Pursall, commanding officer of the 3rd Battalion, greeted the 100th Battalion when it returned to Hawaii in 1946. *U.S. Army*

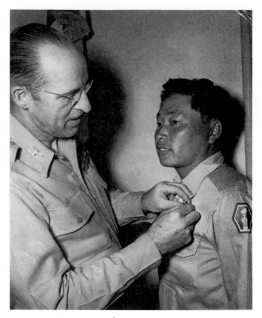

George Sakato's Distinguished Service
Cross was upgraded to a Medal of Honor
in 2000. *U.S. Army*

(From left to right) 442nd Medal of Honor recipient George Sakato later met Eliel
Archilla, one of the successful resupply aircraft pilots. *Courtesy Elliot Archilla*

he lacked the firepower and the ability to transport his wounded off the ridge.

—⊰◉⊱—

WAR IS LONELY. THOSE WHO SURVIVE LEARN HOW TO FILET THE humanity out of their souls. Battle veterans viewed replacements as potentially dangerous rather than newcomers who deserved empathy. Replacements were potential threats to combat veterans because they were naive, anxious, and wholly unprepared for war's horrors. The Germans a few dozen yards away were faceless threats to be eliminated as quickly and efficiently as a coyote threatening a herd of sheep or a rat infesting a family's kitchen.

The killing and maiming among and by all three 442nd battalions throughout the day had become impersonal. Combat veterans in the 442nd had learned that sentiment and compassion could threaten their survival if either gave a man a moment of pause when aiming at the enemy. Yet sometimes humanity had crept into battle.

Earlier in the day, Company K's Sergeant Ken Inada had been part of a four-company assault against German positions. Inada was a particularly reserved and resolute man. The twenty-one-year-old had been raised in an affluent Hawaiian family that quietly instilled Japanese values in their children. He spoke to his parents in Japanese and knew he was expected to become a man of integrity, one who could be trusted, and one who was sincere. He was not to become a disruption. Bringing shame to his family would be a grievous offense. He was taught the value of life and to value the interrelationships between people. Those values made killing even more difficult. To always remain dispassionate was impossible.

Inada had spotted German machine gunners firing off the side, pinning down an American unit. They didn't see Inada approaching from the other direction. He slammed a new clip into his weapon, jumped up, unloaded it into the Germans' position, and then dove to the ground. He waited. Silence. Almost a half hour later, his unit began climbing a hill toward the enemy's foxholes. He remembered the machine gunners and broke away to make sure they were dead. The stench left no doubt. A freshly gutted human body has a cloying vegetal smell. There is a hint of unnatural sweetness. It's a foreign smell, except, perhaps, to those soldiers who had grown up deer or elk hunting. The pungent aroma of death startled Inada. He stared at a dead German, sprawled on his back, his arms outstretched, his head thrown back, his mouth open.

When his unit was ordered to remain in place, he noticed a bulge in the German's left breast pocket and violated a cardinal rule of combat: he looked inside. He wanted to know this German he had killed and made stink. Inada pulled out a worn photo of a very attractive woman in her early twenties. She stood next to a child. The little girl had to be this man's daughter. A family that would never see him again, perhaps never know he had been killed by a stranger following orders. In one instant, this father had been firing his weapon; in the next, his body had been ripped apart, killed as he defended a patch of French forest. Inada had killed a father, a husband, and had ruined a family with a single clip of ammunition. He put the photo back in the dead man's pocket. He sat next to the dead German, waiting for orders to climb out of the death pit and advance again toward more fathers and husbands. Inada never forgot the human destruction he had inflicted in a matter of seconds. "It was revolting to me. I killed this guy," he recalled after the war.[20]

Not far away, radioman Rudy Tokiwa waited for orders for Company K to advance. He was already haunted by death because, for a brief moment, he had let humanity appear on the battlefield. He had spotted a German sniper about to ambush a patrol. Tokiwa shot him dead. Perhaps it was because the German was the first man Tokiwa had killed in combat. Perhaps because Tokiwa had not listened to the veterans who told him to turn cold toward men in battle, to never look at a man he killed. Tokiwa pulled the dead German's wallet out of his pocket. He found a photo, this one of three small children between the ages of two and seven. Another father from a nameless

German city or village had been killed. Tokiwa couldn't know if the mother and her children were still alive, whether they had survived Allied bombing and possible starvation by that point in the war. He had learned only that he had killed the father of three small children and made their mother a widow. He said later:

> I never should have went through his wallet [and] then I'd have never known he had these kids. . . . [I realized] I'm the one who took him away from them. . . . [W]hat I should have done was taken the picture out and see if I could find something with an address, because even today, once in a while, I think about it and think, I wish I can go back there and tell the kids, "I'm the one that killed your father" . . . apologize to them . . . and I try to tell myself that it was all part of the war. But I have children of my own and I know how it must be.[21]

But by now Tokiwa had steeled himself against compassion. At five feet eight, he was one of the largest Japanese Americans in the outfit. He was one of the few who could carry a radio so frontline units could stay in contact with Pursall. He approached a gully, about three feet wide and about the same depth. It was a natural drainage for two converging slopes. A German lay silently on his back in the bottom of gully, looking up at Tokiwa. "Just as soon as I saw him, I raised up my gun and put about four of five rounds into him and killed him right there. But that same guy—I've thought about this many times—I think [all] he wanted to do was give up. He probably threw his gun away but how [could] we know these things? He could have been shooting at us ten seconds before, see? And he was just lying there as quiet as—you know, but that's war."[22]

———⚬———

EVERYONE ON THE BATTLEFIELD WAS HUNGRY. SO WHEN FRONTLINE units of the 442nd dug in for the night, some men could not rest.

Soldiers were selected to hike to the rear, where supply personnel had established temporary depots not far from the front line, and return immediately with the next day's rations for their units. The trails between the foxholes and supply depots could become congested when the fighting stopped. Nightly traffic was universal, predictable, and easy targets for enemy artillery batteries. Heading out on a ration detail in the middle of the night could be as dangerous as confronting a machine-gun nest at midday. Sergeants Ken Inada of Company K and Shiro Kashino of Company I were ordered to select five men from each of their companies for a twelve-man ration detail.

It was as if the Germans were waiting. Perhaps they were. Their units had been in the area for weeks and knew the exact location of the logging road and paths that supply details would travel at night. They knew the routes that jeeps and stretcher bearers would take to aid stations and then to field hospitals in the rear. And their artillery units likely had precise coordinates. They waited. The day's fighting was not yet over.

The twelve-man detail had walked only about two hundred yards when the forest flashed brilliant white and men were knocked onto their backs and bellies, yards from where they had stood moments before. Some were thrown against tree trunks, and others were hurled onto boulders, breaking bones and pulverizing organs. Shrapnel slammed into their bodies, and limbs turned slick with flowing blood. The direct hits decimated the detail.*

Those with minor wounds hobbled back to Companies I and K positions to get medical supplies for those more seriously wounded. Inada waited for Norman Kimura to return with medical supplies to where he lay, seriously wounded. The smell of blood, singed skin, and sulfur drifted in the night air. So, too, did a thin voice, one that haunted Japanese American soldiers when the shelling stopped and a young man knew he was dying.

---

* Postwar survivor reports vary as to how many were killed and how many were wounded.

"I listened to a most haunting and agonizing cry for his mother by a dying soldier," Inada later recalled. "He kept repeating in Japanese *'okaasan, okaasan.'* His voice became weaker and weaker and finally trailed into nothingness."[23] Isamu Minatodani had called for his mother as he lay on a cold, wet forest floor. For his mother to reassure him that, somehow, everything would be okay . . . or perhaps to praise him for facing death honorably. That he had placed honor before glory. That he had not brought shame to his family. Perhaps an honorable and shameless death was what he had sought most at that moment. But he bled to death, alone, on a moonless night. Seven men from Companies I and K died on October 28. They were among the 117 young men in the 442nd who would die and another 639 who would be wounded in only two weeks' fighting in October 1944.

Although Higgins's men had finally received some badly needed supplies, some of his wounded were becoming critical, and the overall health of his troops continued to ebb. Meanwhile, the price among the 442nd's battalions paid to reach Higgins's men had reached gut-wrenching levels. And for General Dahlquist, panic would soon supplant his anger and frustration.

CHAPTER 6

ABOUT TO DIE

"Keep them moving and don't let them stop. There's a battalion about to die up there and we've got to reach them."

"Yes, sir," the field commander answered crisply.[1]

General John Dahlquist's exchange with Lieutenant Colonel Gordon Singles revealed how dire Dahlquist considered Martin Higgins's position to be on October 29. The third-generation West Point graduate who looked younger than his age knew better than to argue with Dahlquist. Apparently, Dahlquist didn't think the previous day's air and resupply missions to the 1/141 had bought the surrounded men much time. At the start of the fifth day of the rescue mission, Dahlquist wanted a full-court press, now that the 100th and 3rd Battalions were nearly a mile from Higgins's men.

Both battalions had been stymied by a major logging-road roadblock and adjoining minefields at Col de la Croisette. The two battalions were abreast, with the 3rd on the north side of the road and the 100th to the south. Both remained vulnerable to German artillery from across the valley to the south. German artillery units knew the exact location of the 3rd and 100th, and the battalions' excruciatingly slow advance made them nearly stationary targets. Jim Okubo and the other medics had faced casualties within minutes of jumping off shortly after daybreak. On the northern flank, George Sakato, Kelly Kuwayama, and others in the 2nd Battalion waited for Kats

Miho's artillery battery to stop shelling Hill 617. The hour was approaching for the major attack on Hill 617 that Hanley had carefully staged. Lieutenant Colonel James Hanley finally had his companies in position.

A few minutes after contacting Singles, Dahlquist called Lieutenant Colonel Alfred Pursall's 3rd Battalion headquarters. For two hours, Pursall had been preoccupied by his men weaving their way through another German minefield. They had advanced only about 250 yards against enemy opposition. Pursall also needed tank support. A tank with a bulldozing blade on the front could clear the stacks of German-felled trees that blocked the road. Another tank or two could support the ground troops as well. The dense forest limited the American tanks' mobility. They generally stayed on or close to the logging road and had to get close to the enemy to be effective against heavily fortified German tanks.

Dahlquist pressed home his sense of urgency with each of his 442nd battalion commanders. He repeated the same order to Pursall by radio. "Let's keep them moving. Even against opposition. Get through to them. That battalion is about to die and we've got to reach them."[2]

The interrogation reports from prisoners taken in recent days confirmed that a well-entrenched German force still separated Higgins's men from the rescuers. At least three companies of the Germans' 936th Grenadier Regiment—upwards of 200 men—and German artillery remained in the Americans' path. New reports from the 36th Division's intelligence section indicated a column of 250 Germans had been spotted marching toward the ridge. They were beyond American artillery range. Dahlquist and all three 442nd battalion commanders needed to know the status of the German positions in the forest as well as the location and progress of any approaching enemy reinforcements.

The 36th Division had a Strategic Services Section (SSS) team assigned to it from the day it had landed in southern France. It was a team of secret agents. It had infiltrated German lines during the advance toward the Vosges, coordinating French Resistance activities and recruiting residents as spies. Local employees of the Bureau of Water, Forests, Roads, and Bridges were especially helpful to the agents in mapping German-held territory and identifying targets for American artillery units.

The day before, three SSS agents had tried to slip through German lines and reach Higgins. The mission failed when they were caught by the Germans. The agents had hidden their incriminating radio equipment but now were on their way to German prisoner-of-war camps, where they would remain until the end of the war.

LIEUTENANT COLONEL HANLEY'S 2ND BATTALION WAS FINALLY ready to ambush the Germans holding Hill 617 on the left flank of the rescue mission. The hill gave the Germans a commanding view of the valley to the north, where Companies E and F had tried to cross in hopes of ambushing the enemy. Frightening losses from enemy mortars had forced both companies to mount trucks at night and swing farther to the north before turning south toward Hill 617. To the west, Company G had attempted to draw the Germans' attention, but the result had been several days of casualties and almost no progress.

But now Hanley was ready. After a failed attempt at dawn, two Company G platoons attacked Hill 617, advancing up a narrow creek bed shortly before noon. Elevated German positions on both sides rendered the creek a killing zone. Bloodied, both platoons pulled back. It had been a diversion. George Sakato, Kenji Ego, and the rest of Companies E and F then attacked from the north. Company G simultaneously attacked again in force, against an estimated two hundred German soldiers on the west side of the hill. Enemy artillery pummeled the American battalion on both sides of the hill. Progress was measured by the distance between trees. The price was measured by the increasing number of casualties as the Americans slowly advanced uphill over the course of several hours' fighting.

Medic Kelly Kuwayama had a unique view of the battle, peering over a boulder or from behind a tree. The intellectual Princeton graduate knew how to dissect a battlefield. Scan the scattered open areas where a man was more likely to be shot as he advanced. Watch for movement because when soldiers were moving, they were more vulnerable. Unconsciously run his hands around his belt, making sure medical-supply packs had not fallen off somehow. Look for stands of trees, mounds of rocks, and foxholes that might offer shelter if a man fell wounded and Kuwayama had to drag him to safety. The shorter the distance, the better. A medic couldn't be searching the forest for a safe haven *after* he had reached a wounded soldier. Listen, especially between the mortar detonations. Men would call for help, most likely for buddies who had been wounded.

"Medic!"

Kuwayama saw a rifleman lying in the open, motionless. German mortars were landing dangerously close to the defenseless soldier. Kuwayama ran across bare ground, oblivious to the shrapnel and bullets splitting the air around him. The thud against his head must have felt like a heavyweight's punch. Blood from the shrapnel gash nearly blinded the medic. He paused, dragged a shirtsleeve across his eyes, and then resumed his dash toward the wounded man. The first thing he did was to check the man's eyeballs. If they didn't move, Kelly would know he was dead. Not this time. They moved. He administered rapid-fire triage before dragging the man thirty yards across open ground and through wicked enemy fire. Litter bearers were nearby, ready for the wounded soldier. Kuwayama needed immediate treatment, too.[*]

---

[*] Kuwayama was awarded the Silver Star for his bravery.

Companies E and F finally reached the top of Hill 617, but it was clear the German units in the area were not defeated. Veteran combat soldiers had learned that a cleared enemy was not necessarily a vanquished enemy in the Vosges. Now the Germans had to drive the Americans off the hill. Trees exploded and the forest floor quivered as Company E's George Sakato dove into a German foxhole. A solder from Company F joined him. George thought he recognized the man, despite the grime and exhaustion that coated his face.

"Hey, you're Mas Ikeda from Mesa, Arizona," he said.

"Yeah."

"What have you heard about home?"[3]

In the middle of the raging battle, they shared tidbits of life a world away, where families endured barbed wire and armed guards. Caucasian America called it internment. Many Japanese Americans called it incarceration where their sons had volunteered to fight America's war.

The artillery attack finally paused, and Ikeda left Sakato in search of more ammunition. Then Sakato spotted the lead elements of the enemy's infantry counterattack. The onetime sickly boy named after a samurai had become a battle veteran whom replacement troops relied upon. Could the 2/442 hold the hill? A German approached Sakato, grenade in hand. Sakato grabbed a German Luger he had found days earlier and killed the German. Now he had only a few seconds to fill his Thompson submachine-gun clips. He had taped two together, giving him a forty-round capacity. As he did, Germans passed him on their way back up the hill. No one noticed the five-foot-four American in the bottom of the foxhole.

Not far away, Saburo Tanamachi led a squad through the trees. He had grown up on a family farm in Texas. He had run the business side of the farm, planning crop rotations and supervising crop deliveries to market. He had promised his sister, Yuri Nakayama, that he "would bring home Hitler's moustache."[4] He and his squad faced four machine-gun nests and twelve German riflemen. An enemy squad advanced toward him.

Oh my God, Sakato thought before he yelled, "Watch out for the machine guns! They're taking the hill back!"

Tanamachi inexplicably stood. "Where?"

The answer was a German machine-gun burst that ripped into Tanamachi. Sakato ran to his friend, who had fallen into a foxhole. Sakato held his friend, blood soaking both uniforms.

"Why'd you stand up?"[5]

Tanamachi gurgled in reply. Seconds later he died, limp in Sakato's arms. Sakato cried in the middle of battle. They had shared a Waldorf Astoria room in New York City when on leave, carefree and happy, looking out the window for a few hours when they discovered they had no money after paying for the room. Now they had shared death. His friend's blood coated Sakato's hands. Tears blurred the battlefield for a few seconds before they evaporated in rage.

"You son of a bitch," Sakato yelled as he, too, rose to his feet, in full view of the enemy.[6] He could hardly have frightened the Germans. Sakato, the smallest and sickliest of five brothers, zigzagged toward the enemy, firing his Tommy gun from his hip, spraying the forest as Germans fell on one side and then the other.

His suicide charge so unnerved the Germans that several raised hands and white handkerchiefs fluttered. Sakato had nearly single-handedly halted the counterattack and taken prisoners. He had killed twelve Germans, wounded two others, and taken four prisoners. But he had lost a friend. Sakato had only thirteen days' battlefield experience when he mounted his charge up the hill. As a replacement soldier, he had halted a flanking attack by the enemy, taking charge when his squad leader had been killed.

The previous day, Tanamachi had told Sakato that he felt sick to his stomach. Sakato had told him to report to an aid station. Tanamachi refused, picked up a grenade launcher, and reported to his assembly area. Once the 2/442 had secured Hill 617, Sakato walked back to Tanamachi's body, soaked with blood and mud. Tanamachi's blood on Sakato's hands had crusted and then been rubbed off by his still-warm submachine gun. Sakato removed Tanamachi's lucky 1921 silver dollar that he had carried in his pocket. After the war, Sakato gave the silver dollar to Tanamachi's mother.[*]

———◦———

UNCERTAINTY CONTINUED TO GNAW AT HIGGINS'S MEN. THE Germans had probed their perimeter regularly for five days. Short of an all-out attack, they nonetheless inflicted casualties and kept the surrounded battalion on edge. By now the Germans knew the exact location of the battalion, so its artillery barrages had become increasingly deadly. When Higgins made his morning rounds, his men reported three more had been killed overnight. Slowly, brutally, the Germans were chipping away at Higgins's force, killing a soldier or two with an artillery attack, wounding a few more by machine gunners and snipers. But on October 29, the war of attrition became one of potential decimation. The Germans launched an all-out attack, from nearly every side of the perimeter. Small-arms fire, machine-gun bursts, and mortar shrapnel tore into the battalion's foxholes. For the first time, German soldiers appeared everywhere throughout the forest as they slowly advanced.

In the next few minutes, Eason Bond would have to decide whether he would lay down his rifle and accept capture. A few yards away, Jack Wilson and Burt McQueen kept their machine gun on single shot, saving precious ammunition and waiting until the advancing enemy crowded together enough to justify bursts of death.

---

[*] Saburo Tanamachi was one of four brothers who served in World War II and on June 4, 1948, became one of the first two Japanese American soldiers to be buried at Arlington National Cemetery. General Jacob Devers, chief of the army field forces, and General Dahlquist, deputy director of army personnel and administration, were two of the five generals who attended the ceremony. Colonels Virgil Miller, Charles Pence, James Hanley, and Charles Owens were pallbearers.

The battalion's riflemen had kept the Germans at bay in previous days. Now it would be up to the machine gunners to turn back the German assault. The supremely confident Martin Higgins knew what he had to do as he looked down at the letter he was writing to his wife when the attack started. He took just a second or two to jot down one more thought—"Time out for a while, Marge. I've got work to do," he wrote before carefully folding the letter inside a piece of orange parachute and tucking it into his wallet.[7]

Once again, however, the 1/141 repulsed the Germans' most aggressive attack. As the forest settled, a now familiar droning hum off to the south slowly emerged. Soldiers looked up into a blue sky they had not seen in days. Another American resupply mission by the 405th was approaching the surrounded men. The first group of aircraft arrived over the battalion's position at 1045. By now the pilots knew exactly when to drop their loads. Fifteen aircraft bombed the battalion with medical supplies, plasma, and ammunition. According to Major John Leonard, who had again led the mission, twenty-two tanks fell within the perimeter. Four others had landed only fifty yards outside the perimeter, and another two tanks were one hundred yards from Higgins's position. Red parachutes laid on the ground, as if they were the remains of Christmas packages torn apart in glee. Red silk—draped across mossy boulders, waterlogged pine needles, and freshly dug craters—became festive slivers of hope in a forest of gloom and desperation.

Once again, the men broke open the tanks and carried all the supplies to a central distribution point near Higgins's foxhole and not far from a handful of medics who were treating the wounded. The medical supplies and plasma gave them hope that at least a few of their casualties might survive grimy wounds and infections. Everyone else waited until Higgins and the other lieutenants determined how the new supplies would be rationed. "They brought the food, piled it up, and looked at it. It was the strongest discipline I ever saw," Higgins said after the war.[8]

Then disappointment returned. They still needed batteries for the FM-frequency SCR 610 radios used by other men attached to Higgins. With fresh batteries the radios had a range of five miles and enabled entrenched observers to communicate directly with their artillery batteries. That was far more effective than routing messages through Blonder. Higgins's men also could not find nearly enough Halazone tablets to disinfect the putrid water they were drinking. The tablets and 610 batteries may have had been in the tanks that had irretrievably fallen into German territory. Food was good, but safe drinking water was critical. Higgins reported that he still needed a supply of tablets and batteries.

ANXIOUS AND INCREASINGLY DESPERATE, GENERAL DAHLQUIST couldn't stand not being at the front line. About the time that Sakato and others launched the attack on Hill 617 and Higgins's men prepared for the airdrop, Dahlquist and his aide Lieutenant Wells Lewis drove east across the ridge. They followed the logging road and used the latest field reports to find Lieutenant Colonel Singles's position. Dahlquist wanted to know what was keeping the 100th from greater advances and apparently didn't accept the explanations he was getting over the radio.

Lieutenant Colonel Singles walked over to Dahlquist's jeep. When Dahlquist asked for a map of the ridge, Singles didn't have one. Lieutenant Boodry, his operations officer, typically had carried the battalion command map, but he had been killed the day before. Lieutenant Lewis offered his. Tall and handsome with wavy, flaxen hair, Lewis looked like the prototypical general's aide. He had graduated Phi Beta Kappa from Harvard with honors five years earlier. The twenty-seven-year-old was the eldest son of novelist Sinclair Lewis and had published his first novel while in college. He was the "golden boy" of the Lewis family.[9]

As Lewis unfolded his map on the jeep's hood, a German only forty yards away took aim. The bullets slammed into Lewis's back. Some soldiers nearby thought they came from a sniper, but others were sure it was a short burst from a machine gun. Blood splattered onto the general's uniform. Lewis staggered and fell into Dahlquist's arms. Almost in slow motion, Dahlquist dropped to one knee to lay him on the ground. Dahlquist greatly admired Lewis, even though he had been Dahlquist's aide for only three months. Lewis was dead. Shock washed across Dahlquist's face. He would later acknowledge that it was if he had lost a son. That was evident when Singles approached Dahlquist.

"Lewis is dead," said Dahlquist.

"I saw that," said Singles. Perhaps Singles had seen so many men die in recent days that another loss meant little when more men would die soon, possibly within the hour. Another lost life that perhaps had been avoidable. No one questioned Dahlquist's personal bravery. He was willing to meet with a battalion commander within a stone's throw of the enemy, even at the cost of his aide's life.

A few minutes later, when the commanding officer of the engineers, Colonel Oran Stovall, arrived to investigate the burst of gunfire he had heard, Dahlquist still held Lewis. "They were shooting at me and killed this fine young man," said Dahlquist.[10]

———◦◦◦———

GERMAN MAJOR FRANZ SEEBACHER HAD SEEN COMBAT IN POLAND, Greece, and Russia. It's unlikely he had experienced the situation facing him on October 29. The commanding officer of the 201st Mountain Battalion faced an overwhelming American force. Like Pursall, Singles, and Hanley, his units were understrength and an uncertain supply of ammunition was a constant worry. And, like Dahlquist, there was a missing battalion.

The 201st and 202nd Mountain Battalions had arrived in the Vosges only a few days earlier as reinforcements for Lieutenant General Ernst Haeckel's 16th Volksgrenadier Division. Each comprised about one thousand men. These were mobile, semi-independent divisions that carried nearly everything they needed for battle. They comprised three rifle companies, a weapons company with machine guns and mortars, a headquarters company, and platoons of light artillery, engineers, and medical personnel. These had been elite battalions at the start of the war. But five years later, replacement troops generally were only young volunteers and men convalescing from Eastern Front injuries. They were critically needed by Haeckel. Haeckel's division numbered three thousand on October 1 but had lost an estimated six hundred during the rescue mission. By November 1, only nine hundred would be left.

The two mountain battalions, elements of the 16th Division, and Lieutenant General Wilhelm Richter's 716th Volksgrenadier Division had been the primary enemy force the 442nd faced. In recent days, the 442nd had learned from captured German prisoners that the enemy faced similar issues of command uncertainty. The commanding officer of the 202nd Mountain Battalion, Captain Erich Maunz, had been killed six days earlier. The 202nd had been cut off by the Americans. Worse, there were no communications, which left the fate of the 202nd very much in doubt.*

German soldiers who had been captured near Hill 617 the day before by Hanley's men confirmed that five companies from the two mountain battalions had arrived a week earlier. The newcomers were disorganized on the battlefield. Training had been minimal, and esprit de corps was almost nonexistent among the men who had been thrown together. They had not expected Lieutenant Colonel Hanley's attack from the north, and several dozen had surrendered to soldiers of the 3rd Division, not far from Hanley's men. Hanley learned that one of them was a battalion commander who was up on the ridge on

---

*The 202nd ultimately lost so many men in October, its first month in combat, that it was disbanded two months later, with the survivors absorbed by the Germans' 338th Division.

a reconnaissance mission. Another had a German map that showed precise locations of defensive positions as well as a regimental command post in the town of Vanemont, about two miles to the east.

The captured Germans also painted a dire picture of defenders as depleted and desperate as the rescuers. One German company had entered the battle with sixty men, but now had only thirteen who were equipped with two machine guns. Four companies in another German battalion had a total of only one hundred men. Those still fighting from their foxholes were relying on horse-drawn supplies and had been low on ammunition for two days.

They also reported that German replacement troops had been positioned on both sides of the logging road leading to Higgins's men. Now there could be no element of surprise. The Germans and Americans knew the locations of each other's units, where their command posts were located, and where artillery batteries were established. Both knew when, where, and how each side resupplied its frontline troops. Both had concentrated their forces on the only route to the surrounded battalion.

———◦◉◦———

YET EVEN WITH SUCH CERTAINTY, POTENTIALLY HORRIFIC MISTAKES could still be made, particularly by men who were exhausted and perhaps in shock over the loss of a best friend, a respected squad leader, or a trusted aide. Not long after Dahlquist had left Lewis's body to others, the 522nd Field Artillery Battalion received orders from Dahlquist at 1400 to fire on position 345573.* Many officers who

---

*Topographical-map coordinates produced specific numerical designations for precise locations. For example, 522nd Field Artillery Battalion at 255569 was near Bruyères, about five miles from the front line. Almost directly east, Lieutenant Colonel Hanley's objective, Hill 617, was at 326606. The massive German roadblock at Col de la Croisette confronting the regiment was at 334588.

heard the order referring to "345573" knew it was Higgins's position. The general wanted his artillery to fire on Higgins?

"345573. I want clearance from 1st Battalion, 141st on the hill," radioed Captain Moyer Harris, a forward artillery observer.[11] Harris was responsible for a seven-man observer team that accompanied the lead elements of the rescue force. All seven had volunteered for the mission and were led by Staff Sergeant Don Shimazu. At one point, they had crept through a minefield unknowingly until they looked back and saw the *Achten Minen* signs. Dahlquist's order didn't make sense to Harris. He wanted Higgins to "authorize" the general's order.

"We'll have to check with them. That plots right in the middle of the lost battalion," replied Lieutenant Colonel Baya Harrison, the commanding officer of the 522nd Field Artillery Battalion.[12] If the American artillery could drop shells from several miles away onto a target of perhaps 50 yards in diameter, it didn't make sense to put deadly artillery inside Higgins's 350-yard perimeter.

"The General wants us to fire on that [Higgins] point. I wish you would check. We had a call from the forward observer that General Dahlquist wanted some shoot on Hill 345573. Isn't that in right in the middle of the lost battalion?" asked Harrison.

"Yes, it's in the middle of the lost battalion," replied another divisional officer.[13]

The record is unclear whether the 522nd radioed Blonder to ask Higgins to confirm Dahlquist's order. But the 522nd never fired at 345573. It also is not recorded if Dahlquist learned that the 522nd never fired on Higgins's men. Less than an hour after he had ordered the artillery bombardment, Dahlquist sent an entirely different message to Higgins, one that the supremely confident lieutenant had already refused on several occasions. "Start patrols out to contact [the advancing 442nd] on the trail you were on. If enemy attempt to interfere, get to work on their rear flank."[14]

Higgins and Huberth must have been flabbergasted by Dahlquist's order. They canvassed their respective companies and those under

Nelson and Kimble. Despite the arrival of some supplies, their men were weak, dehydrated, and sleep deprived, and dozens were in excruciating pain from trench foot. Some had only a handful of ammunition left. They had lost a major part of their fighting force on an earlier Dahlquist-mandated breakout attempt. Daily enemy infantry attacks and nightly artillery bombardments had added casualties and litter cases sometimes by the hour. To make matters worse, the fighting so far on the twenty-ninth had been the most vicious Higgins's men had endured since they had been surrounded nearly a week earlier.

How the hell are we to attack the Germans from the rear? And what about their tanks? Even if they could mount an assault, the logging road leading back to the Germans' roadblock at Col des Huttes crossed open stretches of forest and swales of boggy, open ground. The enemy would have deadly fields of fire if Higgins's men tried to cross the stretches of chest-high willows that offered almost no natural protection against mortars and machine guns. Higgins and the other lieutenants may have discussed Dahlquist's order before replying. Twenty minutes later, Higgins sent his response—again refusing an order by his superior officer.

"Received 5,000 rounds of M1 and 800 rounds of carbine ammo. Patrol would necessitate large force, impossible to spare men due to German patrolling and attacking. Also have too many men with bad feet."[15] Although Higgins's men presumably had some ammunition left before the resupply, the ammo recovered from the 405th's resupply missions gave him only enough to maintain his weakened defensive position for a limited time. It was far short of what was necessary to mount an attack. If five of Higgins's riflemen each fired their M1 rifles six times a minute, they would exhaust five thousand rounds of ammunition in only two and a half hours. Higgins had once again told Dahlquist he didn't have enough men and ammunition to do what the general wanted. They would have to remain hunkered down in a battle of bloodletting attrition as the 442nd advanced, one tree at a time.

A FEW HUNDRED YARDS AWAY, MUTT SAKUMOTO COULD HEAR the firefight deeper in the forest. He was a member of a Company I reserve platoon in the rear. This likely would be the last chance that Sakumoto could have one of his cherished cigarettes for quite a while. The men were sitting around a tree, waiting to be called forward, when Dahlquist approached. Sakumoto was stunned that Dahlquist was at the front.

He looked directly at Sakumoto. "What are you boys doing sitting down?"

"We're the reserve platoon."

"Let the other boys do that. Flank the enemy! Flank the enemy!"[16]

Sakumoto and the others got to their feet, moved across the road, and promptly ran into soldiers of the 100th. The flank was already covered by units of the 100th. Dahlquist didn't know the precise locations of his units, but that apparently didn't stop him from prowling the front line while his aide's body was taken to the rear.

Dahlquist spotted Shig Doi, also of Company I, looking in another direction. Doi had volunteered from an Arkansas internment camp and been told he would be assigned to the artillery because of his mathematical ability. Instead, he was lugging a rifle a few yards from Germans. Dahlquist tapped Doi on the helmet and told him to move forward immediately. "You can't do anything here," said Dahlquist.[17]

Dahlquist continued to make rounds, acting more as a company commander than a division's commanding officer. He approached the 100th Battalion's Lieutenant Allan Ohata. "How many men do you have here?" he asked.

"One company sir."

"That's enough. Here's what you do. We've got to get onto that hill and across it. You get all the men you have and charge straight up that hill with fixed bayonets. That's the only way we can get the Krauts off it."

"You want my men to charge up that hill, sir?"

"Straight up. It's the quickest way. There's a battalion going to die if we don't get to it."

"You realize what this means to our men, sir? They'll be slaughtered climbing a hill in the face of heavy fire in full daylight."

"It's got to be done."

"I refuse to accept your order. You can court-martial me. You can strip me of my rank and decorations but I refuse to accept your order."

"You refuse? I'm ordering you. Take your men and make a bayonet charge up that hill and get those Krauts off it quick!"

"We'll get them off it our way and try to save as many of our men as possible."[18]

Those watching the confrontation said Dahlquist walked away wordlessly, without challenging the twenty-six-year-old lieutenant who had already proved himself as a courageous soldier dedicated to his men.*

Dahlquist wasn't finished. He headed toward the 3rd Battalion's headquarters in search of Pursall. For three days, Pursall's battalion had absorbed horrific losses. His Companies I and K had been on the point, usually abreast, advancing directly into a dug-in enemy. Ration details back to the rear at night had been pounded by German artillery. Pursall's men had suffered through nearly constant fighting under his command. Their respect for Pursall had been one reason they had fought so valiantly and accepted so many casualties. A largely disrespected general countermanding Pursall threatened that devotion. That wasn't Dahlquist's concern when he confronted Pursall as his messenger Rudy Tokiwa stood nearby.

---

*A year earlier in Italy, Ohata had led a three-man squad against forty Germans. At one point, he killed ten Germans as he rescued one of his men when his gun had jammed. After the soldier found another gun, the two of them killed twenty-seven more before capturing the remaining three Germans. Later in the day, they held their position, killing four and wounding three. A half century later, Ohata received the Medal of Honor for his heroism.

"I want you guys to charge! Charge! Charge!" yelled Dahlquist.

Pursall tried to explain why his leading companies' advance had been stalled by intense enemy fire and what a brazen charge up the hill could cost. Pursall knew the hill ahead was heavily defended, with a massive roadblock at Col de la Croisette behind it. The surrounded battalion was more than a mile on the far side of Croisette, and there was a second major roadblock at Col des Huttes, about midway between Croisette and Higgins. A suicidal charge now could leave the 442nd without enough men and firepower to breach the two roadblocks and reach Higgins.

Dahlquist would have none of it. He wanted the 3rd Battalion to mount an all-out assault along with the 100th, just as he had told Sakumoto, Doi, and Ohata. Pursall grew madder by the second. All three 442nd battalion commanders had seethed with frustration over the meddling Dahlquist. But now Pursall had reached the breaking point. "You can go to hell! These are my boys you're trying to kill. You don't kill my boys. If there's any orders to be given for my boys to attack, I'll give the orders personally and I'll lead them," said Pursall, risking charges of insubordination and possibly dereliction of duty. "If you think it's that simple, come with me and take a look," added Pursall.

Dahlquist and Pursall walked toward the gunfire, away from Tokiwa. After a few minutes, they returned, both of them livid, according to Tokiwa. The towering Pursall nearly shook with anger, his face red and wireless glasses steamed. As Dahlquist continued down the hill away from the front, Pursall followed him, yelling at Dahlquist.

Dahlquist turned to face Pursall. "Colonel, you heard what my orders are. You don't carry out my orders, I'll have you court-martialed."

"You know what you can do with your orders. . . . I don't want to see you up in the front lines again where I'm at. You stay out of our way," said Pursall.[19]

Pursall didn't have many options. Two companies would have to advance on a one-hundred-yard front straight into German positions. At first Pursall thought that Company K might be able to flank the

Germans. Within minutes of the flanking attempt, soldiers on both sides were only a few yards apart in a riot of gunfire, ricochets, and explosions.

It became clear that Company K could not flank the Germans' dug-in position. Companies I and K would have to mount a charge up a long slope pockmarked with foxholes and craters. Toppled trees had fallen into haphazard stacks of rain-slick logs, some as tall as a man. Jim Okubo, Jim Tazoi, Jim Oura, and the rest of Company K faced the steeper portion of the ridge. Next to them, Barney Hajiro, Joe Byrne, Shuji Taketomo, Matsuichi Yogi, Mutt Sakumoto, and the rest of a battered Company I faced a longer, slightly less steep climb. They all waited for the order to stand, fire, and advance.

For some, it became known as the "banzai charge." Those who survived referred to this stretch of forest as "Suicide Hill" or "Banzai Hill." Accounts vary as to how it started. But every man from Companies I and K agreed on one point: the commanding officer who always had the best interest of the Nisei at heart, Lieutenant Colonel Alfred Pursall, led the charge. The towering, paunchy Caucasian must have lumbered up the hill, a pistol in his hand, yelling at his men to follow, as his chubby cheeks reddened and perhaps his steel-rimmed glasses fogged.

Chet Tanaka remembered Pursall approaching Tanaka's foxhole, where he had taken cover from enemy fire. Simply approaching Tanaka's position on foot by a man as large as Pursall was an enormous risk.

"Let's get going, sergeant," Pursall had said.

"I looked up at him from my prone position and thought, *My God, if that dumb son-of-a-bitch is going to walk up into that fire, I guess we better too.* I called to the some sixteen men of [Company] K to get up and get going. I was the first up. All the others got up. No yelling. Didn't want the enemy to hear us. Pursall led the way."[20]

Perhaps fifty yards away, Sergeant Joe Shimamura saw Pursall leap to this feet and say, "Okay boys, let's go!" Shimamura noticed Pursall wasn't wearing a helmet. Previously, Shimamura hadn't thought much of Pursall. Maybe he was wrong. "I guess he is going to die with the rest of us," recalled Shimamura. Shimamura jumped to this feet and followed Pursall up the hill, yelling, *"Make! Make! Make!"* (A battle cry for the multilingual Shimamura, it meant "death" in Hawaiian and "lose" in Japanese.)[21]

Forward artillery observer Ed Ichiyama's recollection was similar. His team had been attached to Pursall. He was alongside Pursall and Tokiwa when the frontline troops had been pinned down and Pursall had to make a decision. Should he try to slowly bleed the enemy faster than his men were getting picked off or force the issue and risk even greater loss of life?

"So finally, Colonel Pursall . . . took out his pistol and said, 'Infantry, charge!' . . . Then from the forest, we saw the infantry guys just standing and starting to go. You know, shooting from the hips and just go." Armed with just a carbine, Ichiyama stood and charged. A carbine had a fraction of the firepower of an M1 rifle. He thought his weapon looked like "a toy," but he had orders to follow, regardless of the dangerous situation.[22]

SOME VETERANS REMEMBER COMPANY I's BARNEY HAJIRO, THE former malcontent desperate to show he was a good soldier, as one of the first to charge ahead toward the Germans, nearly one hundred yards in front of his company. In a sense, Hajiro had a running start after a brief exchange with Takeyasu Onaga, his BAR ammo man, a few hours earlier.

"Barney take care, if I die, take my P-38," he said.[23]

Hajiro had been surprised at Onaga's sadness earlier that morning. He had known the usually upbeat Onaga since basic training. Perhaps the relentless fighting since October 15 had begun to take its toll. The prospect of advancing up another exposed hill toward entrenched two-man machine-gun nests tested a man's faith and hope for survival. "What are you talking like that for? If I die, you take my Luger," said Hajiro. Words of more meaningful encouragement failed him, other than to offer Onaga his prized German souvenir. An exchange of weapons was a time-honored demonstration of mutual respect among men on the battlefield.

Pursall's order spread among the troops. "Let's go!" yelled Sergeant Goro Matsumoto. A sniper killed Matsumoto minutes later.

Hajiro was among the first to step out of his foxhole and into the enemy's line of fire. Gunfire erupted and the ground shook as enemy machine guns raked the Americans' path. Hajiro crawled over to Matsumoto, but there was nothing he could do. He took a sip from Matsumoto's canteen just as another man in his unit, Sergeant Shiro Kashino, was shot in the back. Hajiro considered him "a good mainland boy, a good soldier."[24] Yelling over the gunfire and explosions, Hajiro told Kashino to get back to an aid station. Hajiro then turned to face the Germans.

After helping load Hajiro's BAR, Onaga was searching for a good firing position when an enemy shell hit nearby, toppling a tree onto a buddy. Onaga somehow lifted the tree so the wounded man could crawl to safety. Then Onaga, Hajiro, and dozens of others continued their advance up the hill. Each man confronted a personal hell where the margin between survival and death was measured in split seconds.

After killing several Germans with a grenade, a sniper's bullet pierced Onaga's throat. He staggered, steadied himself, and ran nearly fifty yards to an aid man so the medic could remain behind cover. Then Onaga collapsed and bled to death.

Several yards away, Hajiro watched his friend die. A hollow, aching rage erupted from the gut of a man who had grown up poor, insecure, and desperate to prove he was worthy of his fellow soldiers' respect and trust. The enemy had killed his foxhole buddy. A stranger in basic training who had become a trusted friend, one who liked beer and had kept Hajiro out of trouble. A man in whose hands Hajiro had placed his life. Hajiro would find the enemy who had shot Onaga and kill him. He would not allow his friend's killer to surrender. For Hajiro, there was no room for compassion in war, no room in his heart for forgiveness on the battlefield.

Hajiro stood and faced the Germans, perhaps blinded by the rage of loss, by the horror of the carnage around him. He ran ahead of his unit, up the slope toward the enemy. Somehow he reached a two-man German machine-gun position guarded by a sniper. They raised their hands, unnerved by Hajiro's charge. "They want to surrender, but I cut 'em down. . . . [T]here's no prisoners, you know, at that time because you don't have time, eh?" Hajiro recalled after the war.[25] The foxhole was covered in German blood as Barney raced ahead. When a German sniper missed Hajiro as he ran, Hajiro stopped, swung his BAR to the side, and killed the sniper.

The distinct sound of another German machine gun pulled at him. Somehow hundreds of bullets missed him as he wove his way toward the enemy. A few yards away, Lloyd Tsukano was struck by Hajiro's dirty senninbari sash wrapped about Hajiro's waist. The traditional battlefield Japanese cotton sash had been sewn with one thousand stitches by women where Hajiro had grown up.* He fired, forcing the enemy to pause and duck for cover. "I pin 'em down again and I wipe 'em out," he said.[26]

Hajiro never saw the enemy as he approached a third machine-gun emplacement. A burst thundered into his body. The massive invisible punch sent his helmet flying in one direction and splintered his automatic rifle. Hajiro had taken direct hits in his arm and face. Covered in blood and in shock, Hajiro was told by a medic that he had to go back down the hill to an aid station. Now. Hajiro looked around. Had he found a functioning weapon, he would have refused. He would have found a way to attack with a bloody face and blood-slick hands. But he could find none. He looked back down the hill and made a decision. He would walk off the battlefield. He would not

---

*Some Nisei soldiers carried their senninbari in their packs or helmets, concerned that wearing them would imply their empathy for Japan. It appears that wasn't an issue for their commanding officer, Al Pursall, as several members of his 3rd Battalion wore their senninbari on the battlefield.

give the Germans the pleasure of seeing him carried off. He still wanted to prove to his buddies that he was a good soldier. Only then would he allow the medics to take care of him.

———◦———

THE POUCHES ON THE TWO VESTS WORN BY COMPANY I MEDIC Victor Izui were growing lighter by the minute. He called his pouches *shobai dogu*, tools of the trade. The company's charge up the hill had produced an overwhelming number of casualties. Every wounded soldier prayed an experienced medic like Izui would appear at his side. Izui had made the transition from fresh medic to combat veteran in Italy several months earlier. Perhaps it had been a little easier because he had worked in an internment camp hospital. His family had been evicted from the Japantown neighborhood of Seattle and sent to Camp Minidoka, in the desolate high desert of southern Idaho.

Treating his first casualty on the battlefield had been far different from treating a patient on a cot. "Feeling the first quiver of panic, I wanted to be sick. Aw, jeez! But, somehow, training takes over. Hey, don't freak out, stay cool, stop bleeding, watch for shock, watch for lung puncture, ease pain, jab morphine syrettes, dust wound and compress with sulfa, dressing on, tag him, and try to get him the hell out of there," he recalled after the war.[27]

Now Izui faced scores of wounded men across the battlefield. He sprinted fifty yards to a wounded man lying in the open. As the ground around him churned with enemy fire, Izui spread half a pup tent on the ground, pulled the man onto it, and then dragged him to a sheltered location. *Okay, that's all I can do for him. Do I leave him for a litter team? No, too far away.* Izui picked up his patient and carried him farther back to a medical-collecting station. There, litter teams took the wounded soldier down to an aid station. Izui turned, scanned the battlefield, and ran toward the next man he would rescue. By the end of the day's fighting, Izui treated thirty wounded men in Company I.

Most of them were taken to an aid station that was part emergency room, part morgue. There was an eerie calm among the stretchers in the small cave created by digging into a hillside and then placing a few timbers on top. But far more men lay in the open than inside. Medics, a chaplain, litter bearers, unscathed men who helped the wounded reach the aid station, and transport drivers walked among them. If there was a sense of urgency among any of them, it was well concealed. A dying man carried enough fear. Most of the medics moved slowly and methodically, checking watches and making notes as they worked. When one of Izui's wounded men arrived at the aid station, clothing was cut away. Then Izui's bandages were cut or peeled off, exposing the man's raw meat whose sulfa powder had hardened along the edges.

Some men grinned at the medic treating them. Their joy at being alive triumphed over their pain. Others lay with their eyes closed, responding to questions as minimally as possible, their heads perfectly still, lips barely moving. Veteran medics knew to pay closer attention to the quiet ones. Perhaps their systems were shutting down. Internal bleeding could be invisibly draining their life. The loud ones, those who were yelling, crying, or groaning, usually were the less seriously wounded men. Tags containing critical triage notes were attached to Hajiro and the others bound for a field hospital closer to Bruyères or Belmont in the rear.

In the midst of battle, dead men at the aid station could not always be immediately separated from those still fighting for survival. One difference: dog tags were removed from the dead bodies. After that, notes were taken for the official record. Each was wrapped tightly in a tarp. When time allowed, they were carried to a stand of trees next to the logging road, out of sight, if possible, from the wounded. The steady rain splattered on their death shrouds and left random patterns of droplets. They were aligned in neat rows, as if they had already reached a cemetery. Young men had become face-less, silent mummies, waiting for the rough ride on trucks down off the ridge. Their buddies up on the hill could only wonder who was still alive back at the aid station and who had been laid out with the other corpses.

———◆———

SLOWLY AND BRUTALLY, THOSE REMAINING ON THE FRONT LINE pushed the Germans back up the slope and finally off the strategic high ground. The firefight had stretched to nearly two hours. Pursall must have been horrified when he radioed his report to Dahlquist's operations officer. "We have no officers left in K Company. We are up on the hill but may get kicked off. There is a roadblock, and we are having a lot of casualties. K Company CO [commanding officer] is gone, but we are using an I Company officer for K Company," reported Pursall.*

"Blue [3rd Battalion] of 141st is on your left flank," the operations officer replied.

"They are nowhere near us. We have to get that roadblock knocked out."

Dahlquist broke into the exchange. "Blue 141st started a patrol to La Croisette [forest location of roadblock]. They say they are getting tank fire. Is it yours?" Dahlquist asked.

"It could be but we have to shoot up our way. Enemy tank is coming up from the south."

"You have TD [tank destroyer]."

"The roadblock has those stopped," said Pursall.

---

*In dire circumstances, companies, platoons, and squads could be reorganized on the battlefield when one or more units had suffered extreme losses of men or officers.

"We are sending an engineer company toward you. How is Singles doing?"

"He is up against the same thing. I questioned a PW [German prisoner] and he said they were well dug in. . . . How about some infantry help?"

"I can give you only engineers," Dahlquist offered.[28]

Dozer drivers would have been little help to Pursall, and Colonel Stovall needed every man in his engineering crew. They trailed the front by a few hundred yards, rebuilding the logging road and responding to calls to clear minefields and roadblocks under enemy fire. The unit had built more than a mile of planked road, hauled and dumped more than one hundred truckloads of gravel, and installed dozens of culverts.

The roadblock at Col de Croisette, nearly adjacent to the hill Pursall had just taken, was massive. The Germans had felled dozens of trees whose trunks were one to three feet in diameter. They formed a massive pile, blocking Pursall's route. Mines were planted on both sides of the roadblock to prevent his men and vehicles from skirting it. The engineers had to clear a path if the rescue mission was to continue its advance.

Mines and downed trees were so interlocked that the engineers needed to devise a clever solution to remove both as quickly as possible and with minimal loss of life. They welded large hooks onto the heavy equipment and connected them to cables that in turn were attached to the largest limbs of the downed trees that they could reach. Then as those trees were dragged a short distance, they detonated the unseen mines. One trunk at a time, the engineers cleared a path for Pursall and Singles. Stovall's men had plenty to do. Pursall and Singles would have to fight with the men they had left. Both were fiercely devoted to their men, and neither relished the prospect of battle without reinforcements.

———◦◉◦———

As night fell, the battlefield was as fluid and blood soaked for the Germans as it was for the Americans. According to after-action reports, the Germans had lost approximately 150 dead and captured men in the day's fighting on Hill 617.

Dahlquist's intelligence officers learned the Germans had placed up to four 88mm artillery guns to the north of Higgins's position. Higgins reported that three prisoners had told him that German reinforcements were proceeding to a point more than a mile northeast of his position and that they were reinforced by artillery, mortars, and machine guns. But like the Americans, they were low on ammunition.

Enemy machine gunners were digging in at various points between the roadblock at Col de Croisette and Higgins, less than a mile away. Enemy troops had been spotted coming up from the valley to the south, and enemy artillery was confirmed in Corcieux, a village four miles south of Higgins and well within range of the lost battalion.

Were the Germans planning an all-out assault when the sun rose? Higgins's men were exhausted from enemy attacks that had lasted throughout the day. It had been, by far, the toughest fighting since the 1/141 had been surrounded.

Perhaps the Germans sensed they could not hold off the 442nd much longer. Perhaps they concluded they had to press their advantage before more supplies reached Higgins's men and fortified them into a more formidable fighting force. A coordinated attack against Higgins, reinforced by artillery, would be critical if the enemy was to destroy the 1/141 before the 442nd reached it.

The Germans had lost an estimated 350 men in recent days. But a final assault could come in the morning. Higgins had 45 men left in Company A, 71 in Company B, and 95 in Companies C and D. All told, he had about 100 riflemen left. He still needed more supplies.

The day's final resupply mission by air took off at 1600, in fading daylight. Within an hour, seven more tanks had fallen within the 1/141's drop zone. Flight leaders like Lieutenant Eliel Archilla had overcome both the enemy and the weather. Archilla was perhaps one of the most talented pilots who delivered supplies to Higgins. He had trained as a glider pilot and flown P-51 Mustangs before transfer to the 405th. Archilla recalled after the war that he had flown so close to the ground that he could see the GIs he was resupplying.

Seven resupply missions had now been flown within forty-eight hours. On at least one occasion, the 405th had caught Germans by surprise in a clearing near Higgins. They strafed the enemy, adding to its mounting casualty list and the 405th's confidence that it could keep supplying Higgins's men.

The 1/141's morale lifted as bellies were filled with rations most soldiers had disdained only a few weeks earlier. Higgins believed that if he could keep his men supplied, they could hold off the Germans indefinitely. Higgins calculated that he had about three days' worth of supplies but needed Halazone for water purification and more ammunition. Higgins had used the high ground he occupied to maximum advantage. Many foxholes now had log roofs. And the enemy had fallen into a somewhat predictable pattern of attack.

However, Higgins needed to get his wounded to a hospital as soon as possible. He also needed dry socks. Too many of his men were in excruciating pain from trench foot. Many would not be able to move out of their foxholes if an assault in the morning resulted in hand-to-hand combat. If Higgins's men made it through the night, the 36th Division planned another airdrop in the morning, this time with seven hundred pairs of socks, one hundred cans of foot powder, Halazone, batteries, and ammunition.

Those supplies might buy Higgins enough time because the 442nd was planning renewed attacks at 0900 the next morning. But the regiment had suffered horrific casualties in recent days. The survivors in the 100th Battalion's three companies numbered about 220, less than 40 percent of the companies' authorized strength. The losses suffered by Companies I and K were hard to fathom. There were only 20 men left in Company K and even fewer in Company I. Nearly every officer had been killed or wounded. A soldier previously on a food detail was now the acting sergeant for Company K, a unit that had a prewar authorized strength of about 190 men. Company I had suffered 4 dead and 40 wounded in a day's fighting. But when enemy fire finally ebbed at sunset, danger never departed the battlefield.

As evening fell, some men were once again ordered to go back over the ground they had just captured to bring supplies forward for another day's fighting. At Company I, Captain Joe Byrne turned to Sergeant Tak Senzaki, a soldier with an uncanny sense of direction. Senzaki and 14 others headed back to the rear. And directly into a pocket of Germans. Muzzles flashed in the grim darkness as heavy clouds muffled the detonations. Senzaki's men fought their way through. Shortly after the gunfire stopped, Senzaki heard a distant explosion, back where Byrne and the remnants of Company I were digging in, an odd, isolated blast in an unexpected portion of the forest at an unexpected time.

When the supply detail returned with its rations at midnight, the word spread. Captain Byrne had been worried about the exchange of gunfire he had heard. According to Senzaki, he had started out in the direction of Senzaki and stepped on a mine. He was killed instantly. Company I's survivors were horrified. They had lost one of the most respected men of the 442nd.*

Officially, he was listed as killed in action on October 30. But for many men, such as Company I's Mutt Sakumoto, he was the final casualty on a day that survivors would relive in nightmares for the rest of their lives.

---

*Another soldier's recollection was that Byrne was headed toward the battalion's command post in the early hours of October 30 when he was killed by the mine.

CHAPTER 7

NEED ANY CIGARETTES?

EICHI WAKAMATSU WOKE UP TO A BONE-CHILLING RAIN. THE rifleman in the 100th's Company B had closed to within about six hundred yards of Higgins's men. The 100th and 3rd Battalions remained abreast, the 100th on the south side of the logging road and the 3rd on the north. A few yards ahead lay another German roadblock at Col des Huttes. An estimated fifty Germans were waiting for Wakamatsu, Okubo, Sakumoto, and others to summon another day's courage.

Wakamatsu had grown up in the Hood River, Oregon, area, where a handful of Japanese American families grew apples and stone fruit. He didn't know that a few days earlier, the Hood River American Legion post had decided to erase his name from an honor wall of local residents serving in uniform. His was one of sixteen Japanese American names that would be taken off the memorial in the coming weeks as a protest against some Japanese American families who were about to return to what might remain of their homes, farms, or businesses. The American Legion post's goal was to exclude all Japanese Americans from the county.* As he scanned the misty forest on

---

*In late 1944 the War Relocation Authority began allowing some Japanese American families to return to their homes. The Supreme Court was considering a case that challenged the constitutionality of the relocation program.

October 30, he had no idea he would become the lightning rod of a national controversy before Christmas.

He was one of only fifty-five men left in Lieutenant Colonel Gordon Singles's Company B. Singles had sixty-five men in Company A and seventy-two in Company C. He had only about one-third the fighting force of a fully manned battalion. Lieutenant Colonel Alfred Pursall had only a few more men in his 3rd Battalion. It was a bloodied and beleaguered force that rolled out of slit trenches and carefully got on its feet behind trees to stretch aching muscles and stiffened spines. The first order of business was to "count noses," to see how many men might have been killed by enemy artillery in the night.

They had tried to sleep through heavy American artillery directed at the roadblock on the road ahead. The Americans had left a trail of blood on the logging road as they had overcome a series of enemy strongpoints along the ridge. Colonel Virgil Miller couldn't be sure how many more enemy roadblocks his men in the 442nd had left in them.

But Miller knew the 442nd was getting close to Higgins's men. The 442nd had been averaging about six hundred yards' advance each day. They had fought for every foot, as the Germans had pressured each step with gunfire and then pounded night positions with artillery. But on this morning, his men jumped off at 0900 with little resistance. Surely, the counterattack would come soon. Regardless, his thoughts turned to a completed mission. Miller ordered his personnel staff to write citations for "Colonel Singles and Colonel Pursall for a DSC [Distinguished Service Cross] for getting through to that battalion. I also want at first rest period FO [forward observer]

President Roosevelt, among others, was openly discussing the merits of allowing Japanese Americans to return to the West Coast or perhaps require relocation elsewhere in the country. Some organizations in Hood River, Auburn (California), and elsewhere publicly threatened retaliation against any Japanese Americans who returned home.

of artillery written up."[1] Miller also wanted Pursall and Singles to recommend any men they thought worthy of citations for bravery.

———◆———

AT ABOUT THE SAME TIME, HIGGINS SURVEYED HIS REMAINING men. He had forty-five men in Company A, seventy-one men in Company B, eighty-one men in Company C, and fourteen men in Company D. But after discounting for casualties, he figured he had about one hundred riflemen and a handful of machine-gun crews. He calculated he had enough basic supplies for about three days. Although he was out of water-purification tablets, he begged off any more airdrops for fear they were pinpointing his men's positions for the enemy. Its artillery attacks had become more precise once the 405th had begun hitting the drop zone with regularity. He knew that Germans still controlled the roadblock at Col des Huttes, about five hundred yards to the west. Perhaps worse, German prisoners told him more enemy troops were approaching from the northeast with artillery, mortars, and machine guns. About the only good news from the prisoners was that advancing troops were low on ammunition, too.

Yet as dire as the situation Higgins faced had become, Dahlquist again issued what seemed to be his standing order: attack the enemy! Once more Higgins was told to prepare to attack the German roadblock from the rear. Higgins had about forty minutes to organize his men and then, if he had fresh batteries, start listening for additional instructions at 0900. Higgins and the other lieutenants must have been stunned to receive the same order they had rebuffed earlier. As usual, the order was incomplete, leaving them to wonder if Dahlquist expected an all-out assault by those still standing or whether it was to be a more modest diversionary attack.

"What about disabled? German patrol harassing our position," Higgins radioed.

"Remain in position. Await further orders" was the quick reply from headquarters.[2]

Colonel Charles Owens clearly shared Higgins's concern and made his case to Dahlquist's operations officer against an attack. "If 1st Battalion advances, it will mean for them to split their forces and if they are met by a strong German patrol they may be wiped out completely," radioed Owens.

"Leave [a] detachment of weapons platoon to protect [your] casualties and be prepared to attack back along original route to northeast side of road so as to contact 3rd Battalion, 442. . . . Remain in position until time and direction given for attack."[3] Now it was clear. Dahlquist wanted an all-out attack.

Dahlquist may have thought the 442nd was running out of firepower and lacked the strength to reach the 1/141, in which case an attack by Higgins from the rear might be necessary. Whether Dahlquist believed Higgins's reports of his weakening men is open to question. Many times in the past, Dahlquist had overruled his frontline officers and nearly called some of them liars. Certainly, the other two battalions of the 141st were in no position to take over the rescue mission. Regardless of his motivation, he wanted the 100th and 3rd Battalions of the 442nd and the 1st Battalion of the 141st to fight toward each other with the few men who remained on their feet.

Shortly thereafter, enemy fire shattered midmorning preparations as Higgins stood not far from Blonder's radio. Sergeant Bill Hull's machine-gun position was suddenly confronted by Germans on three sides. *This is the last fight*, Hull thought. "It was like the enemy was determined to wipe us out one way or another. That was the first time I thought I was going to die. The only thing in my head was, if I'm going to die then I'm going to take as many of them as I can."[4]

The attack was ferocious, and some Germans closed to within thirty yards. Hull's machine gun ripped through wide swaths of the forest after he switched from single shots to automatic fire. Eason Bond, Arthur Cunningham, and others fired at the slightest movement. The crack of rifles and pistols reflected how intimate the

battlefield had become. Germans fell in what appeared to be a suicidal charge.* More Americans slumped in their foxholes, dead or
wounded.

And then the forest disappeared.

Higgins's men smelled it seconds before it filled the forest. Smoke.
Around midmorning, the Germans had begun laying smoke south
and east of Biffontaine, in the valley below the south side of the ridge.
As it drifted, the smoke consumed the valley and crept up the ridge. It
cloaked man and tree. Was this the Germans' cover for their last desperate attack? Was this another all-out assault that the lieutenants had
been waiting for? Higgins believed a final massive enemy assault was
about to begin. For days he had prepared his men, marshaled his meager resources, and now could rely on only their resolve. Would Cunningham, Bond, Wilson, and the others remain at their posts even if
they couldn't see a German charge? Six days of stalemated battle
might be determined in the next handful of minutes. What were the
Germans up to?

If Higgins's men were blind, perhaps artillery might save them
from the Germans. American artillery batteries began pounding the
blanket of smoke in the valley. Higgins asked for the same in the forest surrounding his men. The closer, the better.

Six minutes later, at 1120, Higgins tactfully refused Dahlquist's
attack order. "Not trying to beg off. Situation here gets worse. 22 litter casualties, 11 trench foot cases, 10 walking wounded, need transportation. Efficiency low. Enemy patrols active on flank and front
with automatic weapons. Mines at Point 10. Require engineers to
clear. Can send [reconnaissance] patrol to feel out the rear of enemy.
Awaiting orders."[5]

---

* War correspondents later reported that as many as 120 dead Germans were
found in the vicinity of the lost battalion's position.

BY MIDMORNING THE 442ND'S TWO VANGUARD BATTALIONS HAD reached a point only four hundred yards from Higgins's men. They had encountered some enemy resistance, but it had become clear that overnight artillery fire directed at the roadblock had been extremely effective. Abandoned German clothing and equipment littered the logging road. They passed the Col des Huttes roadblock and then cautiously entered the relatively open stand of willows where Higgins's men had suffered some of their most serious losses a few days earlier. They discovered two of Higgins's men who had been killed. They had been "manning a machine gun," according to a division report.

When Dahlquist told Higgins shortly before noon to send a patrol toward the Germans' roadblock, he inexplicably added that the 442nd was one and a quarter miles from Higgins. But if the 442nd had reached the roadblock at Col des Huttes, it was less than a half mile from the lost battalion.

Miller received reports that his battalions' slow advance continued to produce casualties. Eichi Wakamatsu was one of them. He was taken to an aid station along with others. Medics, chaplains, and support personnel had advanced behind the frontline troops, establishing command posts and aid stations along the logging road as engineer crews cleared it of mines.

Masao Yamada, a chaplain in the 100th Battalion, witnessed a new development among the combat veterans of the 442nd who were coming off the front line. Combat stress had begun taking a toll, according to a letter from Yamada to his wife:

> Up to now we had a very small portion of shell-shock cases. We are beginning to receive serious cases of shell shock in greater numbers. Many of them break down due to the loss of their best friends. In many cases when they see their buddies go, the going becomes a mental strain, and the enemy shelling becomes a mental disturbance of greater fear than usual. When shelling continues for days and

nights, mental hope diminishes and the accumulation of fear increases in proportion to the degree hope vanishes. The result is finally a close call—a complete breakdown.

Those that were once wounded also have a difficult time adjusting themselves in combat. The fear of being hit again, the sense of suffering, the dread of physical pain, all sensitize the soldier mentally to avoid combat. Hence with the intense shell fire around, one normally dreads the experience. If the fear continues long enough, one cracks up. It is one of the tragic episodes of combat.[6]

A prolific letter writer to the War Department, Yamada's letters in late October and early November reflected the creeping malaise that threatened the rescue mission:

I am spiritually low for once. My heart weeps with our men, especially those who gave all. Never has any combat affected me so deeply as this emergency mission. I am probably getting soft, but to me the price is too costly for our men. I feel this way more because the burden is laid on the [442nd] combat team when the rest of the 141st is not forced to take the same responsibility. In spite of my personal lamentations, our men are facing their enemy with the courage that comes from the heart. When we complete this mission, which we will today or tomorrow, we will have written with our own blood another chapter in the story of our adventures in Democracy.[7]

THE CHAIN-SMOKING MUTT SAKUMOTO HAD ONLY A FEW Chesterfields left in his pocket when he faced another day of fighting. As he looked around each morning, he also noted fewer and fewer men left in his Company I. On the morning of the thirtieth, there had been only two men in the second platoon and ten men in the first platoon. So the two from the second joined Sakumoto and the others in the third platoon. As they had every morning since the rescue mission had begun, scouts took the point and crept ahead to gauge the enemy's positions. On missions of such extraordinary danger, the soldiers on the scouting patrol took turns in the lead, the place where the enemy would first take aim.

The slightest sound might give them an advantage. Perhaps a careless German's voice might be heard. A mess kit might bump against a machine-gun tripod. Even the scrape of a boot across a bare rock could reveal the enemy's position. When the enemy was spotted by those at the front, hand signals would be used to pass the word to the rest of the patrol. Not many soldiers wanted to be assigned to a scouting patrol. Fewer wanted to take the point.

On this morning, the scouts had an unusual guide to determine their route of advance. At their feet was an American communications wire, a black tar-covered strand about the width of a round shoelace that followed the logging road. It stretched east into the forest and toward the lost battalion's position. It must have been laid by Higgins's men as they had advanced nearly a week earlier. Would it lead to Higgins's position on this day? Colonel Pursall ordered Sergeant Takahashi Senzaki to take nine others and follow the communications wire.

The patrol headed out shortly after first light. The squad advanced slowly and silently along the wire. By late morning, the mist and smoke had dissipated. Sakumoto and Henry Nakada had taken the lead, following the wire. Less than a half mile ahead, they estimated, they heard gunfire. After passing the roadblock, they saw a small rise ahead. Nakada heard grumbling a few yards behind him. He left Sakumoto in the lead, as Nakada fell back to tell Fred Ugai to stop complaining about being assigned to the mission. Nakada was worried the Germans would hear Ugai. It was getting difficult for Nakada to keep pace, as a case of trench foot made walking more and more painful. But after a short distance, Nakada nearly caught up with Sakumoto.

By late afternoon, most of the smoke had cleared in the forest. The scouts had not heard any meaningful gunfire in the forest. Perhaps Higgins had not faced the all-out enemy assault that he suspected would accompany the smoke screen.

Up ahead, someone peered out from behind a tree and looked directly at Sakumoto. He quickly stepped back behind the tree. *Who was that?* Sakumoto stopped. He was sure that he had seen a man appear and then duck back behind cover without firing. *Why?*

"Hey, Hank. There's a guy out there looking at us."

"Where?"

They kept moving forward, more slowly and alert than ever, their eyes locked on that tree.

"Hank, this guy is looking at us again!"[8]

Technical Sergeant Edward Guy couldn't be sure what he had spotted from his machine-gun position. The replacement soldier and high school dropout from Indiana stared at the three men out in the forest as they approached his position. They were holding rifles across their chests. They seemed pretty small. It took a few seconds before he could identify their American uniforms.

"Hey!" was all he could muster before he ran down the hill toward them.

He stopped a few feet short of Sakumoto. They stared at each other for a moment. Neither knew what to say. Sakumoto looked up at Guy. A few years earlier, the poor kid from a Hawaii sugar plantation had to convince a recruiting sergeant to let him volunteer, despite his size. Now he didn't weigh much more than the 110 pounds he weighed when he had entered the army. The soldier who once stole cigarettes from his father stuck a hand into a pocket. "Need any cigarettes?" asked Sakumoto.

With that, the lost battalion had been saved.

THE SMOKE SCREEN HAD BEEN LAID TO COVER THE GERMANS'
retreat. For six days they had trapped Higgins's men, suffered horrific
numbers of casualties, and brought reinforcements into the battle.
Finally, the 442nd had overcome a dug-in enemy almost within sight
of Germany.

After a few puffs, Guy escorted Sakumoto to Higgins.

"Sir, this is the first man who came up to us," said Guy.

Sakumoto looked at Higgins. Grime blended with a week's beard
growth gave Higgins a gaunt look. A shelter half was wrapped around
Higgins. Twice in the previous hour he had called division headquarters, asking whether the 442nd was getting closer to his position. The
cold, exhausted lieutenant simply said, "Thank you," and asked Sakumoto if he had any more cigarettes. Sakumoto emptied his pocket
for Higgins and his men.[9]

As the men of the 442nd approached Higgins's men, reactions
varied. One of the men on the scouting patrol, Masao Furugen,
walked up to a small group of men. "They had tears in their eyes
when they came up to thank us for breaking through. They could
hardly speak, they were so happy. Maybe, but we didn't do anything
unusual. We just did our jobs as soldiers, that's all," he recalled after
the war.[10]

Not far away, one soldier of the 1/141, machine gunner Gene
Airheart, watched a 442nd soldier approach. "But when that young
man got within three feet of us and said something about 'go for
broke,' that was my first encounter with Japanese Americans, and he
was one of the greatest I've ever known," explained Airheart fifty
years after the war.[11]

As he approached Higgins's men, Kazuo Takekawa heard someone yell, "Here come the Japs!" Not every man who had been surrounded for nearly a week knew that the 442nd had led the battle to
reach the 1/141. As he and the rest of Company I arrived, Takekawa
shared his water, cigarettes, and food. There were no formal greet-
ings, no joyous backslapping. Just relief.[12]

Forward artillery observer Susumo Ito had a similar experience. When the logs covering foxholes had been packed with mud and brush, they blended with the landscape so effectively that their narrow openings were almost impossible to spot. That, of course, had been one of the objectives of every foxhole digger. As Ito "approached the incredibly deep and cave-like foxholes the trapped men peered out and seemed relieved or perhaps shocked at seeing us. They greeted us with appreciation, but they seemed in no mood for any celebration," said Ito.[13]

Soon Company K reached Higgins's position. One unnamed soldier began scanning the forest in every direction. He saw an American climb up out of a hole in the ground. His complexion was almost the same as his uniform, as a gray-green filth covered him. The two exhausted men approached each other silently, just staring. A cigarette was offered. A simple "Thanks" followed.

Others on the ridge were not as reserved.

After the first quiet minute the whole place erupted. "Hey, the 442nd guys are here!" The guys started coming out of the ground like you don't believe. We didn't know that there were that many GIs out there. We had been pounding all alone up that deadly trail for days, finding nothing but Germans, gunfire and barrages. Then all of a sudden we hear these guys, and there's no more fighting here. And they found they didn't have to fight because we were allies. You know, it takes a little while for a simple thought like that to sink in after all the days of terror and the fighting. We were together and we were happy.[14]

Pursall ordered a defensive perimeter be established, as the realization of being rescued settled on Higgins's men. There would be no more whispered funeral services for the 1/141's dead who had been buried in shallow, sodden graves within sight of the enemy. Higgins would no longer have to lead groups of men into enemy territory, fighting their way to resupply tanks that had fallen outside the 1/141's perimeter.* It was over.

———◦———

No one wanted to stay. Al Tortolano, the rifleman who had been told by his parents he was no better or worse than anyone else, greeted the 442nd with vacant silence. "I heard one guy say, 'Oh my God, we're fighting the Japs.' All we wanted to do was get out of there. We didn't stop to say 'thank you' then or anything. All we wanted to do is get our butts off that mountain."[15]

For some men of the 100th and 3rd Battalions, it was no occasion for celebrating. Entrenched Germans remained in the forest. Too many friends had been left along the logging road either for medics to treat or for grave-registration units to collect. At dawn Hiromu Morikawa, Tadashi Takeuchi, Joseph Byrne, Kosaku Isobe, and George Omokawa had prepared for another day's push toward Higgins. By midafternoon when the 442nd reached Higgins, all five had been killed. Probably not far away, George Takahashi of the 100th and medic Niroku Dochin were guarded by Germans. They had been captured the day before and were on their way to Stalag VII-A in Germany.

Many of the rescuers were in shock. Only eight remained in Company I, and only seventeen still stood in Company K. Chet Tanaka, Company K's clerk who had found himself in command of K's survivors, was witness to Company K's near destruction. "My pencil was worn down to a stub trying to keep track of the people we lost. We

---

* In July 1945, Martin Higgins was awarded the Silver Star for his leadership. In part it reads, "Lieutenant Higgins worked tirelessly and courageously to maintain the morale of his men and, bravely exposing himself to hostile fire, directed elements of the battalion in repelling attacks. . . . [H]is courageous and resourceful leadership inspired his men and kept them well-organized and encouraged until help arrived."

kept asking for replacements. None came up. We were lucky to get just food and ammo. Nothing could come up through that barrage the Germans put down on both sides of us."[16]

The relentless fighting for nearly a week had forced Tanaka and others to stow their compassion deep inside themselves. One night during the mission, Tanaka and a sergeant were counting their men to determine how many they had lost during the day's fighting. When they were finished, Tanaka sat down on his helmet. Not far away, the sergeant sat on the stiff body of a German soldier. Both started eating their K rations, oblivious of the callousness that draped their meal. Each man was so exhausted and numbed to death that the only things that mattered were food and then a little sleep before the next day's killing began again.

Some survivors of the rescue force depended upon a callousness that numbed every thought, every action. When Sergeant Tak Goto of Company K was asked by a member of the lost battalion for a drink of water from his canteen, a direct "No" was his answer. No hesitation, no explanation, was offered. The rescued soldier could only speculate why the volunteer from a relocation camp might want to keep his canteen on his hip.[17]

The leader of the lost battalion, the young confident lieutenant knew better than anyone what the 442nd had accomplished. "Chills went up our spines when we saw the Nisei soldiers. Honestly, they looked like giants to us," said Higgins.[18]

At 1600 General Dahlquist finally received the news in a simple radio transmission that he had desperately sought for several days. "Patrol from 442nd here. Tell them we love them."[19] Only about fifteen minutes later, Higgins radioed, "Anxiously awaiting orders." It was clear the 1/141 couldn't move off the ridge fast enough. But there were dozens of wounded men to take care of and others who were too weak to walk off the ridge under their own power. He was told to wait for Major Claude Roscoe, the officer who had replaced Lundquist as commanding officer of the 1/141, to reach Higgins.

Meanwhile, a skeleton 3rd Battalion pressed ahead on the ridge, fighting for every yard, until it reached Higgins's original objective. More men would be killed or maimed before the Americans finally secured the strategic vantage point high above the valley leading to the German border.

———◆———

DARKNESS FORCED THE 1/141 TO SPEND ONE MORE NIGHT ON the ridge while the wounded were taken off. It was the first time the men of the 1/141 slept secure in the knowledge that others stood lookout posts and had formed a perimeter to guard against enemy attack. As they slept, litter squads and transport vehicles were brought forward to the 1/141 to evacuate the wounded as quickly as possible.*

At the same time, some soldiers in the 442nd were ordered to begin carrying their dead off the hill on stretchers. They would have to be careful when they approached a dead Nisei who had lain undisturbed in the forest. Combat veterans of the 442nd knew Germans sometimes rigged dead American bodies with mines, making the corpses macabre booby traps. It was a trick of the enemy the veterans of 442nd had learned earlier on the Anzio beachhead in Italy.

The wounded were carried or driven to nearby aid stations, where medics checked them, jotted a few notes, and then sent them back down the ridge to field hospitals near Bruyères. Dozens of men suffered from wounds inflicted by the enemy, trench foot, dehydration, and exhaustion, including many who had never left their posts. After thanking Higgins, Erwin Blonder finally set his radio aside and was carried off with a severe case of trench foot. The thoughtful young

---

* The 111th Combat Engineer Battalion had built four and a half miles of road through the forest that had been utilized by seven battalions, three companies of tanks, medical personnel, and an antiaircraft unit.

man who had volunteered one month before college graduation never left his radio post and would not see Martin Higgins again during the war.

As the wounded and dead were taken back along the ridge, Colonel Charles Owens sent Higgins one final message at 1830:* "Best wishes and God bless you."[20]

———◦◉◦———

AT 0915 ON OCTOBER 31, AN ESTIMATED 108 MEN OF THE 1/141 marched off the ridge. About an hour later they loaded onto trucks. Just before noon they reached Deycimont, about two miles southwest of Bruyères. It was the first time the 141st had withdrawn since it had come ashore in France on August 15. Signal Corps videographers were on hand to record many soldiers walking and then riding in jeeps and transports back down the logging road. War correspondents waited, as the saga of the "lost battalion" had become big news back home. When Higgins's men arrived, hot soup was ready and followed by a hot meal about an hour later. It had been eight days since they had enjoyed a full, hot meal.

A noted BBC war correspondent, Colin Wills, was one of several reporters who interviewed Higgins. The interview was broadcast on *Radio Newsreel*, a BBC program aired in England and the United States within a week of the 1/141's evacuation. Higgins and Sergeant Harold Kripisch were also interviewed for another radio program, *Army Hour*, which was broadcast nationally on Sunday afternoons to more than 3 million listeners.

Throughout November a video newsreel report of the rescue riveted American moviegoers. Many of the newsreels showed Higgins

———

*Owens had intended to join Higgins's men before nightfall but reported that his French guide had led him the wrong way, so he could not join the 1/141 as he had intended.

and his men grinning and shaking hands with other GIs and the 141st's medical officer Captain Charles Barry. None had rescued the 1/141.* Some reporters were stunned at Higgins's description of what the 1/141 had endured. In one interview, he pulled his canteen off his hip and emptied its filthy water. "That's what we drank, or worse," he said.[21]

MEANWHILE, THE 442ND HAD NO TIME TO SAVOR ITS ACCOMPLISHment or mourn its dead. As those interviews took place on October 31 and in the days that followed, the 442nd had to reach and secure the 1/141's original objective, which was the eastern end of the ridge. It was about a quarter of a mile beyond where the 1/141 had been surrounded. Once again, Jim Okubo and the rest of the 3rd Battalion took the lead, with the 100th on the south side of the ridge to protect the 442nd's supply road it had just opened. George Sakato and the rest of the 2nd Battalion moved off Hill 617 and closed in on the 3rd, protecting its left flank. Inevitably, the Germans were waiting.

The day's advance began shortly after dawn, and by 1100 another firefight with the Germans developed at a newly discovered roadblock. The 442nd captured a handful of Germans, pulled back slightly, and called in the artillery. A short time later, the roadblock was neutralized by a renewed attack. That marked the end of German resistance. Shortly before dark, the 442nd reached Hill 595, giving those still fighting a commanding view of the Corcieux Valley and the hamlet of La Houssière at the foot of the ridge. Shigeki Nishimura, Albert Sunada, Tadashi Kubo, Ben Masaoka, Renkichi Matsumura, Ned Nakamura, and Minoru Yoshida were part of the final push early in the day. By the time Hill 595 had been cleared of Ger-

---

*The author could not find any newsreels showing the 1/141 personally thanking members of the 442nd. The 442nd remained on the front line when the 1/141 was transported off the ridge to waiting war correspondents and the Signal Corps.

mans, all seven of them had been killed. Seven more entries in the tally to take the ridge from the Germans.

The valley below would become one of the principal routes of the Allies' advance toward the strategic city of St. Die, on the Alsatian plain, and then to the German border. On that final day of fighting, Bert Akiyama of Company I and others found piles of K rations that had been retrieved by Germans from the supply tanks that had landed far from Higgins's position. Most of their contents were un-eaten by the hungry enemy, leading Akiyama to conclude, "The Germans knew what was inside and they didn't want any of that crap."[22]

In the days that followed, the chaos of battle was transformed into an orderly occupation. Supply trucks moved forward to support the Americans at the far end of the ridge. They brought food, ammuni-tion, medical supplies, and replacement troops. On their return trips, they ferried the dead and wounded off the battlefield. Litter teams carried dead men to where they could be loaded onto trucks and jeeps. The processionals stopped some men in their tracks.

> Four men came slowly up a trail along which was strewn with the debris of war. . . . The four were carrying a dead [100th] comrade on a litter. It was not so much the weight of their burden as it was the weight of the sorrow in their hearts that made them tread so slowly on their way. Toward them came a lone [American] soldier, of a dif-ferent division and of a different race. When he noticed the funeral process he stopped, stepped off the path, removed his helmet, and stood with bowed head as the men bore the dead past him. I shall never forget how the white soldier of the 45th Division took the time to honor one of our Japanese Americans. In reverence, he stepped off the road and let the dead pass by.[23]

VICTORY AND DEATH HAD COATED THE RIDGE. THE GERMANS' 933rd Grenadier Regiment had been destroyed. Fewer than 100 men remained in a force that a few months earlier had numbered ten times that. The Germans' back had been broken in this stretch of forest in the Vosges. The Americans had finally punched a hole in the German line. It would become the first time that any army in recent history had broken through the Vosges against entrenched defenders.

Two hundred eleven men had been rescued by the 442nd's three battalions and their support personnel. The exact number of Japanese American soldiers killed, wounded, or missing during the mission is not known. However, one after-action report showed more than 800 442nd total casualties for the month of October. Nearly all had occurred in approximately two weeks' fighting, beginning with the campaign to liberate towns west of the ridge and then the mission to reach Higgins's men. Another 442nd report for the month of October shows 756 men killed or wounded in combat. For every soldier killed, 5 were wounded.

The son of Martin Higgins, who has spent much of his life researching the mission, has written that 54 Japanese Americans were killed and 156 were wounded in reaching the 1/141. Research by the army's 34th Division shows 52 battle deaths during the rescue mission.* If the October killed-to-wounded ratio is applied to 52 deaths, approximately 280 soldiers were wounded during the rescue mission as well, for a total of about 330 rescue-mission casualties.

That figure is comparable to an estimate by Chaplain Yamada, who had served at aid stations, hospitals, and the 100th's headquarters.

Our AJA's [Americans of Japanese ancestry] in this particular rescue mission had approximately 350 wounded in action. Two of our assault companies have only a platoon and a half left in strength. Some say it's strange that the other two battalions of the 141st did not push so vigorously as the 442nd did. Our K Company men saw some of the 141st men run during a counterattack by the Jerries,

---

*The 442nd had been attached to the 34th Division in Italy prior to deployment in France.

thereby exposing them to danger. Others say that the first battalion could have fought their way out with additional supply of ammunition. In many ways, they were in better condition than our own battered battalions, for they have had less casualties and more officers and men. . . . I hope that a human story as such would bring a deeper understanding of the AJA's spirit.[24]

That burden also weighed heavy in the hearts of many who had been surrounded. "No one will ever be able to convince me that the men killed and wounded in our rescue can be justified. We should have been bypassed," Higgins told a group of 442nd veterans more than five decades after the war. "I am not sure if I could have done what you did. To volunteer to fight for the country that took away your constitutional rights. In my lifetime, no other group was ever persecuted as badly as you were. Every one of you deserved the Distinguished Service Award."[25]

It would be another year before the entire 442nd came home. More than five decades would pass before some 442nd soldiers received the credit due to them for reaching the lost battalion.

CHAPTER 8

PATHS TO PEACE

THE SMOLDERING AMERICAN TANK HAD BEEN AN EASY TARGET for the Germans in the dense forest. On November 4, medic Jim Okubo saw that an American tank had been damaged, but not destroyed. Had the crew inside been injured? There was only one way to find out. He ran toward the tank and the enemy's small-arms fire. Others watched him dart in one direction, then another, as he approached the tank. Ricochets off the tank echoed through the forest.

Unharmed, Okubo made himself an easy target when he pulled a wounded crewman out of the tank. But he couldn't treat the wounded man under such heavy fire. He had only one choice. Okubo steadied his legs in the mud, ignored the rain on his face, picked up the man, and found his balance. Then, without pause, he carried the wounded soldier seventy-five yards through enemy fire back to his men. Another American soldier had been lifted out of enemy territory and delivered to a place in the wet forest that offered a chance for survival.

AFTER REACHING HIGGINS AND HIS MEN, MOST OF THE 442ND had pushed ahead, nearly to the eastern end of the ridge, and then dug in. For four days they had expected an enemy counterattack and sent patrols out to probe enemy strength and position. Although the 1/141 had been evacuated to the rear, a significant German presence remained on the ridge, and enemy artillery pounded the 442nd's positions. The casualty list continued to grow. So many men had been lost to enemy fire, trench foot, accidents, battle fatigue, and other causes that members of the 232nd Engineers were alerted that some of their road-building crews might have to move forward, pick up a rifle, and join the 442nd on the front line.

On the day Okubo rescued that tank crewman, the 442nd began receiving its winter-weather gear. Overcoats and heavy jackets offered protection against the rain. Wool sweaters and heavy socks sparked hope for warmth. The seriously depleted 442nd had suffered for weeks in the cold rain and was one of the last units in the sector to receive its winter clothing, only three days before heavier snow arrived.

For a week following the rescue of the 1/141, the 442nd stayed on the ridge, clearing out the enemy, protecting supply routes from the valley to the south, and enduring enemy artillery attacks. By now battle-weary veterans had learned to dread the artillery barrages that often came at dusk, producing more wounded.

Men like John Tsukano struggled with not knowing if in the next split second artillery shrapnel would slam into his body. He could hear chunks of jagged steel flying through the air and slamming into the ground like buzzing bees as he lay in his slit trench. He never knew when he might be hit in the spine, head, neck, shoulders, buttocks—perhaps paralyzing or killing him. Horrific possibilities flashed through his mind after having seen others horribly wounded and then listening to them suffer at night.

Tsukano recalled one night incident in particular. A replacement soldier who was seriously wounded lay in a trench next to Tsukano. His eyes had swollen shut, and there was nothing more the medics could do for him. In shock, he moaned through most of the night. Tsukano and the other battle veterans suspected he would die before morning. At dawn, Tsukano looked at him. He had died with his hands clasped together over this chest, as if he had been praying before he died.

Finally, on November 8, relief came to the 442nd. No more could be asked of these Japanese Americans. The 100th was relieved by the 142nd Infantry and headed back down the ridge toward Bruyères. The following day, most of the remaining 442nd pulled out and headed for Lepanges, a French village not far from Bruyères. A hot bath, clean clothes, pay for October, a movie, hot food, and a beer ration awaited the 442nd. In less than thirty days of combat, the 442nd had lost 25 percent of its men: nine hundred officers and enlisted men.[1]

Sorrow also awaited the 442nd in the days following the men's first bath and clean clothes in weeks. On November 11, George Sakato and the rest of the 2nd Battalion stood motionless in a corner of a snow-covered farm field, shoulder-to-shoulder, their heads slightly bowed. Their shoulders slumped under their newly issued overcoats, belts pulled tight. Helmets that had been tipped jauntily back when they had first hiked into the Vosges had been replaced by skullcaps and helmets pulled hard and square onto their heads. Vacant stares were frozen on expressionless faces. Even in the blustery winter cold, few felt the need to blink. Heavy gray clouds, full of snow, hovered at the top of leafless stands of trees bordering the field.

Wintry sadness hung in the air. It was a day of reflection. They had come to honor eighty-two men who had been killed in recent days. Perhaps some survivors looked to those who had led them in battle to help make sense of the carnage. Colonel Virgil Miller and Lieutenant Colonel James Hanley stood in front of the men. Miller had served with some of these men back in Hawaii before the war. The quick-smiling officer who once favored ascots bore little resemblance to the man standing before them. Miller's and Hanley's pale faces exuded shock and exhaustion. When a chaplain ended his invocation, Miller wiped away a tear. Silent film footage of the brief ceremony did not capture the words Miller and Hanley spoke to their men following the twenty-four haunting notes of taps played by a gloved bugler. But when they concluded their comments and dismissed their men, no one looked relieved or inspired. They broke ranks, almost in slow motion, and walked back across the field's furrows toward their quarters. After they had left, the light dimmed as snow began falling. The ghostly footprints left in the mud by the survivors who had gathered to pay their respects to the dead slowly disappeared.

The following day Major General John Dahlquist came face-to-face with the losses suffered by the 442nd. The entire combat team had been summoned to another farm field, freshly covered in snow. Again the men stood in neat rows, bundled up and motionless. One more night's sleep had no discernible effect on their exhaustion. Dahlquist faced the 442nd, the two white stars on the front of his helmet gleaming in the winter-gray light. Only a few hundred stood before him. He scanned the ranks before turning to Miller.

Accounts of their exchange vary to some degree. But all witnesses agree that Dahlquist once again was angry. Hadn't he ordered the entire 442nd to assemble so he could read its Presidential Unit Citation and pin awards on winter coats? He asked Colonel Miller why he hadn't assembled the entire regiment. "This is all that is left of the 442nd, sir," replied Miller.

Some men present that day say that shock washed across the general's face. They almost took grim solace in witnessing the exchange with Miller. Dahlquist could not ignore how much 442nd blood had been shed in the Vosges campaign in less than one month.

Dahlquist made his comments to the assembled troops, read the citation, and then pinned awards on the lapels of young soldiers standing in motionless rows. Some looked up at the taller general with unblinking eyes when he stood in front of them. Others stared straight ahead, seemingly oblivious to Dahlquist. A few looked away. Dahlquist shook the hand of each, before moving on to the next man as an aide pulled another award for bravery out of the box he cradled in his hands.

The implications of the 442nd's mission to reach what became widely known as the "Lost Battalion" would not be lost. An army analysis undertaken shortly after the war was a blunt postmortem—what led to Higgins's men becoming surrounded, how effective was Dahlquist's command of the mission to reach them, and what price was paid by the 442nd? The mission was characterized by "a very evident lack of any clear cut plan either on the part of the regiment or the Division in the initial phase. . . . The action of the 141st Infantry in not closing all battalions in forward assembly areas in the first day of the operation is not understandable as there was no scarcity of motor transportation or hindrance by division."[2]

The analysis was equally critical of the working relationship between Dahlquist and his corps commanding officer. "At one time in the regimental command post the Corps Commander and Division Commander both made suggestions as to methods of operation that were completely unrelated."[3]

Just as damning, the entire operation was hamstrung because mountainous terrain reduced the effectiveness of tanks. Unit journals and after-action summaries delicately referred to the unavailability of armor, sometimes hinting that commanders refused to take their tanks off reinforced roads and into the waterlogged undergrowth. The analysis, however, concluded, "The use of armor was at best haphazard. . . . The major derelictions of armor were more the fault of infantry in not understanding and planning with armor than it was a lack of aggressiveness on the part of the armor."[4]

Of all the battalions used to reach Higgins's men, the postbattle analysis praised the 442nd in particular. "No mention of this operation can be complete without words of praise for the splendid work of the Japanese American (442nd Infantry) Regimental Combat Team. The spirit of cooperation with the units of the 36th Division, the aggressive, determined and relentless drive of the 442nd Regimental Combat Team, was in a large measure responsible, not only for the relief of the 1st Battalion, 141st Infantry but for the success of the entire operation."[5]

After the lightning advance north from southern France in a few weeks, the 36th Division advanced only ten miles over the next month following the events of the last week in October.

———————◆———————

ON CHRISTMAS EVE, GEORGE SAKATO; JIM OKUBO; LIEUTENANT Colonels Hanley, Pursall, and Singles; and the rest of the 442nd Regimental Combat Team looked forward to a hot turkey dinner near Nice, France. Colonel Charles Pence had recovered from his wounds and returned to command the 442nd as it established a defensive position in the Maritime Alps on the France-Italy border.

The 442nd had been reassigned to southern France and left the Vosges Mountains on November 19. The regiment had suffered 261 additional casualties in the first two weeks of November before the ridge was finally cleared of Germans. According to the 442nd October and November operations reports, 856 men had been killed or wounded in battle during the Vosges campaign. The 442nd required a relatively modest convoy of about forty trucks to transport the remainder of the regiment to southeastern France.

In the French Alps they had dug in for the winter, guarding the extreme right flank of the Sixth Army. The 442nd had been temporarily assigned to this backwater of the war where minimal enemy action was expected. Patrols periodically engaged the enemy, and Germans sometimes fired artillery from Italy across the border into the 442nd. However, the battered 442nd was to rest, recover, and assimilate hundreds of replacements into its thinned ranks. The assignment became known as the "Champagne Campaign."

Higgins's men were given only a few days' rest before they were sent back to the front line in the Vosges Mountains to join the push toward Germany.

———————◆———————

THE MOST THAT MARTIN HIGGINS COULD HOPE FOR ON CHRISTMAS Eve when he arrived in Szubin, Poland, was a Red Cross package that hadn't already been looted by his German guards. Higgins was a prisoner of war. He and seventy-seven others, the entire Company A, 1st Battalion, 141st Infantry, had been captured in the Alsace two weeks earlier. In the five weeks since the 442nd had broken through to the 1/141, Higgins's Company A had advanced about twenty miles.

In early December the American offensive had reached the eastern side of the Vosges. A number of towns and villages in the remaining Vosges foothills were in their path toward the Rhine River and the German border. On December 9 Higgins's unit approached the outskirts of Sigolsheim, a battered village of largely vacant buildings by that point in the war. He opted to consolidate his men in the small town rather than fight a larger enemy force supported by tanks in the foothills. Then, similar to the episode on the ridge, the battle plan unraveled.

Company B, led by Higgins's friend Lieutenant Harry Huberth, took "friendly fire" from American units, suffering unexpected casualties. Huberth wasn't able to protect Higgins's left flank, as Higgins had expected. Dating back to their days as cavalry soldiers in California, Higgins had always been able to rely on Huberth. Also, for unknown reasons, Company C had never left the line of departure, making Higgins's other flank vulnerable. Finally, a communications team that was expected to lay wire from battalion headquarters to Higgins's position never appeared. Higgins had to use runners to reach battalion headquarters at a time when he couldn't spare a single man. His company once again had become the isolated spearhead, virtually surrounded, and in danger of being destroyed.

On December 10, the Germans swept one house clear after another until they reached Higgins and his men, who had been herded into the southwest corner of the village. Enemy fire pounded the house Higgins had commandeered. Shrapnel from a German tank hit Higgins in the knee. He maintained command from an upstairs bed. By midafternoon Company A was surrounded and nearly out of ammunition. Higgins made the only decision he could: surrender his men to the Germans so they could take their chances in a prisoner-of-war camp somewhere in Germany or farther east.

Higgins's enlisted men were sent to one POW camp in Germany, while Higgins and his officers were shipped to the officers-only section of Oflag 64 in Poland. When he arrived, perhaps there was a Red Cross Christmas package or two still unopened. If so, it would contain plum pudding, boned turkey, deviled ham, small sausages, strawberry jam, candy, cheddar cheese, nuts, canned cherries, and twelve bouillon cubes. A few personal items would include chewing gum, playing cards, cigarettes, tobacco, a pipe, a washcloth, and two postcards of American scenes.

On January 20, 1945, Higgins learned he would not spend the rest of the war in Oflag 64. The Russians were approaching from the east. The following day, he and fourteen hundred other prisoners were shepherded into an enormous column of twos and marched out of camp. The temperature was barely above zero. Their ultimate destination was Stalag VII-A at Moosburg, Germany, 350 miles away.

The death march during one of Europe's most brutal winters in recent memory littered the countryside with dead bodies. Medic Jimmie Kanaya was part of the odyssey across frozen Germany. He had been incarcerated in Oflag 64 since Kanaya and the rest of his group of wounded men on stretchers had been captured at the outset of the mission to rescue Higgins. After subsisting on eight hundred calories a day, Kanaya, Higgins, and the others walked twelve miles a day through the snow. Most had only a wool blanket for protection, and they usually slept in abandoned barns at night. They were fed boiled potatoes and beets. Polish officers who had been confined much longer than Higgins and Kanaya died during each day's march. Kanaya passed many as they lay dying along the road. "I still see their hands sticking out of the snow. I think knowing the same thing could happen to me gave me incentive to keep going," he recalled after the war.[6] Only one-third of the prisoners, about four hundred, including

Higgins and Kanaya, reached Stalag VII-A six weeks later. The POWs in Germany's largest prisoner camp barely noticed their arrival.[*]

———◦———

As spring began to warm southern Europe, machine gunner Hank Yoshitake of the 100th Battalion, medic Jim Okubo, and the rest of the 442nd embarked on a secret mission in late March 1945. The Champagne Campaign had come to an end when the 442nd had shipped out of Marseille on transport ships bound again for Italy. Their transport ships took a circuitous route to avoid German spotters. Secrecy was paramount as they headed back into battle.

After disembarking in Leghorn, the 442nd gathered in Pisa. All identifying insignia were removed from their helmets and uniforms. No one could know the 442nd had arrived in Italy. The replenished battalion had been assigned to be the western spearhead of a massive attack to break through the Germans' foremost Italian defensive line. The Gothic Line stretched from the west coast a few miles north of Pisa east across Italy to Pesaro on the east coast. Attacks against the Gothic Line had produced only casualties and a stalemate. The Allies had made almost no progress in Italy since the 442nd had left for France seven months earlier.

General Mark Clark, who commanded the 15th Army Group, had developed an ambitious plan to break through the Gothic Line. Major General Lucian Truscott's Fifth Army would make a frontal assault to the west. The British Eighth Army would attack to the east and then turn west to trap the fleeing enemy. It was a massive pincer movement across the width of Italy. The 442nd would face at least four divisions of enemy soldiers that had reinforced the western portion of the Gothic Line.

---

[*] Estimates of the number of POWs at Moosburg in 1945 vary greatly, from fifty thousand to more than one hundred thousand, in a camp designed to hold only about ten thousand prisoners.

Much like what it had faced in the Vosges five months earlier, the 442nd faced a seemingly impregnable ridgeline held by the enemy. This time the south–north ridgeline was riddled with deep ravines and defined by a series of mountains. Mount Cerreta, Mount Folgorito, Mount Carchio, and Mount Belvedere loomed in their path. The eight-hundred-foot ridges of the Vosges had been replaced by mountains nearly four times taller. The 442nd would have to climb up into the series of mountains, cross minefields, evade enemy artillery zeroed in on mountain paths, and drive the Germans out of hundreds of bunkers.

Secrecy and a surprise attack were essential for success against the dug-in enemy. The 100th Battalion would make a frontal assault at the westernmost end of the enemy line, while the 3rd Battalion would attack about four miles to the east and then swing west to meet the 100th. It was to be a mini-pincer movement within the overall campaign. Battle planners for the 442nd believed, "All the theory of security, [a] night approach, and the frontal attack coordinated with a surprise flank assault from the least expected source, were wrapped up in this action. . . . The flanking movement [by the 3rd Battalion], made with the eyes of the enemy looking down from 3,000-foot heights, had only a 50–50 chance of success."[7]

On April 3 the 100th and 3rd Battalions loaded into trucks for a seventeen-mile journey north toward Pietrasanta under the cover of darkness. Slowly and quietly, they disembarked. Hundreds of unidentifiable men, their gear carefully packed to avoid noise, formed into units and began hiking. The 100th headed toward Vallecchia, eight miles away, while the 3rd Battalion marched four miles to Seravezza and then another eight miles up to Azzano, a mountainside village on the final hill before enemy territory.

The climb to Azzano was terrifying. Local guides led Okubo and the others up narrow trails carved into the hillsides in the dark. Switchbacks were especially treacherous, and unseen rocks on the path could become as deadly as a land mine. Most men carried enough K rations for three days, one pouch for a canteen, another to carry grenades, more grenades attached to a shoulder strap, their weapon, extra bandoliers of ammunition, spare socks stuffed inside their shirts, and toilet paper tucked into their helmet liner. Loaded down with the equipment tightly strapped to their bodies, twenty-five men fell off the trail, sliding and rolling uncontrollably down the hill. Two had to be hospitalized from the injuries they suffered in their fall. None uttered a sound as they caromed off rocks. The Germans could not learn of the sneak attack.

The 3rd Battalion reached Azzano shortly after midnight. Everyone was exhausted as they settled into houses and other buildings. Okubo and the other medics made rounds to check on the troops as the eastern sky lightened. The 100th and 3rd Battalions rested, out of sight, most of April 4. That night just before midnight, the 3rd Battalion headed out again. The men still had to cross one final valley after leaving Azzano and then make another brutal climb up toward Mount Folgorito and Mount Carchio. "The trail skirted drop-offs of 15 to 150 feet high and was so steep that the troops were forced to practically scramble up on hands and knees," stated an after-action report.[8]

Finally, just before dawn on April 5, the 442nd was ready to attack. At 0500 Hank Yoshitake was at the forefront of the 100th's assault. The machine gunner supported the second platoon of Company A. When Company A led off the attack, all was quiet for a few minutes. Quietly, slowly, they advanced about the length of a football field until a man stepped on a land mine. The battlefield erupted. Germans raked the minefield with gunfire and lobbed grenades into the Americans. Many fell wounded or dead.

Like many others, Sadao Munemori's squad was pinned down when its leader was killed. Munemori summoned a courage that would make him legendary. He mounted a one-man charge at the enemy. He single-handedly knocked out two machine-gun nests under intense fire. As he withdrew to a crater that held two American soldiers, a German grenade bounced off his helmet and rolled toward them. Munemori dove onto the grenade a second before it exploded. He died instantly as he saved the two men's lives.[*]

In only thirty minutes the 100th took its first objective, a hill designated "Florida." By the end of the day, twelve German bunkers had been destroyed.

To the east, the 3rd Battalion had also caught the Germans by surprise. Believing a major assault force could not climb the precipitously steep mountainsides undetected in the middle of the night, the Germans miscalculated. When dawn broke, the 3rd Battalion attacked almost at point-blank range. By midday Company L had captured Mount Folgorito to the south, and Company I had taken Mount Carchio to the north.

Vicious fighting persisted into the night along the length of the ridgeline and in the surrounding area. At one point, Okubo's Company K was called out of reserve to reinforce troops up on the ridge. As the men crossed the valley near Azzano and approached the mountains, enemy artillery rained down on Company K. German observation posts high in the mountains had pinpointed Company K's advance. As a result, Okubo's unit suffered more casualties than most of the units up in the mountains. Okubo and the other medics treated forty-two wounded men. Four others were killed.

Only two days later, elements from the 100th and 3rd Battalion linked up as the last enemy resistance was overcome on Mount Cerreta. The western end of the Gothic Line had been breached. Men of the 442nd had accomplished the feat in less than a day's fighting, followed by several days of mopping up isolated pockets of the enemy. Dozens of Germans had been taken prisoner, and the 442nd captured two thousand hand grenades, enough rations for a battalion

---

[*] Munemori became the only Japanese American soldier to receive the Medal of Honor during World War II or shortly thereafter. For others, decades passed before they were recognized.

for two days, one hundred bazooka shells, one hundred boxes of land mines, and other enemy equipment.

THE OPERATION AROUND MOUNT CERRETA WOULD BECOME THE last major battle for the 442nd Regimental Combat Team in Europe. In only two years, it had become the most decorated U.S. Army regiment of its size. In less than ten months, the 442nd had earned a remarkable 7 Presidential Unit Citations, 4 of them for reaching the 1/141. More than 9,000 Purple Hearts had been issued to men who had been wounded on the battlefield. Some wore as many as 4 Purple Hearts on their chest. Before war's end, the 100th was widely recognized as the "Purple Heart Battalion." The 442nd was earning what would forever characterize it as the "Go For Broke Regiment."

In addition to the single Medal of Honor, its 18,000 men earned more than 18,000 awards for bravery and sacrifice. That included 29 Distinguished Service Crosses, more than 330 Silver Crosses (28 men earned multiple awards), and more than 2,000 Bronze Stars.

In the years following the war, many veterans questioned the lack of Medals of Honor for the men of the 442nd. Command decisions that had downgraded Medal of Honor nominations written on the battlefield offered minimal rationale.

George Sakato's award citation stated that he had made a one-man charge against the enemy on October 29 when his unit was pinned down. A few minutes later, the citation recounted, he led a squad that repulsed an enemy counterattack. After running out of ammunition, he picked weapons up off the battlefield and kept fighting. He had killed twelve Germans, wounded two others, captured four, and had assisted the platoon in capturing thirty-four others.

But that wasn't good enough for the Medal of Honor. Three weeks before the assault on the Gothic Line, his nomination had been downgraded to a Distinguished Service Cross. The decision memorandum stated, "It is considered that the recorded acts were not so conspicuous as to clearly distinguish the nominee for gallantry and intrepidity above and beyond the call of duty."*

On April 11, a brief memorandum from General Dwight Eisenhower's command staff downgraded Barney Hajiro's nomination for a Medal of Honor for his legendary "banzai charge" to a Distinguished Service Cross. A month later, medic Jim Okubo's heroism in saving lives in enemy-held territory on different days was downgraded two levels from a Medal of Honor to a Silver Star. Okubo received his Silver Star at a memorial service on May 6, two days before the Germans surrendered.

———◉———

BY THAT TIME, MARTIN HIGGINS AND OTHER MEMBERS OF THE 141st were on their way home. He and four others from Company A had brazenly escaped their POW camp by walking out the front gate. Higgins could remember the French he had learned in school as he watched French soldiers being repatriated by the Germans.† *Could he and others blend in with the French?* The pipe-smoking Higgins had an idea. He swapped his unwanted Red Cross cigarettes to other prisoners for parts of a French uniform. As Frenchmen were released, Higgins and four others fell in with them and simply walked out of camp. One of them was Eddie Guy. Higgins had spotted Guy earlier through a fence that separated enlisted troops from the officer prisoners. Higgins had always considered Guy "one of his rocks" and one of the most reliable men under his command.[9] The five men dodged

---

*Command decisions typically were conveyed in sparse memoranda, in this case by Lieutenant General Ben Lear, U.S. Army deputy theater commander, on March 11, 1945.

†Germany allowed some French prisoners of war—World War I veterans, those with skills in short supply, fathers of large families, and others—to return to France prior to the end of the war.

patrols as they made their way through fifteen miles of enemy territory to the Elbe River and the American line. Once they had reached
friendly territory, they were transported to a rest-and-rehabilitation
camp near Normandy before being shipped home.

The 442nd, however, remained in Italy for nearly a year following
the German surrender, guarding German prisoners and military in-
stallations. First, they were sent to Ghedi, where eighty thousand
POWs were processed. Later assignments included the Italian Alps,
Florence, Pisa, and the Leghorn area, not far from where the 442nd
had entered battle several years earlier. Replacements continued to
arrive following the war, as battle veterans earned enough points to
be discharged and sent home.*

Finally, in 1946, the 442nd sailed into New York Harbor on
July 4. Less than two weeks later in Washington, DC, they paraded
down Constitution Avenue in a muggy rain, bound for a reception
on the White House lawn. President Harry Truman presented a seventh Presidential Unit Citation. He told them:

> You are to be congratulated on what you have done for this great
> country of ours. I think it was my predecessor who said that Ameri-
> canism is not a matter of race or creed, it is a matter of the heart. You
> fought for the free nations of the world along with the rest of us. I
> congratulate you on that, and I can't tell you how very much I appre-
> ciate the privilege of being able to show you just how much the
> United States of America thinks of what you have done. You are now
> on your way home. You fought not only the enemy, but you fought
> prejudice—and you have won. Keep up that fight, and we will con-
> tinue to win—to make this great Republic stand for just what the

---

*Military personnel earned points based on length of service, time spent over-
seas, campaign participation, awards and decorations, and the number of young
children at home. Generally, an enlisted soldier needed eighty-five points to be
discharged from the army.

Constitution says it stands for: the welfare of all the people all the time.[10]

He shared the sentiment of nearly every senior military officer who had any knowledge of Japanese American troops who had served in Europe and in the Pacific. Six thousand Japanese Americans trained as linguists and served as interpreters, interrogators, translators, and radio-message interceptors in the Military Intelligence Service. General Douglas MacArthur considered them crucial in the war against Japan in the Pacific. "Never has a commander gone into battle as did the Allied Commander Southwest Pacific, knowing so much about the enemy."[11]

General George Marshall noted, "The men of the 100/442 took terrific casualties. They showed rare courage and tremendous fighting spirit. . . . [E]verybody wanted them."[12] A week after the 100th entered battle in Italy in 1943, Marshall received a glowing report from General Mark Clark. Clark told Marshall that the 100th had performed brilliantly and asked for as many Japanese American soldiers as Marshall had available. In his postwar memoirs, Clark lavishly praised the combat record of the 442nd, considered it one of his most accomplished regiments, and recognized that the Japanese Americans' acceptance of brutal casualty rates was spawned in part to prove their loyalty.

Perhaps Major General Dahlquist understood what and why the 442nd had endured the missions he had assigned them when he wrote to his wife, Ruth, during the rescue campaign, "It astounds me how the men are able to stand the physical and mental strain under which they are constantly living. It is almost beyond comprehension that the human being can stand so much."[13]

CHAPTER 9

HONOR BESTOWED

LIKE OTHER MEMBERS OF THE GREATEST GENERATION, 442ND veterans likely anticipated plaudits and credit when they returned to America. Some, however, discovered that bigotry trumped patriotism. Some Americans continued to wage their own brand of war against Japanese American citizens in the months following World War II.

Several incidents became national news. A wounded Japanese American soldier, Raymond Matsuda, was ordered out of a barbershop owned by Andy Hale. "I don't want none of their business. They might close me up but I sure as hell won't work on a Jap," he told a newspaper reporter.[1] Others were tolerated silently. A San Francisco–area barber refused to cut future U.S. senator Daniel Inouye's hair when he returned home after losing an arm in the war. On many occasions, restaurant staff took the food orders of Japanese American families and then silently refused to serve their food until they grew tired of waiting and left. Some veteran associations denied Japanese American membership, prompting the establishment of Nisei-only veteran groups.

Such racism proved relatively rare, however, as many Caucasian Americans came to the defense of Nisei veterans. Colonel Pursall's battlefield aide Rudy Tokiwa was confronted by a group of men in Salt Lake City. "Why the hell they let Japs walk on the street for?"

one taunted. But then a policeman stepped in. "Either you guys get on your knees and apologize to this man, or I keep swinging this [billy club]."[2] One day Ushuro Ito's barn near San Diego was burned to the ground by unidentified vandals. It stored tools used in his commercial nursery. The nine-thousand-dollar loss could have been devastating. "In the midst of Ito's despair, his friends descended on his little farm. They came from nearby Vista and Del Mar, bringing material from which they erected a new building for Ito's tools."[3] Ito was able to continue growing stunted cacti.

Similarly, the Fort Hood American Legion post that had erased Nisei GI names from a monument had become the object of national scorn. "Why the dirty, lousy . . . that's the lousiest thing I ever heard of. The men who came off that hill in the mountains know those Japanese aren't as good as the average soldier, they're better," said Lieutenant Joe Kimble of the 141st.[4] Secretary of War Henry Stimson, who had supported the internment of Japanese Americans, was especially critical of the post's action. A week later, a group of Hood River ministers announced plans for a new memorial that would include all local Nisei veterans.*

When General Joseph Stilwell learned of what some Nisei veterans were enduring at home, he exploded with anger. "You're damn right those Nisei boys have a place in America's hearts now and forever. And I say we soldiers ought to form a pickax club to protect Japanese Americans who fought the war with us. Any time we see a barfly commando picking on these kids or discriminating against them, we ought to bang him over the head with a pickax. I'm willing to be a charter member. We cannot allow a single injustice to be done to the Nisei without defeating the purposes for which we fought."[5]

---

*Meanwhile, the local newspaper carried advertisements listing farms still owned by Japanese Americans and encouraging Caucasian residents to make offers to buy them.

By 1948 the anti-Japanese sentiment in the United States existed only in pockets around the country, as the legacy of the 442nd became more widely known. On June 4 two men from the 442nd who had been killed in Europe, Fumitake Nagato and George Sakato's friend Saburo Tanamachi, became the first Japanese American soldiers to be buried at Arlington National Cemetery. The cast of senior military officers attending reflected how much respect the 442nd had earned. Attendees included General Jacob Devers, the commanding officer of the Sixth Army Group in France, and Major General John Dahlquist. Pallbearers included 442nd commanding officer Colonel Virgil Miller and two of the 442nd's battalion commanding officers, Colonel Charles Pence and Colonel James Hanley. The 141st's commanding officer Colonel Charles Owens also attended. They had come from their posts across the country to pay homage to the 442nd three years after the war.

IN SOME WAYS, IT TOOK AMERICA FAR LONGER TO FULLY RECONCILE its treatment of Japanese American civilians in World War II and to acknowledge the legacy of the young men of the 442nd matched or exceeded that of the other millions of Americans who served during the war.

First, Americans needed to apologize to the neighbors they had sent to internment camps. In 1988 President Ronald Reagan signed historic legislation that authorized redress to the Japanese Americans for their internment in World War II. "We must recognize that the internment of Japanese Americans was . . . a mistake. . . . [T]he [442] soldiers' families were being denied the very freedom for which so many of the soldiers themselves were laying down their lives," said Reagan when he signed the Civil Liberties Act of 1988.[6] More than $1.6 billion in reparations was distributed.

Then, on June 21, 2000, seven old men shuffled toward reserved seats inside a pavilion on the White House lawn. A large American flag framed their seating area. The deliberate and haunting sound of Aaron Copland's "Fanfare for the Common Man" added a somber note as the rest of the seats were filled by family members, politicians, and the news media. Everyone waited for President Bill Clinton to arrive. It was time to correct an injustice: the repeated denial of Medal of Honor awards more than a half century earlier.

Only two Medals of Honor had been awarded to Asian Americans during the war. Dozens of nominations had been downgraded to lesser awards. After a detailed review of the record, in 1997 the Senior Army Decorations Board had recommended that twenty-one Distinguished Service Crosses and Jim Okubo's Silver Star be upgraded to Medals of Honor. Nearly all of the Medals of Honor had been earned by men in the 442nd. But only seven of the twenty-two were still alive in 2000.

Barney Hajiro and George Sakato took their seats, not far from Jim Okubo's widow, Nobi. Okubo had died in a car accident in 1967 when he was forty-seven years old. As each citation was read, President Clinton presented a ribboned Medal of Honor to a veteran, widow, or family member. "They did more than defend America," President Clinton told the audience. "They helped define America at its best. . . . Rarely has a nation been so well served by a people it has so ill-treated."[7]

Additional redemption and reconciliation followed the Clinton ceremony. In 2010 President Barack Obama signed legislation awarding Congressional Gold Medals to all Japanese American veterans of World War II. The nation's highest civilian medal was presented to as many living veterans as possible, often in front of friends and grandchildren, in small ceremonies across America and in Washington in the ensuing months. In 2013 the U.S. Postal Service unveiled a stamp series showcasing twelve Medal of Honor recipients, including George Sakato. The series was expected to be so popular that that the normal print run of 30 million stamps was increased to 81 million Medal of Honor stamps.

Meanwhile, the landscape of America was changing. Campaigns were mounted to change the names of Jap Road and Jap Lane in Texas and elsewhere. In Jefferson County, Texas, a Beaumont teacher, Sandra Tanamachi, led a twelve-year campaign to rename Jap Road.* Part of the public pressure came from Company K's Kenneth Inada, who had listened to Japanese American soldiers calling for their mothers as they slowly died in a French forest. "I can really understand the feelings of Beaumont people when they first named the street, 'Jap Road,' in memory and recognition of Mr. Yoshio Mayumi, a pioneer rice farmer. But with language sometimes playing a nasty social and psychological game as seen in the word, 'Jap,' I . . . beg you to consider the matter and simply change the name to 'Japanese Road.'"[8] The county commissioners changed Jap Road to Boondocks Road in honor of a local catfish restaurant that had closed.

Yet as America took steps to reconcile its commitment to freedom with its treatment of Japanese Americans, the scars remained deep and tender for many men of the 442nd Regimental Combat Team— as well as the 141st—until the day they died and for a few who are still alive. Some learned to share the horrors they had endured only in the final years of their life.

For others, memories were carefully locked deep inside. Yet they could surface at the most unexpected times. Martin Higgins kept his awards for valor in the center drawer of his desk at home. About the only time they came out was when his son wore them on his Halloween costume in the late 1950s. Forests unnerved 141st radioman Erwin Blonder following the war. He also had a touch of claustrophobia. Most veterans instinctively ducked when they heard a loud, unexpected noise. Some never wanted to see a war movie.

---

* Sandra Tanamachi was the niece of Saburo Tanamachi, who had been buried at Arlington National Cemetery more than fifty years earlier.

MORE THAN 1 MILLION AMERICANS WERE KILLED OR WOUNDED in World War II. The infantrymen, sailors, personnel clerks, supply officers, marines, medics, and pilots who survived came home to finish school. Others became husbands, doctors, teachers, electricians, fathers, mechanics, lawyers, or small business owners. Some made the military their life's work. Others never fully felt comfortable in their beds at home. Nightmares riddled with screams and body parts haunted some men for the rest of their lives.

As the 2nd Battalion's Kenji Ego recorded his war experience decades later, a dam deep inside broke. A torrent of pain surfaced in an instant.

> We try to forget it, the ugliness of war. And among the things that stopped me from going to [442nd reunions] was the joking about what happened to us. . . . Now I realize it was therapy for them. It would have been therapy for me, too, if I would have joked about it. . . . I guess . . . it's proper to be able to forget a lot of the horrifying things that go on. But if we all forget and if we don't share the horrors of war, how are future generations to know how bad war is? Since the beginning of human beings . . . there have been wars, even to this day. What would be better for all human kind than to stop war? Have peace. I think that should be the primary goal of mankind.[9]

At one point Ego broke into sobs. His faced turned red as he shook his head slowly side to side. His eyes wandered away from the interviewer, off into the distance as his face grew redder. The sobs paused as he wiped a tissue across each eye, holding his glasses in his other hand. Ego's head then rolled back, as if he was about to collapse with grief. His eyes closed, then tightened, just before he violently shook his head side to side. Hard and far to the right and then to the left. "I'm sorry," he whispered a split second before heaving sobs returned and he wiped away new tears. As they ebbed, he was clearly exhausted as he unsteadily reached for a water bottle. For a few seconds, it was unclear if he had the strength to lift it. He managed a sip and dabbed at a final tear. He put his glasses back in place.[10]

Just as he had appeared to center himself, deep, cleansing breaths slowly developed. Perhaps each was a sliver of sixty-year-old pain escaping his soul as he exhaled slowly. He stared off into another decade for a few more seconds before his breathing settled and he reconnected with the interviewer. "I think we can continue."[11]

The soldiers on that nameless ridge in eastern France each took a different life's path, often in anonymity. Few shared their war experiences with their families. Coworkers had no idea. Only at reunions of their military buddies did the memories bubble to the surface, sometimes in whispers and with downcast eyes, sometimes after a couple of drinks that likely were stiffer than what they usually drank at home. Tears and shudders sometimes punctuated their stories. Others joked to mask their pain. Others never had that chance.

The day before Martin Higgins, Harry Huberth, and Joseph Kimble led their men up onto the ridge, the 100th Battalion fought its way to the outskirts of Biffontaine at a horrific cost. Itsumu Sasaoka was captured by the Germans. A month later, he arrived at a German prisoner-of-war camp. In late January 1945, he was killed by invading Russian forces. It is unclear whether he died attempting to flee the Russians or was killed inside the camp. Harry Kamikawa also became a prisoner of war. He was liberated near the end of the war and returned to Hawaii, where he became a grocery store produce manager. He died in 2012 at the age of eighty-nine. William Yamaka was also captured by the Germans and later liberated. One year and a day after George Suyama had been listed as missing in action, he was declared killed in action. His name is etched on an honor wall at the American cemetery near Epinal, France.

The 442nd's founding commanding officer, Charles Wilbur Pence, remained in the army. His final assignment was as chief of staff of the Alaska Defense Command. Pence retired as a general in 1952 and moved to Georgia. He became a bank president and died nine years later, at the age of sixty-seven. It was said he could not utter Dahlquist's name without trembling with anger.

Virgil Miller had helped forge the 442nd as its executive officer at Camp Shelby and then as its commanding officer when Charles Pence was injured midway through the mission to reach the 1/141. Miller served in Italy until 1947 and then became an infantry adviser in Turkey. He came to the defense of Richard Naito after the war when the Japanese American was denied membership by an American Legion post. Miller wrote an angry letter to the post's commander, stating, "When supposedly reputable organizations such as yours violate the principles and ideals for which we fight, these young Japanese Americans are not the only ones to wonder about our war aims. Millions in Europe and Asia, too, will learn of your action and question the sincerity of American policy and ideals."[12] Miller retired in 1954 and became a professor of military science and tactics at Pennsylvania State College and Lehigh University and then was a research associate at the University of Michigan Institute of Science and Technology. He retired from academic life in 1963 and died five years later, at the age of sixty-seven. He stayed in contact with a 442nd reunion association whose members had developed a personal relationship with him and called him by a familiar nickname, Gil.

Alfred Pursall, the 3/442's commanding officer, was on the docks waiting for the 100th in August 1946 when the battalion returned to Hawaii to a massive celebration. He took time to visit the families of men who had been killed or wounded before resuming his army duties. Pursall later served at a variety of posts, including assignments in Korea and with a military assistance group in Vietnam in the 1950s. He later retired as a colonel and died in January 1979 at the age of seventy-three.

Gordon Singles, the 100th Battalion's commanding officer, remained in the army. Following World War II, he served in the Philippines and then in Korea. He graduated from the army's war college in 1952 and then served as a senior training officer in Europe. Singles was an executive to the inspector general when he retired in 1961.

Singles became one of the 442nd's most respected officers among 442nd veterans in the years following World War II. One day several years after the war, Dahlquist visited Fort Bragg, where Singles was stationed, for a parade review. At one point, Dahlquist approached Singles, offered his hand, and suggested that enough time had passed and they should put their differences aside. Presumably, Dahlquist was referring to his controversial treatment of the 442nd. In front of hundreds of soldiers, Singles signaled that the time had not yet come. Rather than shake Dahlquist's stand, Singles's salute remained frozen in place, as required by military protocol. His men stared in shock. Dahlquist paused and then withdrew. Singles forever became known as the Caucasian officer who refused to accept Dahlquist's awkward attempt at reconciliation following the war.

Singles died in December 1979 at the age of seventy-three. When Singles died, Senator Daniel Inouye, a member of his battalion, wrote that in his experience, some officers were excellent trainers of soldiers. Others were fearless heroes in battle. Inouye believed Singles was both.

By the time Young Oak Kim recovered from his wounds, World War II had ended. He returned to Los Angeles, where his family had barely made a living and where he had lived with discrimination before the war. Kim started a self-serve launderette business in Los Angeles. Two years later, he reenlisted and served in the military until he retired as a colonel in 1965. By that time, he had earned awards for valor in World War II, Korea, and Vietnam. He earned a college degree in history following his retirement and served on several non-profit boards of directors until his death in 2006 at the age of eighty-six. His legacy remains a pillar of the Korean immigrant community. The Young Oak Kim Academy (a middle school) in Los Angeles is named in his honor.

Like Kim, medic Jimmie Kanaya served in Korea and Vietnam after he was liberated from a German prisoner-of-war camp in 1945. He served thirty years in the military before retiring in 1974. His last assignment was as deputy commandant of the Medical Training Center at Fort Sam Houston.

James Hanley, the 2nd Battalion's commanding officer, was discharged in 1946. The following year, he applied for an army commission. He returned to active duty in 1947 as an army lawyer. He became the chief of the War Crimes Section, Eighth Army, in Korea. In 1953 he testified in front of Senator Joseph McCarthy on Korean War atrocities. Hanley made the military his career, retiring as a colonel in 1973. After nearly forty years as a lawyer, he then became a project manager for General Dynamics and taught business at San José State University. Hanley died in 1998 at the age of ninety-three.

Miller, Pence, Pursall, Singles, and Hanley didn't live long enough to see the reparations paid to Japanese Americans who had been sent to internment camps or, more important, to see some of their men receive the Medal of Honor that they had recommended nearly a half century earlier.

Medic Jim Okubo's family paid a heavy price in the war. Two brothers and a cousin also fought in World War II. His cousin Isamu Kunimatsu was killed in Italy, and his brothers returned home with war injuries. Okubo never returned to the Seattle area to resume his life after the war. He and his family settled in Detroit, Michigan.* Okubo attended Wayne State University and earned a degree in dentistry from the University of Detroit. He later was a member of its faculty and had a private practice. He was killed in an automobile accident in 1967.

Barney Hajiro, always eager to prove he was a good soldier, never fully recovered from his shoulder and wrist wounds. After rehabilitation he left a Stateside military hospital and paid his way to Hawaii. He later said he had five cents in his pocket when he arrived. He couldn't return to plantation work. He endured racial slurs when he

---

*About 40 percent of Japanese American families who were interned never returned to their homes in California, Oregon, and Washington. Like the Okubos, they settled in states far from the West Coast neighborhoods they had known prior to the war. Many prewar "Japantowns," like that in San Diego, disappeared permanently from the urban landscape.

returned, found work as a security guard at Pearl Harbor, and then got a job at a local airport. Hajiro told his family very little about his war experience and later acknowledged he was proudest of his Good Conduct Medal. He refused to buy a Japanese-built car and died in 2011 in Hawaii at the age of ninety-four.

George Sakato also came home seriously wounded. Shrapnel had pierced his back and ricocheted into his left lung. He endured eight months of surgeries and rehabilitation in England, Washington, and San Diego.* He received his Distinguished Service Cross on his last day in the hospital and then returned to Arizona, where he had picked cantaloupes a few years earlier. On his way home, the bus stopped in Santa Fe, New Mexico. When Sakato tried to order a meal at a local diner, he was refused service and returned to the bus hungry. The onetime lackluster student who had been held back one year and liked to ditch class had a hard time finding work. Sakato learned to be a diesel mechanic before he ultimately settled in the Denver area. At first he got a job extending truck beds in the day and also worked nights, delivering mail to the airport. He finally found a job with the Postal Service, "because there was no discrimination in the post office."[13] For decades, he suffered from nightmares of a German soldier stabbing him in the back. He believed, "Dahlquist used us as cannon fodder, no matter the cost."[14] Sakato died in December 2014. He was the last of the seven Japanese American soldiers who had attended President Clinton's Medal of Honor ceremony.

Mutt Sakumoto remained famous as the first Nisei to reach Higgins's men and offer them his remaining cigarettes. He suffered from the effects of trench foot in the years following the war and quit smoking. He returned to a prewar job as a mechanic with the federal government. He retired in the early 1990s. He died in 2011 at the age of eighty-seven.

---

* Sakato's last rehabilitation hospital was at Camp Lockett, east of San Diego, where Higgins and Huberth had trained. By war's end, it had been converted into a hospital for returning soldiers.

Chaplain Israel Yost returned to the East Coast after he left the 100th Battalion. He taught an indigenous tribe in Papua New Guinea how to read during a two-year mission. He served as a pastor in Pennsylvania, Hawaii, and Maryland churches. Despite his travels, he remained close to many members of the 100th Battalion. All eleven of his children graduated college before he died in 2000. In the latter years of his life, the reflective Yost was plagued by nightmares in which he called out, "Medics! Medics!"

Leaders of the 405th squadron that resupplied the 1/141st met various fates. Major John Leonard kept flying combat missions. Only about two months after the lost battalion missions, he was shot down during a vicious dogfight with enemy aircraft over the city of Worms. He shot down two enemy aircraft before he was hit. Leonard bailed out, but witnesses reported his parachute never opened as he plummeted toward the German forest. He had been promoted to lieutenant colonel before he died on impact that day. Leonard had earned two Distinguished Flying Crosses and twenty-two Air Medals, among other awards. He was twenty-four years old.

Others, like 405th pilot Eliel Archilla, quietly built new careers after surviving the war. After completing three missions over the English Channel and ninety-five more over France and Germany, he came home on VE Day, was discharged from active service in 1947, and retired from the reserves as a lieutenant colonel in 1964. He and his wife, Sue, raised a family, and he worked for decades for a Texas lubricant and fuel-additive company. Widely known as "Arch," Eliel was a longtime and highly respected deacon in his Baptist church until he died in 2015 at the age of ninety-one.

THE GERMAN LEADERS WHO COMMANDED THE ENEMY TROOPS ON the ridge met a different postwar fate.

General Hermann Balck, commanding officer of Army Group G in eastern France, surrendered to the Americans in Austria at the end of the war and remained in prison until 1947. After he found work as a depot worker a year later in Germany, he was arrested and convicted of murdering a German artillery commander in the war. Balck served eighteen months. In the 1970s he participated in panel discussions with senior leaders of the North Atlantic Treaty Organization at the U.S. Army War College. He died in 1982 at the age of eighty-nine.

Major General Dahlquist's nemesis, General Friedrich Wiese, was relieved of his command of the Nineteenth Army after his army failed to retake Strasbourg late in the war. He was captured by the Americans in 1945 and released two years later. He died in Germany in 1975 at the age of eighty-two.

"OLD STONE FACE," COLONEL CARL ADAMS, COMMANDING officer of the 143rd Infantry Regiment, never followed through on his threat to have Dahlquist "busted." He retired as a general in 1966 after serving thirty-eight years in the military. He died in 1987, only three weeks after his eighty-first birthday.

Major General Lucian Truscott never fired Dahlquist. The ambitious general commanded the Fifth Army in Italy at the end of the war and succeeded General George Patton as commanding officer of the Third Army in Germany. He returned to the United States, and in 1954 Congress passed Public Law 83-508 making him an honorary general. Truscott died in 1965 at the age of seventy.

Days after the war ended in Europe, Major General John Dahlquist was ridiculed for his courteous treatment of Reichsmarshall Hermann Göring after he had been captured. He and Brigadier General Robert Stack were filmed shaking Göring's hand, smiling, and posing for a photograph as they welcomed him to a lunch of chicken and peas. At one point, Dahlquist dismissed the group's interpreter and spoke with Göring in German. When the lunch became public knowledge, Stack and Dahlquist were widely criticized over their conduct. General George Marshall was among those critics.

Marshall wrote to General Dwight Eisenhower that he was being "deluged with violent protests and the radical press, as well as numerous conservative papers, carry bitter editorials on the subject. For your information I think the serious error lay in Dahlquist, Stack, etcetera, permitting themselves to be photographed."[15] Eisenhower later stated publicly that he "regretted" the public hospitality shown by Dahlquist, Stack, and other senior American officers in their treatment of Nazi leaders.

Dahlquist left the 36th Division on November 1, 1945, and returned to the United States and to a military life he knew well. He was assigned to the secretary of war's Personnel Board for a year and then became deputy director of Personnel and Administration in the War Department until 1949. Other assignments followed, and in August 1954 he received his fourth star to become a general. He retired from the army in 1956 and died in June 1975 at the age of eighty-nine.

As critical as most soldiers in the 442nd were of Dahlquist, the 36th Division came home with a notable war record. Dahlquist commanded the 36th for all but nine months during World War II. The division earned twelve Presidential Unit Citations. It also had the ninth-highest casualty rate of all army divisions in World War II.

Colonel Carl Lundquist, the commanding officer of the 1/141 whom Dahlquist fired only days after Higgins's men had been surrounded, was assigned to other combat posts. He was chief of staff for the 41st Infantry Division until March 1945 and then became the commanding officer of the 14th Infantry before returning to the United States in 1946. He retired as a colonel and died in 1980 at the age of seventy-six.

Martin Higgins received a battlefield promotion to captain about the time of his capture. Before he reached Oflag 64, he was interviewed by Reichsführer Heinrich Himmler. At the end of the interview, Himmler told Higgins, "Fuer Dich ist der Krieg vobei!" (For you, the war is over!). In later years, he rarely mentioned his Silver Star, two Bronze Stars, Purple Heart, POW Medal, or other citations.

After the war he went to work in sales for a playing-card company, Diamond International. Higgins retired as a regional sales manager in 1979. Thereafter, he earned a master's degree in education and later taught adult literacy. He died in February 2007 at the age of ninety-one. When he was buried at Arlington National Cemetery, the only flowers permitted on his grave by his son were the crimson-red anthuriums presented by members of the 442nd who were in attendance. Higgins always felt his men were "relieved" by the 442nd, not rescued.* But out of respect and deep gratitude to the men of the 442nd who used the term *rescue*, he never argued the point.

Higgins's second in command, Harry Huberth, built a prosperous real estate career in New York following the war. Like many soldiers after World War II, he drifted away from his religious upbringing, and only in the latter years of his life did he again become active in the Episcopal Church. He was an avid and accomplished horseman. Higgins remained close to Huberth, and they went riding together. Late in his life, Huberth said one of his most cherished possessions was a letter Higgins had written to Huberth, saying, "While I received all the credit as commanding officer of the lost battalion, there was not a move I made without consulting you as B Company commander. You are one of the finest and bravest officers I ever saw in combat and I cherish our friendship. . . . [M]ay the bond never be broken." Huberth died in 2009 at the age of eighty-seven.

Machine gunner Jack Wilson went to air-conditioning school in Chicago following the war. He couldn't find a job upon graduation and returned home to Newburgh, Indiana. He became a rural mail carrier and retired on his fifty-fifth birthday, after thirty years of civil service (including his time in the army).

---

*According to his son Michael, Martin felt his men could have held out indefinitely with adequate supplies. Therefore, they were not rescued, in his view, but relieved by the 442nd that then carried out the rest of the mission to the end of the ridge.

Radioman Erwin Blonder was hospitalized in Illinois with the severe trench foot that had developed while he was surrounded for a
week in the Vosges. Gangrene was found in both ankles, and at one
point amputation was considered. Rehabilitation took nearly a year
after Blonder returned home. For a while, Blonder didn't want his
wife or parents to see him, and he wouldn't talk about his war experience. After he recovered, he rejoined the family's successful paint-
and-wallpaper business in Ohio. He retired in 1971 and ultimately
sold the family business. He was active in a number of civic organizations and loved to talk about politics. More than fifty years after the
war, he met some of the members of the 442nd at the Texas Military
Forces Museum and started attending their reunions. Blonder died in
2013 at the age of ninety-two.

For decades following the war, battlefield memories sometimes
haunted Eason Bond, the rifleman who was tempted to leave his station when surrounded in the Vosges. He returned to his native Thomaston, Georgia, to work at the local cotton mill. That life offered
minimal prospects, so he went to technical school. For the next thirty-
five years, he ran an auto-body shop and then retired a few miles east
of Monroe. "I think of the war every day," he recalled more than sixty
years later. Various memories would flash into view. Sometimes he
wondered if a man whose jaw had been blown to pieces and whose
tongue had been shredded somehow regained his ability to speak.
"When I go to bed I think about the ol' boys and what they've been
doing. I don't always remember their names, but I sure do remember
their faces."[16]

Faces of men saved and lost haunted many members of the 442nd
to the last days of their lives. The 100th's Young Oak Kim articulated
an epitaph that spoke for many in the decades following World
War II: "My memories of France still show the bitterness burnt
deeply into my soul."[17]

BIBLIOGRAPHY

PRIMARY SOURCES

Botsch, Walter. *Nineteenth Army: Combat Operations of Nineteenth Army in the Forward Defense Zone of the Vosges, in the Vosges Mountains, and the Alsace Bridgehead.* N.p., 1950.

Haeckel, Ernst. *German 16th Infantry Division, 15 September to 1 December 1944.* N.p., n.d.

Higgins, Martin L., Jr. Family Papers Collection. Courtesy of Michael Higgins.

Peek, Clifford H. *Five Years, Five Countries, Five Campaigns.* Munich: 141st Infantry Regiment Association, 1945.

Reinhardt, Hellmuth. *Withdrawal from Southwestern France, 19 August 1944–15 September 1944.* Germany, 1950.

Roettiger, Hans. *History of Southern France/OB West.* Germany, January 1947.

Seventh United States Army. *Report of Operations.* Vol. 1. Nashville: Battery Press, 1988.

Stewart, E. P. *Investigation of Conditions Affecting General Welfare of Members of the 442nd Combat Regimental Team (Japanese-Americans).* Camp McCain, MS: IX Corps Headquarters, 1943.

Taeglichsbeck, Hans. *The Retreat from Southern France, 19 Aug–15 Sept 1944.* Germany, n.d.

U.S. Army. *100th Battalion Bravery Award Nomination Submission: Kamikawa, Suyama, Yamaka.* N.p., October 26, 1944.

———. *Operational Report of the 442nd Regimental Combat Team Covering the Period 4 to 15 April 1945.* N.p., August 27, 1945.

———. *Seventh Army History, Phase Three: The Drive Through the Vosges and the Rhine*. File N-13215-C. Combined Arms Research Library Archives, Fort Leavenworth, KS.

———. *The Story of the 442nd Combat Team*. Education Section, Mediterranean Theater of Operations, 1946.

U.S. Army, 36th Infantry Division. *G-3 Journal*. October 25–31, 1944.

———. "Operations in France: October 1944 Narrative." File N-11178. Combined Arms Research Library Archives, Fort Leavenworth, KS.

U.S. Army, 141st Infantry Regiment, 36th Division. *History of Operations After Battle Report*. October 1944.

———. *History of Operations After Battle Report*. November 1944.

———. *Operations in Foret Dominale de Champ*, 141st Regiment, 13 October to 7 November 1944.

———. *Operations Report, 1944*.

———. "Regimental History for the Month of October 1944 and Conclusions of Operations." RG 407, Box 9947, National Archives, College Park, MD.

U.S. Army, 442 Regimental Combat Team. *141st Infantry Journal*. October 1944.

———. *442nd Regimental Combat Team and 100th Battalion*. Education Section, Mediterranean Theater of Operations, 1946.

———. "A Challenge to Democracy." Office of War Information, U.S. Government, 1944.

———. *Chronology of Events: 1–31 October 1944*. U.S. Army Center for Military History. http://www.history.army.mil/html/topics/apam/442_chrono.html.

———. *Combat Bulletin #17: Invasion of Southern France, 1944*. U.S. Army, n.d.

———. *FM-105, Field Service Regulation: Operations*. Washington, DC: USBGPO, May 22, 1941.

———. *Handbook for German Military Forces*. War Department, U.S. Government, 1945.

———. "Narrative of Events, 1–31 October 44." RG 407, Entry 427, Box 21250, Location 270/63/18/4, National Archives, College Park, MD.

———. *The Overseas Target War Reports of the OSS*. Vol. 2. War Department, U.S. Government, 1949.

———. "Regimental Journal, October 1944." RG 407, Box 9944, Folder I, National Archives, College Park, MD.

————. *Wartime Exile: The Exclusion of the Japanese Americans from the West Coast.* Washington, DC: U.S. Government Printing Office, 1946.

U.S. Army General Orders. Numbers 317, 360.

U.S. Army Headquarters. *442nd RCT, Monthly Historical Report(s): 25 November 1944, 15 December 1944.* N.p., n.d.

U.S. Department of the Interior. *People in Motion: The Postwar Adjustment of the Evacuated Japanese Americans.* Washington, DC: U.S. Government Printing Office, 1947.

Wiese, Friedrich. *The 19th Army in the Belfort Gap, in the Vosges, and in Alsace from the Middle of September Until 18 December 1944.* U.S. Army, March 8, 1948.

Zerbel, Alfred. *Combat Operations of the Nineteenth Army in the Forward Defense Zone of the Vosges.* Koenigstein, Germany, November 15, 1950.

————. *Operational Report of Grenadier Regiment 933 in Southern France from Begin [sic] of the Invasion in the Bay of St. Raphael to the Vosges.* Germany, June 18, 1950.

ORAL HISTORIES AND INTERVIEWS

141st

Gene Airheart, Erwin Blonder, Eason Bond, Arthur Cunningham, Bill Estes, Martin Higgins, Joe Hilty, Harry Huberth, John Krause, Albert Lasseign, Jack Wilson.

442nd

Nelson Agi, Seitoku Akamine, Tets Asato, George Buto, Kenji Ego, Frank Fukuzawa, Minoru Furuto, Barney Hajiro, Kaz Hamasaki, Ed Ichiyama, Lawrence Ishikawa, Victor Izui, Stanley Izumigawa, Harry Kanada, Enoch Kanaya, Jimmie Kanaya, Young Oak Kim, Larry Kodama, Sadaichi Kubota, Yoshikatsu Maruo, Rocky Matayoshi, Frank Matsuda, Shigeru Matsukawa, James Matsumoto, Paul Matsumoto, Kats Miho, Rocky Miyamoto, George Morihio, Kiyoji Morimoto, Edward Nishihara, Ron Oba, Ted Ohira, Francis Ohta, Yukio Okutsu, James Oura, Mas Sakagami, Ray Sakaguchi, Seichi Sakaida, George Sakato, Larry Sakoda, Eddie Sasaki, Kazuo Sato, Sus Satow, Takashi Senzaki, Jun Shiosaki, Sam Sugimoto, Eji Suyama, Al Takahashi,

Keyo Takahayashi, Shuji Taketomo, Richard Tanaka, Thomas Tanaka, Jim Tazoi, John Togashi, Rudy Tokia, Jim Tokushige, George Uchimiya, Ernest Uno, Kei Yamaguchi, Jim Yamashita, Fred Yasukochi, Hank Yoshitake.

OTHER SOURCES

"Army & Navy, No Problem." *Time*, July 31, 1944.

Asahina, Robert. *Just Americans: How Japanese Americans Won a War at Home and Abroad*. New York: Gotham Books, 2006.

Baer, George. *One Hundred Years of Sea Power*. Stanford, CA: Stanford University Press, 1993.

"Battlebook: The Alsace Campaign." U.S. Army, n.d. http://www.eur.army .mil/pdf/Alsace-staff-ride.pdf.

Bonn, Keith. "Most Underrated General of World War II: Alexander Patch." Marshall Foundation newsletter, July 2003.

Breuer, William. *Operation Dragoon: The Allied Invasion of the South of France*. Novato, CA: Presidio Press, 1987.

Carroll, Andrew. *Letters of a Nation: A Collection of Extraordinary American Letters*. New York: Kodansha America, 1977.

Clarke, Jeffrey J., and Robert Ross Smith. *Riviera to the Rhine*. Washington, DC: U.S. Army, 1993.

Cole, Hugh. *The Lorraine Campaign*. Washington, DC: U.S. Army, 1993.

Comstock, James. *The Farmboy Who Went to WWII*. Self-published, 1995.

Courington, Morris. *Cruel Was the Way*. N.p.: Velletri Press, 2000.

Crost, Lyn. *Honor by Fire*. Novato, CA: Presidio Press, 1994.

Daniels, Robert. "Incarceration of the Japanese Americans: A Sixty-Year Perspective." *History Teacher* 35, no. 2 (2002).

Duus, Masayo. *Unlikely Liberators: The Men of the 100th and 442nd*. Honolulu: University of Hawaii Press, 1987.

Fisher, Ernest F. *Cassino to the Alps*. Washington, DC: Center of Military History, U.S. Army, 1977.

Goodman, Paul. *A Fragment of Victory in Italy: The 92nd Infantry Division in Italy*. Nashville: Battery Press, 1993.

Grossjohann, George. *Five Years, Four Fronts*. New York: Ballantine Books, 2005.

Han, Woon Sung. *Unsung Hero: The Col. Young O. Kim Story*. Riverside: University of California–Riverside, 2011.

Hanley, James M. *A Matter of Honor*. New York: Vantage Press, 1995.

Hawaii Nikkei History Editorial Board. *Japanese Eyes, American Heart: Reflections of Hawaii's World War II Nisei Soldiers*. Honolulu: Tendai Educational Foundation, 1988.

Heefner, Wilson A. *Dogface Soldier: The Life of General Lucian K. Truscott, Jr.* Columbia: University of Missouri Press, 2010.

Herzig, Juerig. "442nd Regimental Combat Team." http://standwherethey fought.jimdo.com/the-vosges-2009-battle-of-bruyères-and-the-relief -of-the-lost-battalion-by-the-442nd-rct/.

Higgins, Michael P. *Crimson Threads: The 405th Fighter Squadron and the Lost Battalion*. Kent: Edon, 2009.

Hosokawa, Bill. *Nisei: The Quiet Americans*. New York: William Morrow, 1969.

Lingeman, Richard. *Sinclair Lewis*. St. Paul, MN: Borealis Books, 2002.

"Lost Battalion Symposium." Austin: Texas Military Forces Museum, 2008.

Ludewig, Joachim. *Ruckzug: The German Retreat from France, 1944*. Lexington: University Press of Kentucky, 2012.

Masudo, Minoru. *Letters from 442nd*. Seattle: University of Washington Press, 2008.

Matsuo, Dorothy. *Silent Valor*. Honolulu: Honolulu Chapter of 442nd Medics, 2002.

McGaugh, Scott. *Battlefield Angels: Saving Lives from Valley Forge to Afghanistan*. New York: Osprey, 2009.

Morita, Col. Hiroaki. "The Nation's Most Decorated Unit, the 100th/442nd Regimental Combat Team." Master's thesis, U.S. Army War College, 1992.

Moulin, Pierre. *U.S. Samurais in Bruyères*. Paris: Éditions Gerard Louis, 1993.

Nisei in Uniform. Washington, DC: War Relocation Authority, 1944.

Parker, Lcdr. Joni I. "Nisei Soldiers in World War II: The Campaign in the Vosges Mountains." Master's thesis, U.S. Army Command, 1994.

"A Pictorial History, 36th Division in World War II." Austin: Texas Military Forces Museum, n.d.

Porter, John D. "The Operations of the 442nd Regimental Combat Team in the Vosges Mountains." Master's thesis, U.S. Army Infantry School, 1947.

Reardon, John. "Nightmare at Rapido River." http://www.redbubble.com /people/warwolf/writing/3571203-nightmare-at-rapido-river.

Shirey, Orville. *Americans: The Story of the 442nd Combat Team*. Washington, DC: Infantry Journal Press, 1946.

Smith, Bradford. *Americans from Japan*. New York: J. B. Lippincott, 1948.

Steidl, Franz. *Lost Battalions*. Novato, CA: Presidio Press, 2000.

Sterner, C. Douglas. *Go For Broke*. Clearfield, UT: American Legacy Historical Press, 2008.

Stewart, Maj. Duncan. "Operation Anvil/Dragoon: The Invasion of Southern France." Master's thesis, U.S. Army Command and General Staff College, 1984.

Tanaka, Chester. *Go For Broke: A Pictorial History of the Japanese American 100th Infantry Battalion and the 442nd Regimental Combat Team*. Richmond, CA: Go For Broke, 1982.

Texas Military Forces Museum, 36th Division Archives. Austin.

Tomblin, Barbara B. *With Utmost Spirit: Allied Naval Operations in the Mediterranean, 1942–1945*. Lexington: University Press of Kentucky, 2004.

"Toughest of the Tough." *Time*, April 17, 1964.

Truscott, Lucian, Jr. *Command Missions*. New York City: E. P. Dutton, 1954.

U.S. Army, Field Artillery Battalion, 522nd, Historical Album Committee. *Fire for Effect: A Unit History of the 522nd Field Artillery Battalion*. Honolulu: Fisher, 1998.

Wagner, Robert. "The Odyssey of a Texas Citizen Soldier." *Southwestern Historical Quarterly* 72 (July 1968): 82–83.

Wakamatsu, Jack. *Silent Warriors*. Los Angeles: JKW Press, 1992.

Watanabe, Nathan K. "The 100/442nd Regimental Combat Team's Rescue of the Lost Battalion: A Study in the Employment of Battle Command." Master's thesis, U.S. Army Command and General Staff College, 2002.

Wellesley, Susumu. *Charlie Company*. N.p.: Roberts Press, 1991.

Yamasaki, Edward M. *And Then There Were Eight*. Honolulu: 442 Veterans Club, 2003.

Yamashia, Jeffrey. "A War Within World War II: Racialized Masculinity and Citizenship of Japanese Americans and Korean Colonial Subjects." Honors thesis, Macalester College, 2011.

Yenne, Bill. *Rising Suns*. New York: Thomas Dunne Books, 2007.

Yost, Israel. *Combat Chaplain*. Honolulu: University of Hawaii Press, 2006.

ACKNOWLEDGMENTS

Over the course of more than three years, the completion of this book would not have been possible without a host of remarkably supportive family, colleagues, and strangers, from San Diego to eastern France. I'm always amazed and grateful when so many people who are strangers at the outset are willing to research, review, revise, and refine to make a project the best it can be on a particular subject.

But I first must start with those closest to me. My wife, Marjorie, is my rock and far stronger than she realizes. Her review of the manuscript was absolutely vital to its clarity. Our cat, Tazi, was a patient and silent wingman during hundreds of predawn writing sessions in our home office. Never a peep, never an edit. And every author needs cheerleaders. Garrett and Sara, my son and daughter-in-law, were unfailing in their enthusiasm and interest in Dad's project. I cannot thank or express the depth of my love and appreciation for my family.

This book would not exist without the expertise, support, and enthusiasm of Bob Pigeon, executive editor at Da Capo Press, and my agent, Scott Mendel. Bob is a crackerjack editor, and Scott is a steadying hand on the rudder of my journey as an author. Project editor Amber Morris and copy editor Annette Wenda organized, finessed, polished, and shepherded my prose from the computer to the bookshelf. I am enormously grateful for their expertise and collaboration. I look forward to more projects supported by the very professional production, marketing, and sales staffs at the Perseus Books Group.

Herve Claudon and Gerome Villain live only a few miles from where the rescue mission took place and have made it their lifework to preserve its legacy. Their knowledge and firsthand research were critical to this project, and I'll forever be grateful to Gerome for accompanying me on the ridge where the rescue mission took place. Herve provided near-scientific data, analysis, and manuscript review that were invaluable. I cannot thank Herve and Gerome enough for their assistance. Juerg Herzig in Switzerland has also researched and written extensively on the subject.

Michael Higgins and Elliot Archilla graciously shared vast information about their fathers' involvement. Michael in particular has contributed significantly to preserving the legacy of this remarkable mission. Evan Archilla has written extensively as well. Similarly, one of the men rescued, Eason Bond, welcomed me into his home and shared his vivid memories—a journey made possible by Mike Bond, Denise Bond, and Rod Davis. Many others, including Barbara Berthiaume, Louie Morrison, Alton Chung, Keith Yamaguchi, and Julian Hiraki, shared their family histories and other story collections with me.

Institutions also contributed. Chris Brusatte, Summer Espinoza, and Benjamin Abbott of the Go For Broke National Education Center opened archives rarely seen by others. Lisa Sharik of the Texas Military Forces Museum was equally forthcoming and helpful at the outset. Lauren Zuchowski of the Japanese American National Museum steered me in productive directions, while Linda McLemore introduced me to the Japanese American Citizen League of San Diego. Tom Ikeda at Densho, the Japanese American Legacy, provided valuable photo input. Tiffany Ujiiye at the Japanese American Citizens League made dozens of World War II publications available.

I must also acknowledge the authors who blazed this trail before me. Although *Honor Before Glory* is based on rarely seen and relatively new oral histories, the work of C. Douglas Sterner, Robert

Asahina, Franz Steidl, Lyn Crost, Mawayo Duus, and others cannot be overlooked.

Others who provided the fruits of their personal research included Roger L. Eaton, Dave Kerr, Junwo James Yamashita, and Matthew Henry. USS Midway Museum volunteer Yaeko Sunada courteously verified my use of Japanese words. She's a great example of the eight hundred volunteers aboard *Midway* who preserve the legacy of those who serve. *Midway*'s military historian extraordinaire, Karl Zingheim, was always at the ready to answer a question or clarify an otherwise arcane military point. Jack Harkins helped me understand the extraordinary demands of a commanding officer on the battlefield.

To be sure, organizations such as the 442 Veterans Club in Hawaii, National Japanese American Historical Society, and Americans of Japanese Ancestry World War II Alliance have all preserved a foundation of documents, oral histories, and writing that makes books such as this possible.

I cannot overlook some of those closest to me. Successful novelist and longtime friend Richard Setlowe has graciously served as my mentor for years. He seized on the central appeal of this book at the very outset and helped chart a course that kept me focused on the essence of this remarkable story. Similarly, my good friends and colleagues at Champ Cohen Design Associates in Del Mar, California—John Champ, Randy Cohen, Jo-lin Govek, and Nick Kass—translated a congested battlefield into maps with clarity that will be of great value to readers.

They have all contributed to helping preserve the legacy of young Japanese Americans who defeated the enemy on the battlefield as well as prejudice at home. I will forever be grateful for their support and encouragement.

NOTES

CHAPTER 1

1. Michael Higgins, interview, Martin L. Higgins Jr. Family Papers Collection, Go For Broke Association.

2. Itsumu Sasaoka Distinguished Service Cross citation.

3. Lucian Truscott, *Command Missions*, 430.

4. Scott McGaugh, *Battlefield Angels: Saving Lives from Valley Forge to Afghanistan*, 84.

5. Harley Kilgore, letter to President Franklin Roosevelt, February 19, 1942.

6. FDR letter to the secretary of war, February 1, 1943.

7. Harrison Gerhardt to Abe Fortas, undersecretary of the interior, July 13, 1944, www.the442.org.

8. "Army & Navy, No Problem."

9. Barney Hajiro, oral history, Go For Broke Association.

10. Ibid.

11. George Sakato, oral histories, Go For Broke Association, Library of Congress, and C-SPAN.

12. Robert Wagner, "The Odyssey of a Texas Citizen Soldier," 82.

13. Susumu Wellesley, *Charlie Company*, 51.

14. William Breuer, *Operation Dragoon: The Allied Invasion of the South of France*, 62.

CHAPTER 2

1. Jimmie Kanaya, oral history, Go For Broke Association.

2. Martin Higgins, oral history, Go For Broke Association; Harry Huberth, oral history, Go For Broke Association.

3. *442nd: Live with Honor, Die with Dignity* (documentary, directed by Junichi Suzuki, 2010).

4. E. P. Stewart, "Inspector General's Report, U.S. Army," in *Investigation of Conditions Affecting General Welfare of Members of the 442nd Combat Regimental Team (Japanese-Americans)*, October 2, 1943.

5. Ibid.

6. Ibid.

7. Mutt Sakumoto, oral history, Go For Broke Association.

8. Kanaya, oral history.

9. U.S. Army, 141st Infantry Regiment, 36th Division, *History of Operations After Battle Report* (October 1944), 31.

10. U.S. Army, 442 Regimental Combat Team, *141st Infantry Journal*, 283.

11. Jack Wilson, unpublished first-person recollection, Gerome Villain Collection.

12. Franz Steidl, *Lost Battalions*, 54.

13. Woon Sung Han, *Unsung Hero: The Col. Young O. Kim Story*, 129.

14. Ibid., 122.

15. Higgins Family Papers Collection, Go For Broke Association.

16. Sakato, oral history, Go For Broke Association.

17. 442 Regimental Combat Team, "A Challenge to Democracy," 305.

18. U.S. Army, 442 Regimental Combat Team, *141st Infantry Journal*, 283.

19. Nathan K. Watanabe, *The 100/442nd Regimental Combat Team's Rescue of the Los Battalion: A Study in the Employment of Battle Command*, 53, 92.

20. U.S. Army, 442 Regimental Combat Team, *141st Infantry Journal*, 288.

CHAPTER 3

1. Edward Guy, oral history, Go For Broke Association.

2. U.S. Army, 442 Regimental Combat Team, *141st Infantry Journal*, 286.

3. James Comstock, *The Farmboy Who Went to WWII*, 20.

4. Erwin Blonder, oral history, Digital Collection of the World War II Museum, http://www.ww2online.org/view/erwin-blonder; Shirlee Blonder, phone interview with the author, May 2015.

5. U.S. Army, 442 Regimental Combat Team, *141st Infantry Journal*, 291.

6. Nelson Akagi, oral history, Go For Broke Association.

7. Kats Miho, oral history, Go For Broke Association.

8. Ibid.; Akagi, oral history.

9. Kelly Kuwayama, oral history, Library of Congress.

10. Rocky Matayoshi, oral history, Go For Broke Association.

11. Kenji Ego, oral history, Go For Broke Association. During his interview he reflected, "I've thought about this insensible war. The horror of war. There is no glory in war."

12. Kuwayama, oral history.

13. U.S. Army, 442 Regimental Combat Team, *141st Infantry Journal*, 295–297.

14. Ibid.

15. Ibid.

16. Jim Tazoi, oral history, Go For Broke Association.

17. Al Takahashi, oral history, Go For Broke Association.

18. U.S. Army, 442 Regimental Combat Team, *141st Infantry Journal*, 302, 298.

CHAPTER 4

1. U.S. Army, 442 Regimental Combat Team, *141st Infantry Journal*, 299.

2. Arthur Cunningham, oral history, Go For Broke Association.

3. Ibid.

4. Rudy Tokiwa, oral history, Go For Broke Association.

5. Ernest Uno, oral history, Go For Broke Association.

6. Jim Tazoi, oral history, Utah WWII Stories, KUED-TV, Salt Lake City.

7. Ibid.

8. Takahashi, oral history.

9. Steidl, *Lost Battalions*, 19–20.

10. Ibid., 21–22.

11. Takahashi, oral history.

12. Morris Courington, *Cruel Was the Way*, 32.

13. Minoru Masuda, *Letters from 442nd*, 103.

14. U.S. Army, 141st Infantry Regiment, 36th Division, *History of Operations After Battle Report* (October 1944).

15. Wick Fowler, "Hell on the Hill," *Dallas Morning News*, November 6, 1944.

16. U.S. Army, 442 Regimental Combat Team, *141st Infantry Journal*, 309.

17. Ibid.

18. Lawrence Ishikawa, oral history, Go For Broke Association.

19. U.S. Army, 442 Regimental Combat Team, *141st Infantry Journal*, 314.

CHAPTER 5

1. U.S. Army, 442 Regimental Combat Team, *141st Infantry Journal*, October 28, 1944, transmissions, 3.

2. Ibid., 2.

3. Al Tortolano interview, KMJ Radio podcast, 2011.

4. Harry Huberth, oral history, Go For Broke Association.

5. U.S. Army, 442 Regimental Combat Team, *141st Infantry Journal*, 317.

6. "Like Something You Would See in the Movies," *Air Force Print News Today*, October 29, 2014.

7. Steidl, *Lost Battalions*, 197.

8. U.S. Army, 442 Regimental Combat Team, *141st Infantry Journal*, 318.

9. Young Oak Kim, oral history, Go For Broke Association.

10. Ibid.

11. "Saga of Lost Battalion," *Stars and Stripes*, November 6, 1944.

12. "Hell on the Hill," *Dallas Morning News*, November 6, 1944.

13. U.S. Army, 442 Regimental Combat Team, *141st Infantry Journal*, 319.

14. U.S. Army, 442 Regimental Combat Team, "Regimental Journal, October 1944," 4.

15. Ibid.

16. U.S. Army, 36th Infantry Division, *G-3 Journal*, October 28, 1944, transmissions, 4.

17. "Toughest of the Tough."

18. U.S. Army, 442 Regimental Combat Team, "Regimental Journal, October 1944," 3.

19. Ibid., 4.

20. Kenneth Inada, oral history, Go For Broke Association.

21. Tokiwa, oral history.

22. Ibid.

23. Kenneth Inada speech, June 11, 2005.

CHAPTER 6

1. U.S. Army, 442 Regimental Combat Team, "Regimental Journal, October 1944," October 29, 1944, transmissions, 1.

2. Ibid.

3. Sakato, oral history, Go For Broke Association.

4. Letter by Yuri Nakyama, http://arlingtoncemetery.net/tanamac.htm.

5. Ibid.

6. Ibid.

7. Higgins, interview, Higgins Family Papers Collection, Go For Broke Association.

8. Ibid.

9. Richard Lingeman, *Sinclair Lewis*, 460.

10. Wagner, "Odyssey of a Texas Citizen Soldier."

11. U.S. Army, 442 Regimental Combat Team, "Regimental Journal, October 1944," 5.

12. Ibid.

13. Ibid.

14. U.S. Army, 442 Regimental Combat Team, *141st Infantry Journal*, 329.

15. Ibid.

16. Sakumoto, oral history.

17. Robert Asahina, *Just Americans: How Japanese Americans Won a War at Home and Abroad*, 180.

18. Lyn Crost, *Honor by Fire*, 190.

19. Rudy Tokiwa, oral histories, Go For Broke Association and Library of Congress.

20. Crost, *Honor by Fire*, 193.

21. Masayo Duus, *Unlikely Liberators: The Men of the 100th and 442nd*, 206.

22. Ed Ichiyama oral history, Go For Broke Association.

23. Hajiro, oral history.

24. Ibid.

25. Ibid.

26. Ibid.

27. Edward Yamasaki, *And Then There Were Eight*, 167.

28. U.S. Army, 442 Regimental Combat Team, "Regimental Journal, October 1944," 6–7.

CHAPTER 7

1. U.S. Army, 442 Regimental Combat Team, "Regimental Journal, October 1944," October 30, 1944, transmissions, 1.

2. U.S. Army, 442 Regimental Combat Team, *141st Infantry Journal*, 334.

3. Ibid., 335.

4. Duus, *Unlikely Liberators*, 210.

5. U.S. Army, 442 Regimental Combat Team, *141st Infantry Journal*, 335.

6. Hawaii Nikkei History Editorial Board, *Japanese Eyes, American Heart: Reflections of Hawaii's World War II Nisei Soldiers*, 260–261.

7. Masao Yamada, letter to Colonel Harrison Gerhardt, October 31, 1944.

8. Sakumoto, oral history.

9. Yamasaki, *And Then There Were Eight*, 175.

10. *JAVA Advocate* (Japanese American Veterans Association newsletter), September 2010, 13.

11. Gene Airheart, oral history, Go For Broke Association.

12. Kazuo Takekawa, oral history, Go For Broke Association.

13. Yamasaki, *And Then There Were Eight*, 85.

14. Ibid.

15. Al Tortolano, oral history, Go For Broke Association.

16. Chester Tanaka, *Go For Broke: A Pictorial History of the Japanese American 100th Infantry Battalion and the 442nd Regimental Combat Team*, 92.

17. Duus, *Unlikely Liberators*, 211.

18. Asahina, *Just Americans*, 192.

19. U.S. Army, 442 Regimental Combat Team, *141st Infantry Journal*, 343.

20. Ibid., 345.

21. Alfred Zerbel, *Operational Report of Grenadier Regiment 933 in Southern France from Begin [sic] of the Invasion in the Bay of St. Raphael to the Vosges*.

22. Letter from Bert Akiyama to James Comstock, a member of the 1/141.

23. Speech by Chaplain Israel Yost at a memorial service on October 5, 1947.

24. Hawaii Nikkei History Editorial Board, *Japanese Eyes, American Heart*, 260.

25. Martin Higgins, speech at the fifty-seventh anniversary memorial service held at the National Memorial Cemetery of the Pacific on March 25, 2000.

CHAPTER 8

1. Asahina, *Just Americans*, 202.

2. Lcdr. Joni I Parker, "Nisei Soldiers in World War II: The Campaign in the Vosges Mountains," 75–76.

3. Ibid.

4. Ibid.

5. Ibid.

6. Renita Foster, "March to Freedom Filled with Danger," MG Keith L. Ware Journalism Awards Competition, 2006.

7. *Operational Report of the 442nd Regimental Combat Team Covering the Period 4 to 15 April 1945*, 1.

8. Ibid., 5.

9. Michael Higgins (son of Martin Higgins), correspondence.

10. U.S. Department of the Interior, *People in Motion: The Postwar Adjustment of the Evacuated Japanese Americans*, 19.

11. George Baer, *One Hundred Years of Sea Power*, 246.

12. *The War* (PBS documentary by Ken Burns, 2007).

13. Steidl, *Lost Battalions*, 91.

CHAPTER 9

1. "Wounded Nisei War Veteran Ejected from Barber Shop," *Pacific Citizen*, November 18, 1944.

2. Tokiwa, oral history, Go For Broke Association.

3. U.S. Department of the Interior, *People in Motion*, 28.

4. "Front Line GIs Condemn Hood River Legion," *Pacific Citizen*, January 6, 1945.

5. McGaugh, *Battlefield Angels*, 100.

6. "Reagan Signs Measure to Pay WWII Internees," *Los Angeles Times*, August 10, 1988.

7. McGaugh, *Battlefield Angels*, 101.

8. Kenneth Inada, correspondence, July 4, 2004.

9. Ego, oral history.

10. Ibid.

11. Ibid.

12. *Puka-Puka Parade* (100th Infantry Battalion Veterans Club news-letter), February 2008, 11–12.

13. Sakato, oral history, C-SPAN.

14. Ibid.

15. George C. Marshall Papers, Pentagon Office Collection, Selected Materials, George C. Marshall Research Library, Lexington, VA.

16. Eason Bond, interview by the author, Monroe, GA, August 2015.

17. Young Oak Kim speech, 1982.

INDEX